MW01627069

SOLSTICE

'A Turning Point'

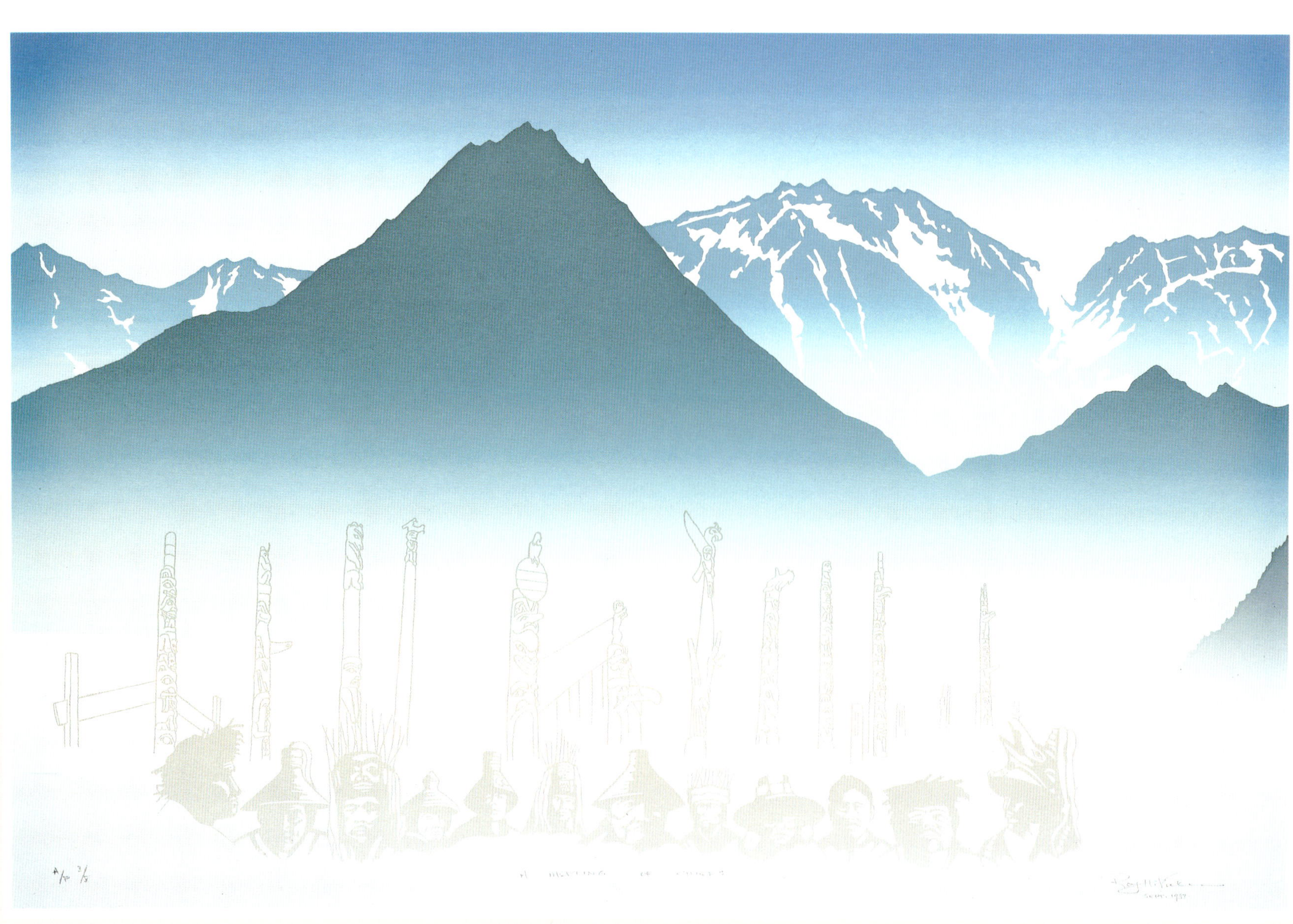

SOLSTICE

THE ART OF
ROY HENRY VICKERS

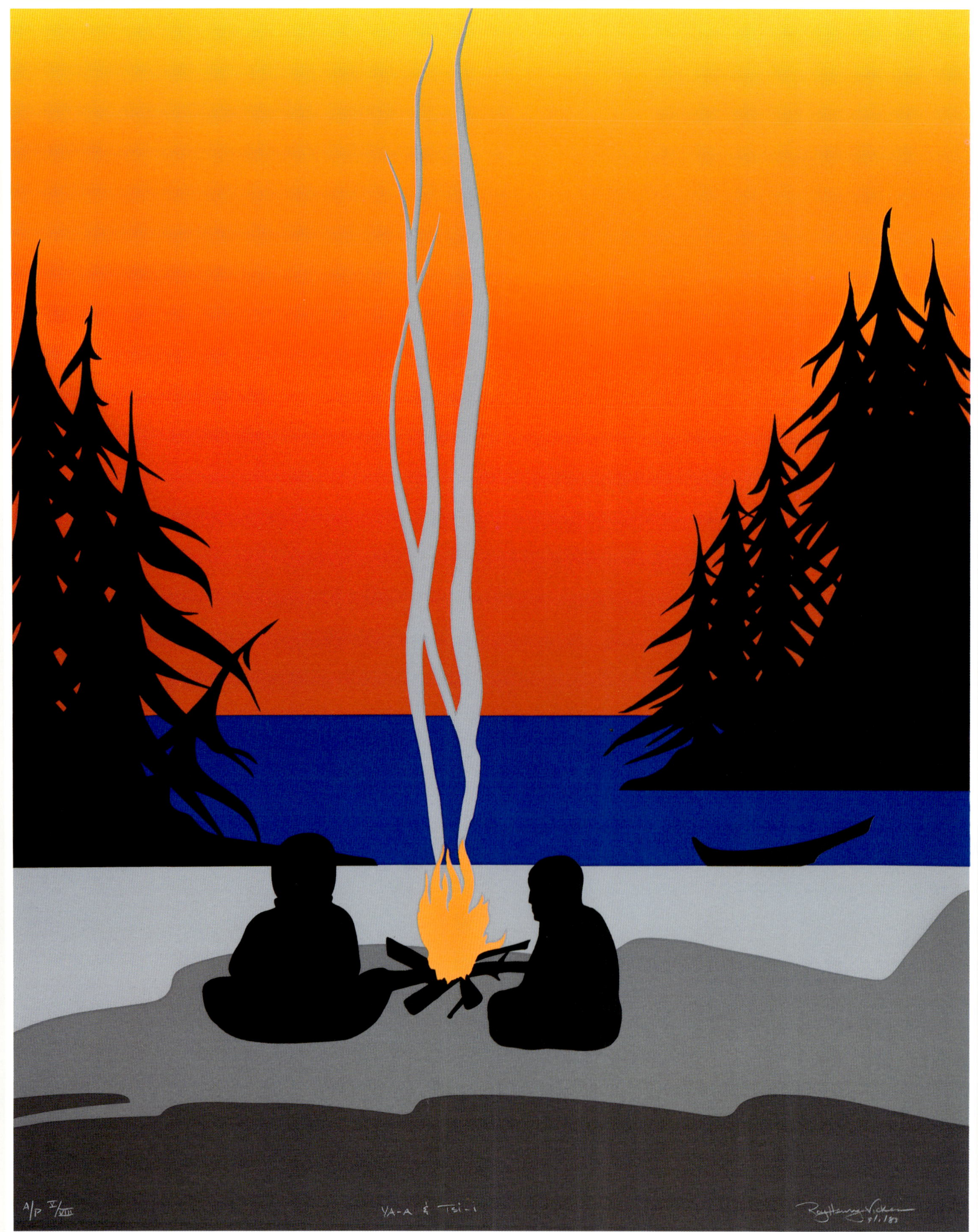
A/P I/VIII
YA-A & TSI-I

To my grandparents
HENRY and KATHLEEN VICKERS
and
JOHN and SOPHIA FREEMAN
and their children, my parents,
ARTHUR and GRACE VICKERS
with love

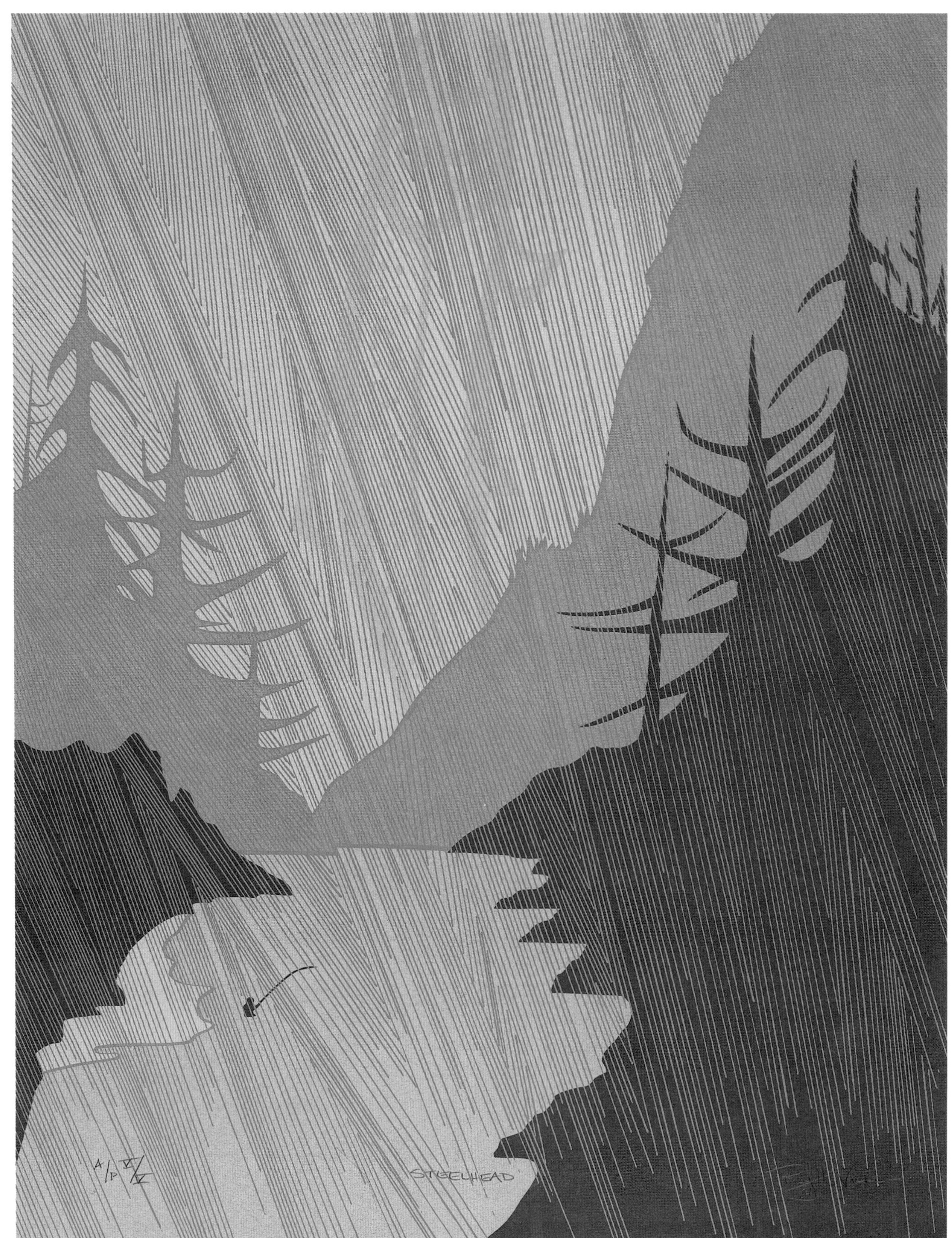
A/P V/V
STEELHEAD

IMPRESSIONS

by Ed Hill

Welcome to the art and adventure of Roy Henry Vickers. Roy's work is a celebration of line and colour that not only depicts the imagery of the West Coast of Canada, but also transmits the feeling that is the West Coast. Roy Henry Vickers is a man of dreams and inspiration and a person with a deep love and respect for his environment.

Roy's earliest expression of artistic talent was in the traditional art of his Indian ancestry. His talent, interest and indeed destiny, led him to the Gitanmaax School of Northwest Coast Indian Art at Ksan, near Hazelton, on the Skeena River. His studies there, coupled with hard work and determination, began to reveal a gift of great potential. Not only could Roy copy many of the fine works of his ancestors, but he could also interpret and create. His work gradually unfolded and progressed to a point where a Vickers' traditional piece is easily recognizable.

His artistic style has since evolved from that of traditional Indian design, to a more contemporary, impressionistic form that has proved unique and appealing to people from around the world.

One of Roy's dreams has been to produce a book of many of his works. He is a unique person in that his dreams become goals, and usually reality. His feelings become paintings and his emotions become lines and colours. This book then, is a collection—not just of pictures, but of sentiments and impressions. It is that part of the West Coast and its heritage that is ingrained in Roy Henry Vickers.

If you view these pages having never been to British Columbia, having never seen the Pacific surf or a cedar snag against the brilliant West Coast sunset, I can assure you that you will touch and experience the West Coast, simply because of Roy's interpretation and artistry. One of his main reasons for printing this volume is to share that feeling, to allow a minute piece of the West Coast of Canada, to come to you wherever you may be.

Haven't we all gazed at a billowing cloud and imagined faces and images hidden within its cotton candy form? Roy, too, allows his imagination to drift and wander, but he carries these visions one step further. Concealed within many of his works are silhouettes, designs and forms. Notice the eagle in the snows of the mountain of 'Megin Lake', find the extra totem pole standing in 'Skedans' or catch the right angle and you'll see the giant steelhead in 'Morning Glory.' I'll leave the rest to you.

One of the very special appeals of a Roy Henry Vickers' print is the participation that it encourages of you, the viewer.

Roy's West Coast Indian heritage has been a strong and important influence in many of his paintings. He feels a sense of loss when he realizes the culture that was, yet he believes that while the culture may be gone forever, the sentiment must be preserved. Traditional song and dance tell of, and reflect the old culture, and now Roy's work preserves even more. He finds and expresses what his ancestors must have felt. He shows with paint and brush what it was that influenced their lives. The West Coast Indian culture was, and is, filled with legend and story. Those legends tell of powerful spirits that guide, protect and direct all of our lives. Hidden in everything around us are spirits and forces.

'Guardian of the Pass' shows just how such legends have come to be. The eagle in the rock has some aura that seems to touch a sixth sense. Roy not only painted a picture of that specific narrow passage on Owikeena Lake, but he locked within the painting a hint of that aura. He found that 'feeling' that must have been felt hundreds and thousands of years ago, and he preserved it for you to take with you to your own home.

Roy's emotions are never expressed louder or in a more obvious way than when he is fishing. His passion for fishing is known to all who have met him or seen his work.

A dark, cool rainforest, shrouded in fog can be a place of almost absolute silence. Only a few song birds and the trickle of the clear, clean water as it finds its way to the ocean, breaks the stillness. Hidden in those pools are cutthroat trout, perhaps salmon on their return trip to their birthplace and soon-to-be spawning beds, or the king of fish—steelhead trout. They ply these waters with silent swiftness and haunt the deep, dark holes. Almost unnoticed on the shore is a fisherman quietly casting, watching, waiting. A loud yell of excitement and accompanying verbal descriptions resounding through the valley, tell all within echo distance that Roy Henry Vickers, artist, has again become a successful fisherman. At such times his emotions erupt.

So important is fishing to Roy that he has dedicated several of his works to that subject. 'Steelhead', 'Cypre River', 'Icy River' and 'Morning Glory' are only a few.

It is fitting that as a collection, these works depict a variety of weather conditions. That is part of the experience. Only those who have stood beside, or in a river in the numbing cold, patiently fishing for hours, can appreciate that Roy's images have captured 'the feeling'.

'Icy River' in particular, presents the solitude and quiet closeness of the West Coast rain forest. Look long enough and you'll see the elusive cutthroat trout hiding in the pool at Roy's feet.

Soaring bald eagles, cool thick rain forests, and the spectacle of a giant grey whale as it breaches—West Coast sights and sounds. A fisherman quietly and patiently pursuing the wary steelhead trout, or a sunset so brilliant only those who see it can believe it. This is the West Coast magic that touches all who visit or live here. Only a select few can capture or recreate the feeling and emotion of Canada's West Coast. Roy Henry Vickers is an artist who has the spirit and heritage of this coast in his blood. More than any photograph, more than any verbal description, Roy is able to paint that feeling. His works are the West Coast. They transcribe through hues and shapes, those intangible emotions that we all feel when we experience this geography—this landscape, seascape and fauna. Roy puts those feelings in colour and line so that those emotions can go with us to all parts of the world, to wherever we may call home.

As the pages of this book turn and the rich colours present themselves to you, take the time to monitor your senses, your feelings, and your emotions. It will become part of you—that feeling that is the West Coast. That's the awe, the sense that you didn't know was there. Once again, welcome to the art and adventure of Roy Henry Vickers.

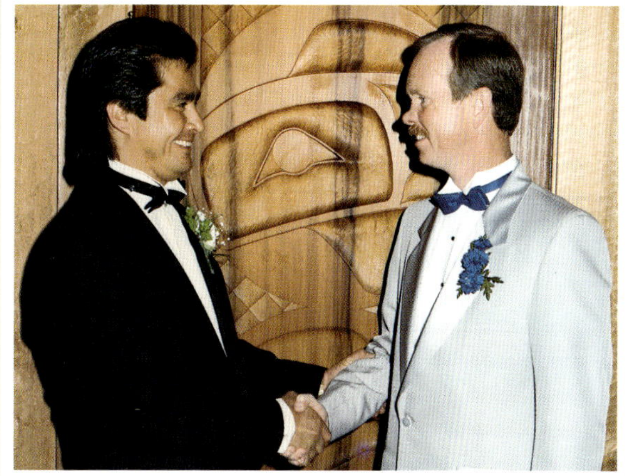

Ian Batchelor

Ed Hill and I are the best of friends. He was best man at my wedding. An artist in his own right, he is developing his own unique style. Whenever possible, we spend as much time as we can chasing the magnificent steelhead.

REFLECTIONS
by Roy Henry Vickers

Kitkatla, the home of my Tsimshian forefathers for better than five thousand years. To this small, isolated village on the North West coast of British Columbia arrived English school teacher, Grace Isabelle Freeman. She would fall in love with Indian fisherman, Arthur Amos Vickers, and together they would embark on a most unusual, often difficult, but always adventuresome life.

It was unheard of for a white, English woman to marry an Indian man in the mid-1940's. The shock though, was soon cushioned by the arrival of myself and subsequently, three more boys and two girls.

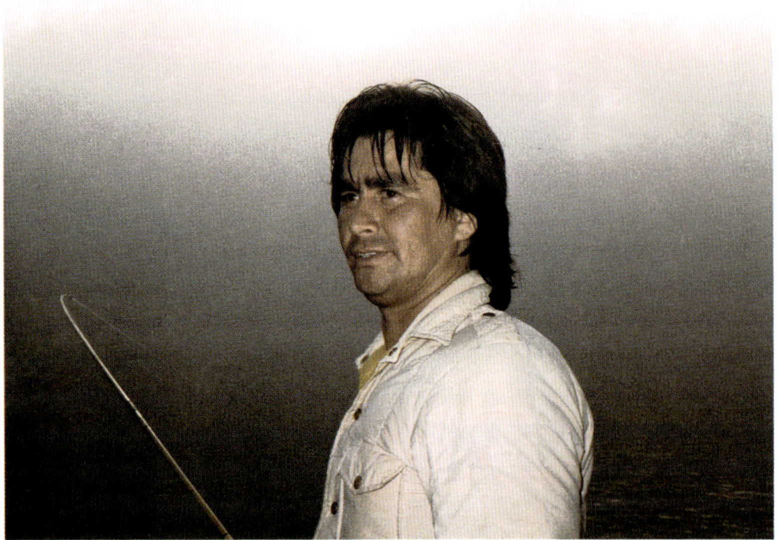

Graeme Wood

I love a grey mist on the sea's face.

The kind of people my parents were also made things easier. My father was a respected fisherman in the village. And the villagers came to love my mother so much they elected her the first white Chief of the Council in a Canadian Indian community. She was also adopted by Matthew Hill, the hereditary Chief of the Eagle Tribe, and we Vickers children enjoyed an extra grandpa.

My earliest recollections are of the feelings of security I had living in a God-fearing home with strict, but loving parents, and of the thrills I shared with my unique environment, and mostly, with my brother Art. He was just fourteen months younger than me, so there was a world of adventure for us to explore together. It is said we were more than two handfuls, always pursuing something out of the ordinary.

As children, our playground was the beach; our theatre was the unfolding of nature around us; and our companions included the village children and pet seals, eagles—even a sea lion.

But there were quiet, alone times too. I spent many an hour at the oceanside with a long, cedar stick and a line attached to the bow of 'Bromada'. I would pretend to be the skipper of my little craft, navigating the dangerous rocks, strong tides and fierce waves that assaulted the beach where we would play all day.

It was a beautiful little boat, hand-carved out of cedar by my grandfather, Henry Vickers and named after my uncle Johnny's real seiner. It might very well have had something to do with my lifelong fascination with the ocean.

Spending summers fishing with my uncle Johnny and his son John, undoubtedly enhanced my love for open water. We used to love to fish with grandfather Vickers too. Aboard his oldstyle gillnet boat, we would answer the call of the sea—the brisk west wind, the sea spray, the cry of the gull and the smell of salt air that never leaves one who is born to it.

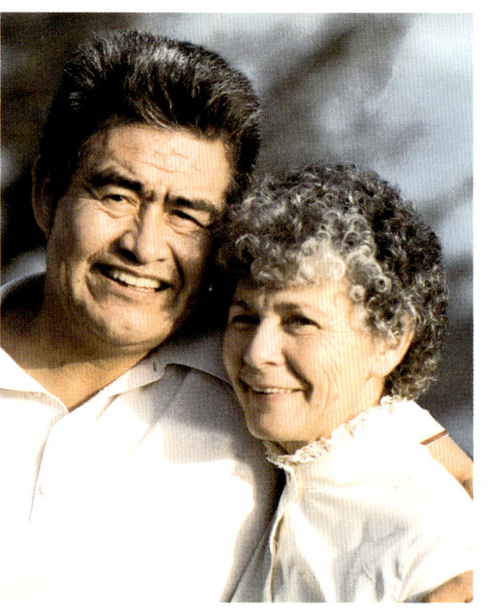

Art Vickers

My mother and father, Grace and Arthur Vickers.

We grew up without electricity or running water. We awoke to the smell of woodsmoke, and sat around the dinner table on dark, stormy, winter evenings in the glow of a coal-oil lamp. We washed in a basin of water heated on the stove, and cut firewood with a handsaw. We carried everything on our backs.

Our only communication with the outside world was a radio run by battery, with CBC childrens' programs on Saturday mornings a very special event.

Mom had two kinds of irons—a fancy one that was kind of scary because it was heated by a flame inside it, fueled by white gas, and the common kind heated on the stove called a flatiron.

I remember the continual excitement generated by the

village's light plant. The power was turned on when darkness fell, and turned off following a warning dimmer at 11:00 pm. It was necessary to conserve fuel because diesel oil could only be brought to the isolated village by the local fishing boats.

But these were not hardships. This was the way of our lives.

The spirit in the community was wonderful. Absolutely everyone played some kind of musical instrument, and we had a marching band. Our large community hall boasted a basketball court, and when a larger generator replaced the smaller one, basketball could be played every Monday, Wednesday and Friday night. Living next to the hall, I remember falling asleep many nights to the drum beat of the basketball as the men's teams played long past our bedtime.

Easter was the high point of life in the village each year. There was a whole range of activities organized throughout the week to celebrate this special time. I remember track and field events, basketball tournaments, boat races, and a large feast at the end of the week where awards and trophies were given to competitors. Friends from other villages were hosted by the people of Kitkatla. It was a very festive occasion.

Easter Sunday was the culmination of the celebrations. We had a beautiful church and an equally beautiful choir that filled the rafters with song. It seemed that the roof would rise to the heavens when the congregation sang.

I remember the old organ whose bellows were operated by a large wheel that had to be turned by hand. The honour student in Sunday School was given the privilege of turning the organ wheel. I got to do it a few times, and it was always a thrill.

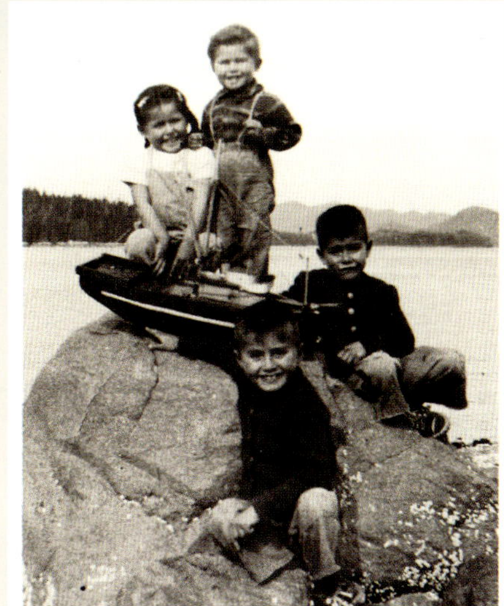

As children, we spent many hours at the oceanside playing with 'Bromada.'

Those were precious times, however all of this was to change soon. Our parents were about to make a decision that would alter the course of our lives forever. To enable the children to have a chance for a 'better life'—more opportunities and a good education, the Vickers family would leave the secluded island.

Hazelton, on the beautiful Skeena River, was to be our new home. Gone was the sea and the seagulls, the boats and the salmon, the beach rimmed with magnificent cedar.

Life was all very new and equally exciting to my eight year old eyes. We found new friends who had horses and taught us to ride. There were cars, and a school bus that picked us up and took us to school each day. We had running water in our house!

People thought Art and I were funny because we called the front of a pick-up truck, the bow and the back, the stern. We were quite confident in ourselves though, and in our ability to learn. After all, we could navigate big boats and foretell the weather by the shift in the wind. We were somewhat fearless, having been so close to killer and humpback whales, wolves, sea lions and even sharks.

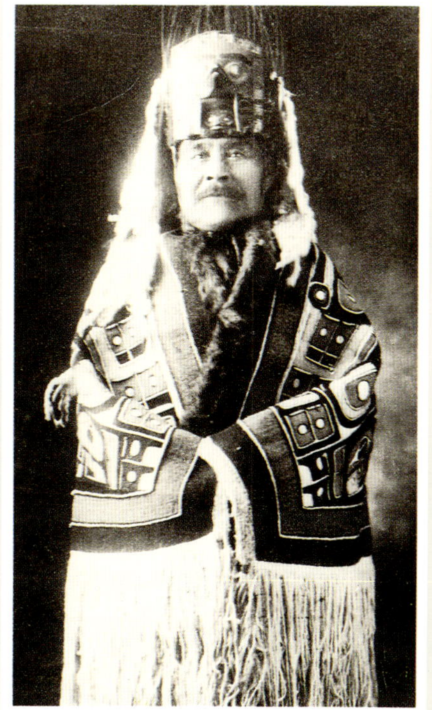

Amos Collinson, whose Indian name was 'Wakais,' was my great-grandfather.

When winter came we were in for a surprise. We had never see that much snow before. We were certain that Santa would appear on a sleigh towed by real reindeer!

One memory of winter involves Art, my sister Margaret, myself, the Vancouver Sun and wolves. The three of us had paper routes, delivering the two-day-old newspapers (it took that long for the train to get the news to our neck of the woods!) to people in Two Mile, a sparse settlement we lived in two miles from the town of Hazelton.

Bitter cold, a blanket of snow smothering everything, and eerie shadows of the trees in the moonlight—that was the setting as we pulled our sleighs along our separate routes.

Our parents insisted that in the winter darkness, one of us go along with Margaret on her deliveries, after we had finished our own. Art helped Margaret one evening. They came home afterwards, very frightened and claiming something had followed them. I was made to look after the route with Art the next night.

He and Margaret had not exaggerated the night before. That evening, fear followed us all the way home as we believed we heard wolves howling in between the creaking of the trees in the wind. The belief was so strong that at one point Art began to run, and when he heard me running behind, he ran faster. He could always outrun me. I did my best to keep up until we rounded a corner in the dark road and felt safe under the light of a lone street lamp not far from our house.

The wonderful aroma of birchwood smoke reminded me that soon we would be safe at home out of the chill of a wintery night, and away from the fear of that experience.

I suspect that was one of the reasons I eventually grew tired of winter, and anxiously awaited a change of season.

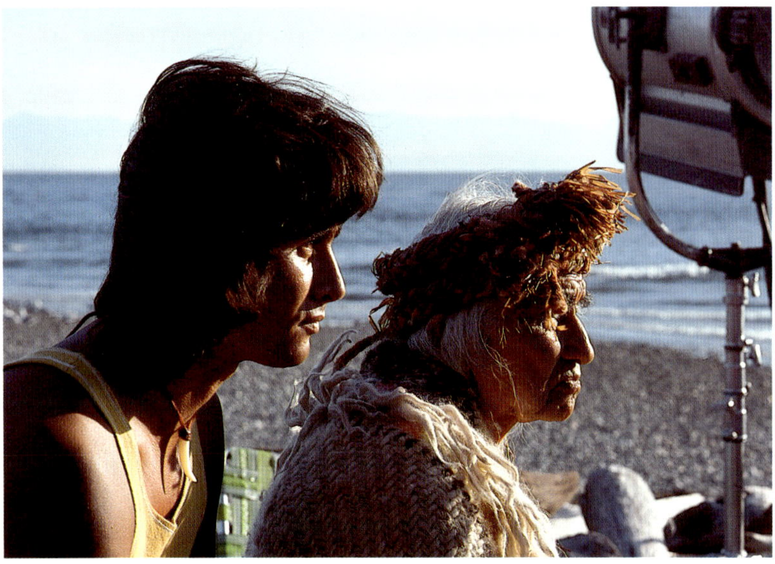

It was a privilege to work with my friend, Chief Dan George.

I think the scent created by leaves unfolding on cottonwood trees in spring subconsciously reminds me of the love and security of family. The peace and comfort that comes over me when I smell this fragrance stems from my memory of springtime in Hazelton.

When summer came and school let out, Art and I would leave our growing family to travel by train and eventually boat, to enjoy a reunion with our cousins, uncles, aunts, grandparents, friends—and Kitkatla.

So it was that in fall, winter and spring we would live on the upper Skeena River, and in the summer, we would reside near the great river's mouth.

That was until I was twelve, when a rancher/horseman asked my parents if I could work for him. He wanted me to learn to ride, train and exercise his thoroughbreds. I would also have to work on the farm cutting, mowing and storing hay. I was allowed to take the job, and for three years I played at being cowboy, jockey and ranchhand.

During this time Art and I joined the Boy Scouts. I soon ended up the Scout Leader of the small troup, and together we learned new skills as woodsmen. It was an exciting day when all of us in the troup achieved the honour of Queen Scout, a distinction of which I am still extremely proud.

By now, the Vickers family was complete: Mom, Dad, myself, Art, Margaret, Matthew, Patricia and Noel—eight in all. It would appear as though we always had the best of both worlds. It occurs to me, however, that we really had the best the world could offer us. Though we were poor monetarily, we were rich in family, relatives and friends.

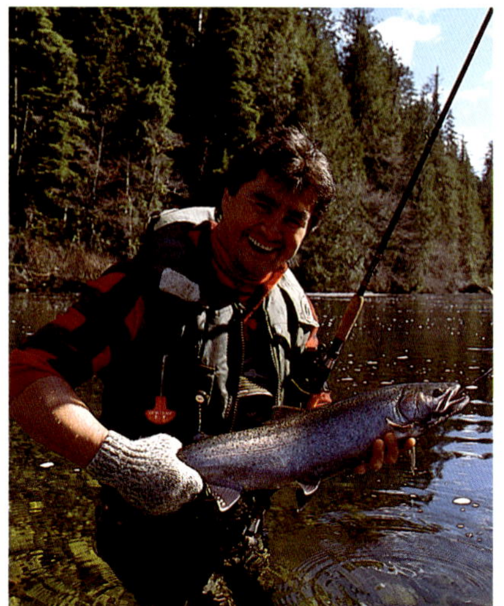

Cameron Young

The reward.

Our move to Hazelton meant new friends. Ward and Jane Marshall, and Jane's parents the Yorks, all but adopted us. People in the community believed we were blood relatives. The kinship between our families continues today.

My early adolescence cemented my relationship with nature. Forays into the forest; fishing with a hook, line and pole to 'work' for trout; and honing my abilities with a gun to supplement our staple diet of moosemeat resulted in my bringing home grouse or rabbit for the table. These were the experiences that represented my youth.

I was sixteen, had a 'real' job for the summer as a carpenter's helper, and had learned to drive our first car when it was decided that the family would move to Victoria.

I made up my mind to help with the move to the city, and then to use my summer wages as tuition to high school at the Prairies Bible Institute in Three Hills, Alberta. With my parents blessing, off I went.

It took less than a month for me to realize that I wasn't ready to leave my family, but it was too late. I had been taught to finish what I started, so I bit the bullet and endured one of the most difficult years of my life.

While there were plenty of activities in Three Hills to keep me busy, I realized that as a growing young man, the segregation between boys and girls was not right for me. The pleasure of dating and friendships with girls was an unknown to me for that year while I went from sixteen to seventeen.

Fortunately, the love of family, and the presence of my uncle Alan and aunt Esther (Mom's sister), and their children, helped me through a very difficult year. The long, cold Alberta winter passed and spring arrived, but there were no cottonwoods in Three Hills to herald the coming months of summer. I yearned to be reunited with my family.

Victoria was a mixed blessing. Our family was a complete unit once more, yet it was disconcerting to be happy at home and to miss my real homeland so much. I longed for the Skeena River Valley and Hazelton. I missed my friends—even the horses. I ached to be back in Kitkatla, on the fish boats and with other family.

In Victoria, I was a young man developing as an artist, but not adjusting at all well from the outdoor life of the North Country to the stress of city living. Through numerous personal trials, I found myself becoming more and more introspective. My soul-searching brought me to the realization that people stereotyped me as an Indian, instead of recognizing me for what I was—a half-breed with both worlds to choose from.

I began to study my Indian roots, and develop a sense of pride in my heritage. Throughout my life, I had always taken the time to draw whatever inspired me. As this new feeling of identity with the Indians of the Northwest Coast grew, so did my interest in their art.

I found myself spending a great deal of time in the British

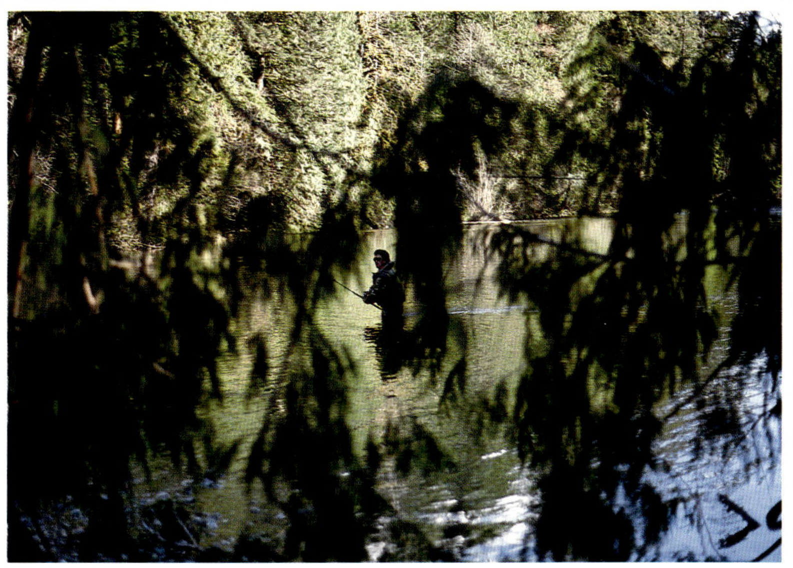

Cameron Young

Fishing gives me many magic moments relaxing in the beauty of our land.

Columbia Provincial Museum where I nurtured friendships with various people involved with ethnology, archaeology and anthropology. All of these disciplines helped me to a better understanding of my personal dilemma. My math, art and social studies teachers were instrumental in helping me complete high school.

It seemed fateful that at this time I met the late Wilson Duff, then curator of the Provincial Museum. He was to have a profound effect on my young life. We met on one of my many sojourns to the old museum in the Legislative Buildings where I used to enjoy seeing the specimens of

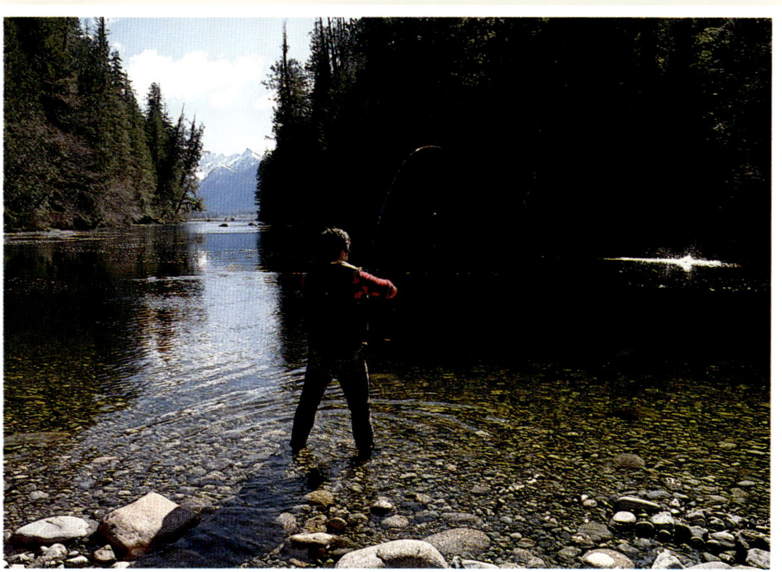

Cameron Young

I thrill to the rush of adrenalin when the fight is on.

wildlife. I was also impressed with the totem poles, canoes and the ceremonial dress of another culture with which I was feeling a strong bond. We became friends and he acted as a great source of encouragement and inspiration for me.

I'll never forget him introducing himself and inviting me into his office. He told me later he had seen me visit this sanctuary many times, and perceived me to be a young man of Indian ancestry, obviously searching for something.

Upon learning that I was a Vickers from Kitkatla, he opened a file drawer and pulled out a handful of papers which shared information on my uncle, my grandmother and my great-grandfather. He was able to tell me that my great-grandfather, Amos Collinson, was Chief of the Raven Tribe, whose ancient Indian name was actually Wakais. He was apparently a Haida man, whose ancestors were from Skidegate in the Queen Charlottes who married a Tsimshian woman. They lived in Kitkatla, nurturing the growth of the most recent branches on my family tree.

The information that I gathered regarding my heritage from Wilson Duff offers enough material for a book by itself. There are intriguing stories of relatives who were carvers and painters. Some belonged to the Killer Whale

Clan, others to the Eagle Clan, and so on. Suffice it to say, I have been blessed with a heritage that is rich and fascinating.

But even with this new understanding of my family's history, my destiny was not obvious. My art was more of a release rather than a career choice.

Attempting to focus on my future, I became a fireman in Saanich for six years which included a year and a half as an ambulance attendant. I developed lasting friendships through those experiences; my work-mates were like brothers. The hardships and human suffering I evidenced had a devastating effect on me though. I needed more meaning in my life, and my art was where I found it.

Those were the factors that helped me decide to enroll in the Gitanmaax School of Northwest Coast Indian Art at Ksan. It was an exciting time for me, and I will be forever grateful to those teachers and classmates who encouraged me to grow and reach those goals that sometimes we have trouble even defining.

In 1974, at age twenty-eight, I began my life as an 'Indian artist'. I was soon to realize that making a living creating 'traditional' works of art could be very frustrating.

I knew I was not a traditional Northwest Coast Indian, nor was there a traditional culture still alive in the Canadian

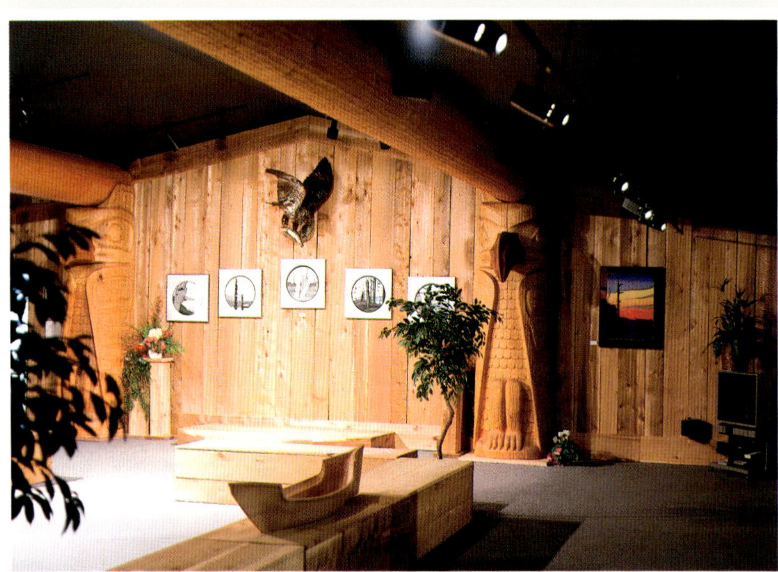

Ian Batchelor

Thanks to many people, Eagle Aerie Gallery is a beautiful creation.

cultural mosaic. I was a contemporary artist who knew academically of the old Indian culture and carried part of that culture within me. The beginning of my artistic expression then, was fraught with the desire to be original and relevant to the world I lived in.

Some of my earlier pieces, 'Creation of Eve' and 'Tuaq—The Only One' illustrated my need to be different. While adhering to the colour and shapes of Northwest Coast Indian Art, I strived to show movement and dimension. Had I been wiser or more aware, I could have seen in 'Oola! Oola!', for example, the emergence of a style and worked with it. I have come to realize how wisdom comes from experience and age.

This struggle for a personal style—indeed identity, could perhaps explain why I felt so disillusioned at this time. While I constantly recalled my art teacher's advice to strive for originality, and received exceptional encouragement from my marvellous friend George Clutesi, things just weren't working out.

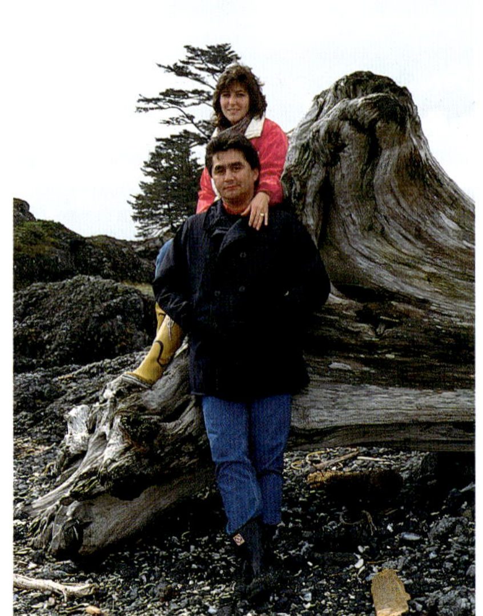

Cameron Young

We love spending time at the beach.

I found myself spending too much time walking the streets of Vancouver and other cities in the Northwest, selling my prints from shop to shop, and not painting and carving enough. I tried using an agent to sell my work, but felt too removed from what I was trying to accomplish. It seemed there was no one who cared how I felt or to listen to what I wanted to say. I felt abused—a commodity related only to money-making. My personal life was also in shambles.

I thank God for friends, especially Bill and Art, two businessmen who advised me to take a break and go fishing. The three of us entered into a partnership, bought a gillnetter from my uncle Clarence and I became a commercial fisherman. Bill was to become a close friend, and his professionalism was to have a profound effect on me. Most of all, he cared.

The year was 1980, and I found myself still fishing, but on a different boat. My brother Art had just commissioned a beautiful forty-two foot troller that he wanted me to skipper. So I left the gillnetter to my uncle up north and fished the West Coast of Vancouver Island.

Bill and I kept in touch, and I continued to take his good advice until I lost him a short time later. I can still get in touch with the pain of that loss, but his positive influence will always be with me.

Those two years of fishing reunited me with Mother Nature and the ocean. Forgotten was my artistic career—the days were long and filled with hard work. I did carry a camera onboard though, and loved to capture the awesome beauty of the sea. I was stunned by the changes in light and colour and the reds, yellows and blues in those exciting sunsets. There was great peace in being rocked to sleep by the constant movement of the waves—as if I was a child snuggled in his mother's bosom, content with the world.

However, these experiences rekindled a desire in me to create, and I found myself longing to be back at my drawing board.

The end of that last fishing season found me tied alongside other fishboats in the picturesque harbour of Tofino. An acquaintance, Henry Nolla, convinced me to stay the winter so we could carve together.

I soon discovered that Tofino had everything I enjoy in life: great fishing, the ocean, and a long drive to the city! I believed I had found my little corner of the world. I felt settled for the first time.

My newly found contentment was to have a significant effect on my art. I felt a freedom to paint whatever inspired me, and I was soon able to express myself in a unique style.

With the support of the community, for which I will always

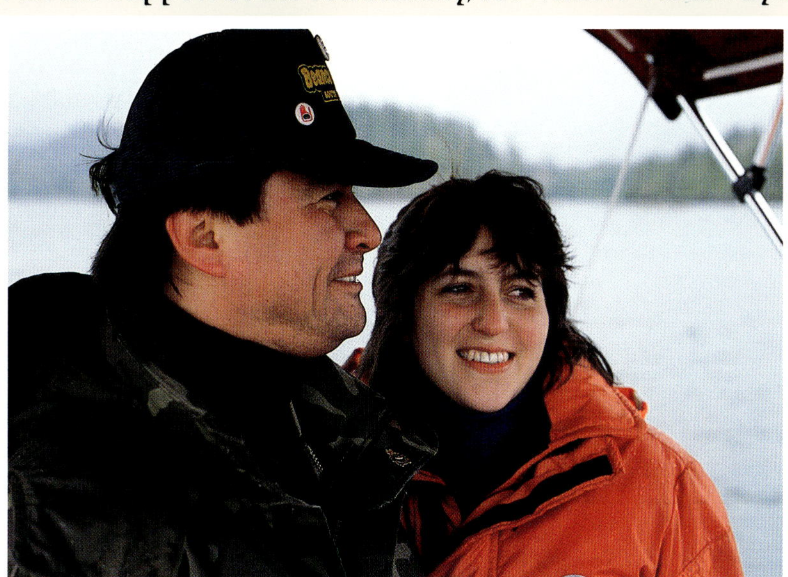

Cameron Young

We enjoy many hours at sea.

be grateful, I opened a temporary gallery. It was very successful and allowed me to realize a dream—to design, build and operate my own gallery fashioned after the traditional Indian longhouse.

I am extremely proud of Eagle Aerie Gallery. The compliments I have received from the tens of thousands of visitors from around the world and the commitment I enjoy from a truly dedicated staff, make me realize what a fortunate man I am.

My life is rich. I am healthy, happily married and a successful artist. I am proud of my heritage and confident that if I use the lessons I have learned wisely, my future will be secure and very exciting. The harmony I feel – outstanding friends, an incredible environment to live in, and the closeness of family, is exceptional. I have experienced a SOLSTICE—a turning point, and I anxiously look forward to the challenges ahead. I am truly blessed.

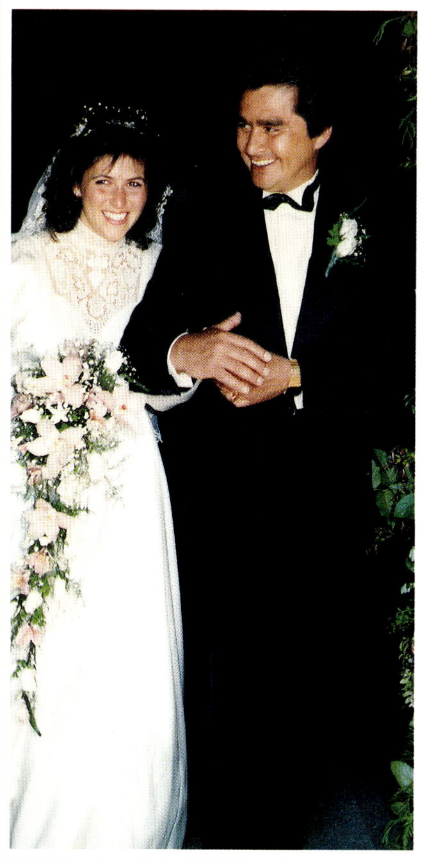

Ian Batchelor

My beautiful bride, Rhonda has made me a happy man.

Roy H. Vickers

THE OWL

I HEARD THE OWL CALL MY NAME—the book, was the seed which set into motion the flow of creativity resulting in my rendition, THE OWL. I had the desire to design an owl, and so began to think of owls that I had seen and experiences that I had concerning owls. My memory took me back to my teen years in Hazelton. The season was winter, a time when I turned my attention to rabbits.

I had learned how to set a snare for rabbits by locating their 'runs' or trails. Once I found their route, I would set the snares as I had been taught and then check them each day. My luck was usually very good—which takes me back to owls.

There were times when I would find a snare tripped, but empty. The only trace of the rabbit were the signs of struggle, blood and a few tufts of hair. This amazed me. I finally went to 'Uncle' Ward Marshall, always an expert trapper, and shared my frustration. He told me it was owls who were stealing my rabbits!

I always wished I could catch an owl in the act, but I was never that lucky. I do remember cornering little owls in the barn. When they had no way of escaping they would bluff you by fluffing up their feathers, stooping low and shaking themselves, as if to attack you. This would always bring a chuckle. As boys, we would leave them alone to let them make good their escape.

I actually did capture that owl—using paints and brush—as he stooped, with head low, tail high and feathers fluffed. It was his 'Owl Dance' that he did for me.

(Released 1975)

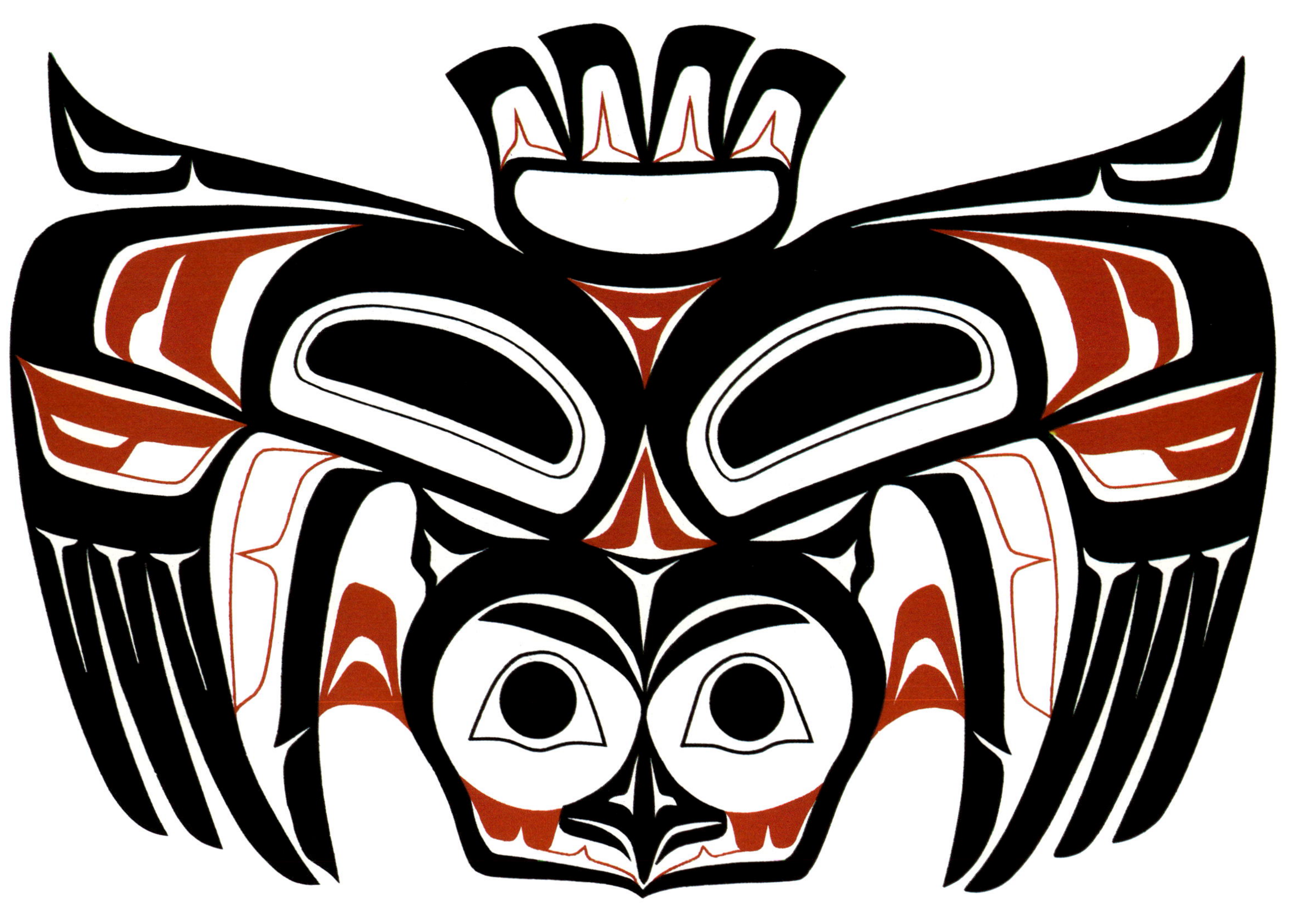

OOLA! OOLA!

This work was inspired by my thoughts of what it must have been like to hunt seals before the white man came to the Northwest Coast. The Indians on the coast hunted from canoes, and used bows and arrows as well as harpoons, clubs and spears. I chose to portray the sea-going hunters utilizing bows and arrows.

The day is blustery, with a frequent downpouring of rain that is so commonly experienced. The stern man is holding the canoe back as the wind tries to blow them forward too quickly. The hunter cries "OOLA! OOLA! (SEAL! SEAL!)" and the bowman readies for the shot.

(Released 1976)

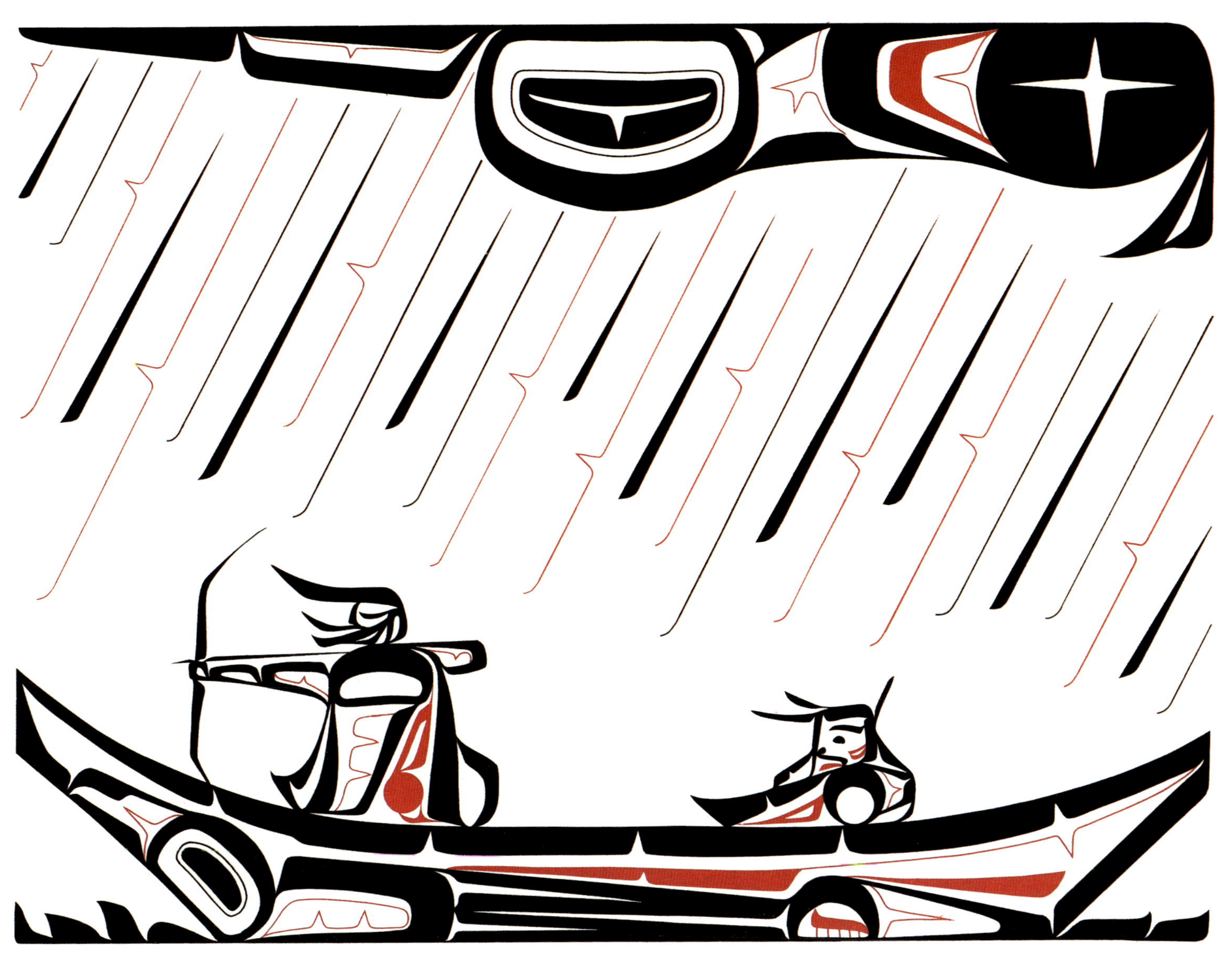

WEGET AND THE WEGET LEGEND

This is the legend of The Origin of Daylight. It is about a big man, and the hero, WEGET. Weget is the son of the Great Chief in the Queen Charlotte Islands. He grew up with extraordinary powers to hunt, fish and do battle.

His father gave Weget a raven's skin. When he wore the skin he was able to fly. He was also given a pouch containing salmon roe, small stones and the seeds of berries.

At this time, the world was still in darkness.

Weget left the islands and flew over the ocean towards the mainland. When he grew tired, he dropped stones from his pouch into the ocean, and they became islands on which he could rest. When he grew hungry, he sprinkled the salmon roe into the water and spread the seeds upon the soil. From this time on, there were all kinds of fish in the ocean and berries on the land.

Weget was not happy with the darkness and remembered a house in the heavens that belonged to the Chief of the Heavens. The Chief guarded a box in which he kept the Ball of Daylight. Weget believed that if he could marry the Chief's daughter, he would inherit the box and bring light to the earth. So he went to the heavens.

(continued)

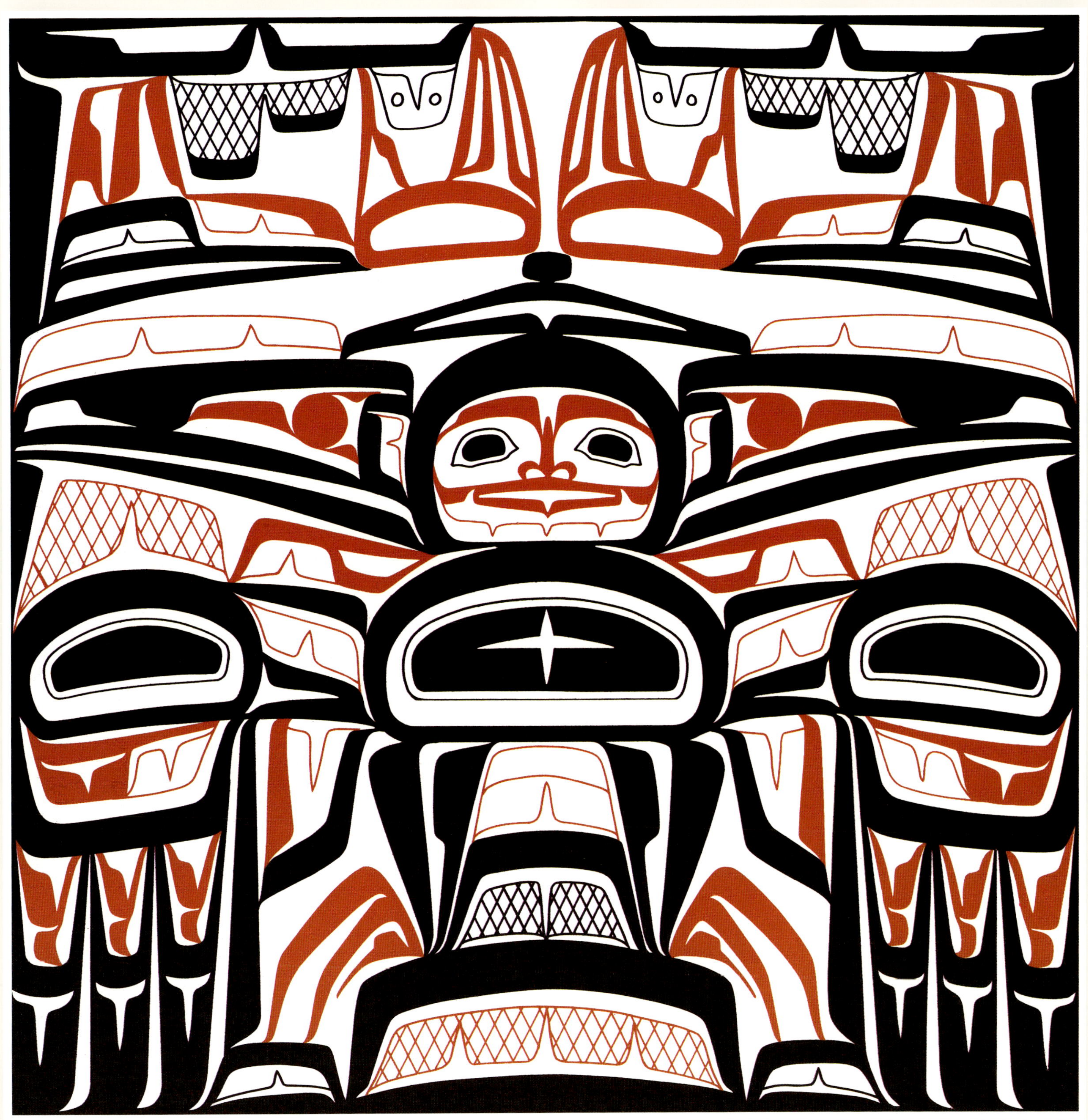

It turned out that the Chief discovered Weget's plan and would not let him marry his daughter.

Weget then plotted to turn himself into a pine needle and drop himself into the stream so that the Chief's daughter would gather him up when fetching water. The daughter drank the transformed Weget and became pregnant.

As the Chief's grandson, Weget grew and was able to get the box with the Ball of Daylight. He put on his raven's skin, took the box and flew back to earth.

The world was inhabited by only frog people—spirits who could work and gather food in the darkness.

Weget was hungry and asked these frog people for a few of the many fish they were catching in the river. He asked four times and four times the frogs refused, so Weget broke open the box and flooded the earth with daylight.

The North Wind blew the frog people down the river to the ocean and turned them into stones.

From that day on, all of the Tshimshians, and others, could fish and gather food.

(Released 1978)

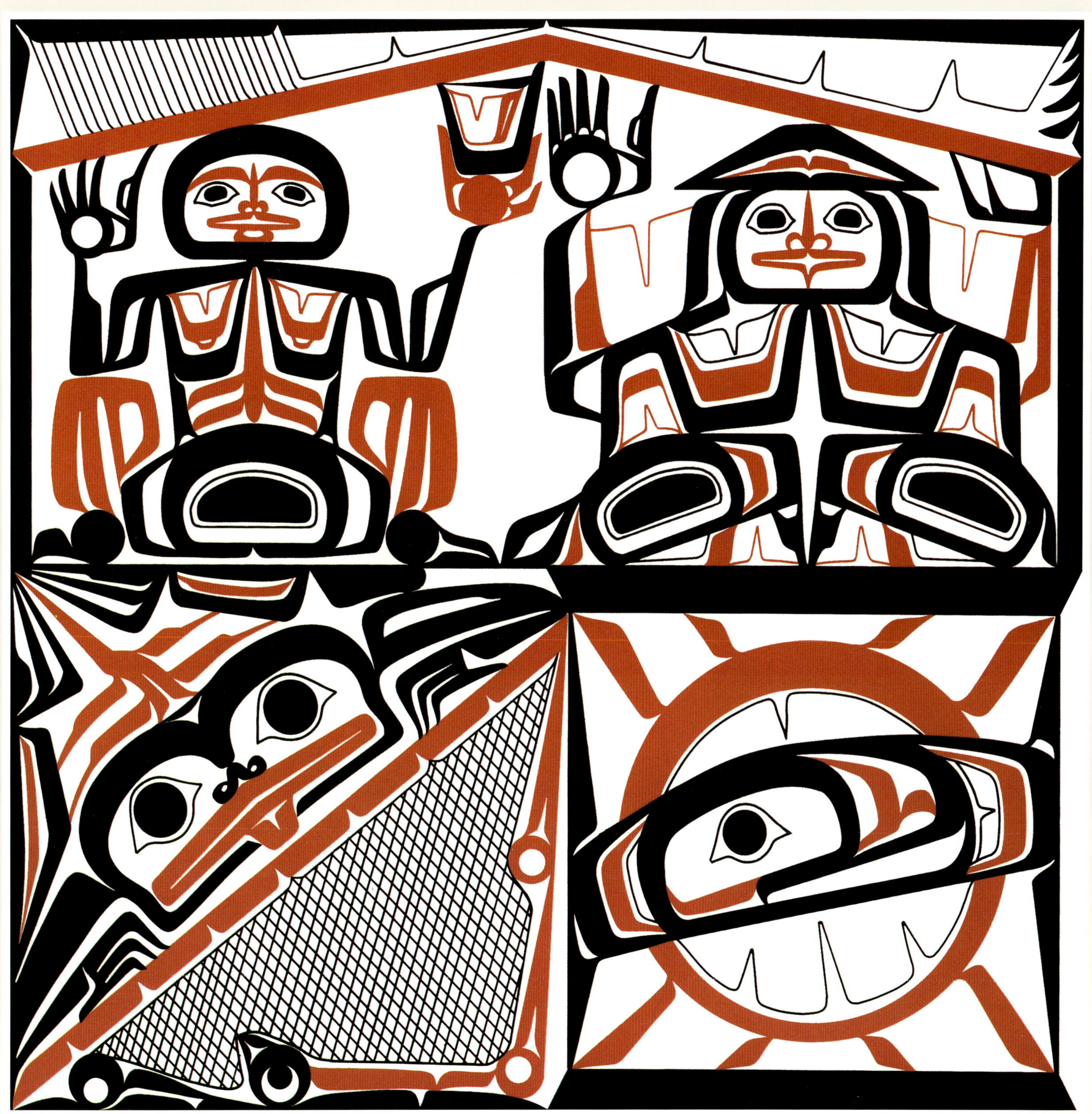

MY GUARDIAN ANGEL

Angels, or spiritual guards, are written and spoken about often in most every culture on the earth. Accounts in the Bible are many. In one, an angel wrestled with Jacob and then disappeared. In another, an angel appeared and told Joseph that Mary would have a baby. It was angels that told the shepherds of Christ's birth.

To portray MY GUARDIAN ANGEL, I chose to dress him in the armour of an Indian warrior. He wears a helmet or hat of wood that has a wooden face guard. On both the protector of the head and face, is painted the eagle. This eagle warrior also wears a breastplate made of wooden slats to which are attached the wings of an eagle. I have placed my guardian angel on a cloud so that he can watch over me.

(Released 1978)

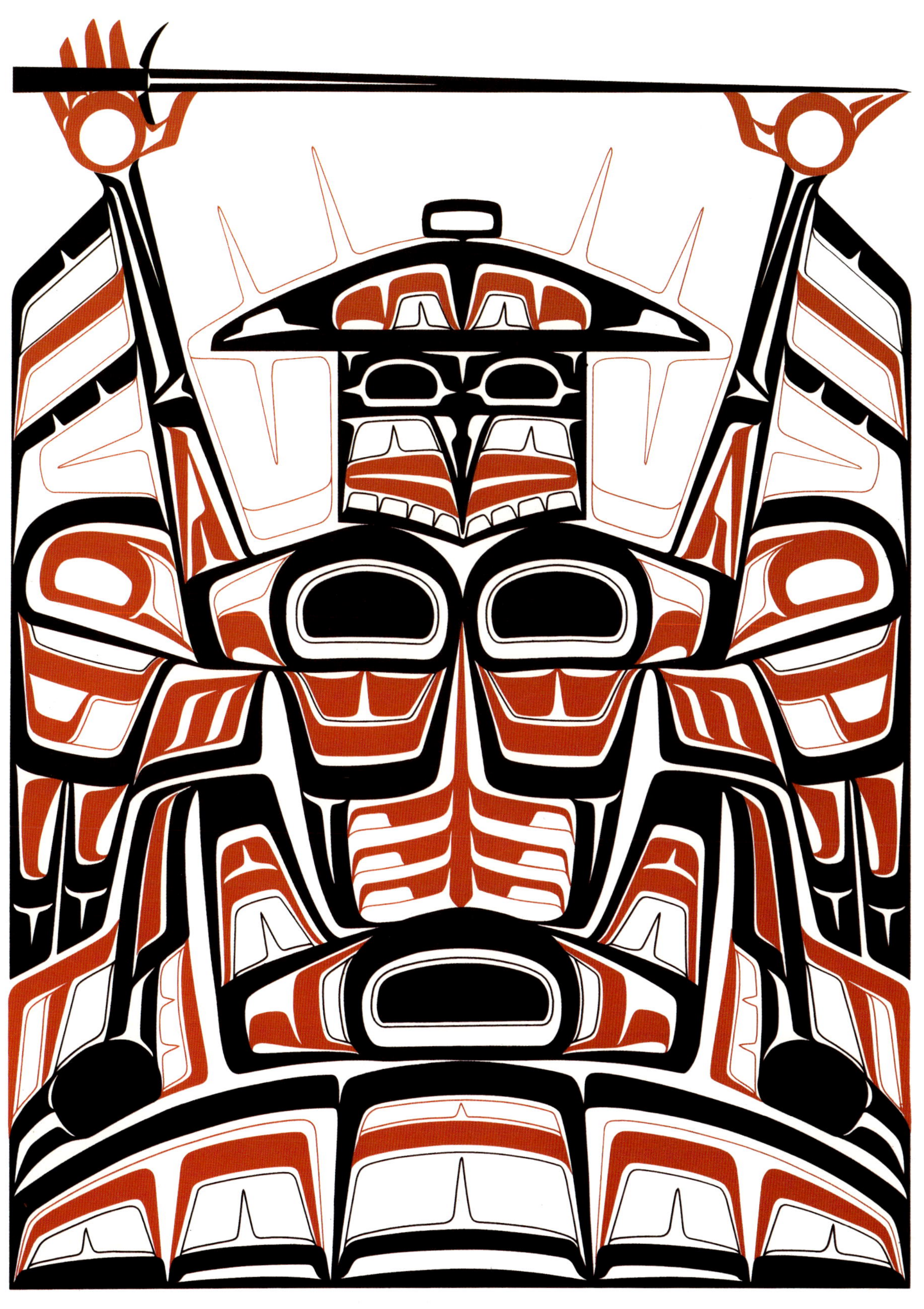

EAGLE—FULL CIRCLE

The eagle is my family crest and this particular creation represents the full circle that I have come in my development as a Northwest Coast Indian. The title of this crest is EAGLE—FULL CIRCLE. It is dedicated to the man, Wilson Duff, whose influence was and still is important in my life. The image 'EAGLE—FULL CIRCLE' is published in the book, *The World is as Sharp as a Knife,* an Anthology in Honour of Wilson Duff.

(Released November, 1982)

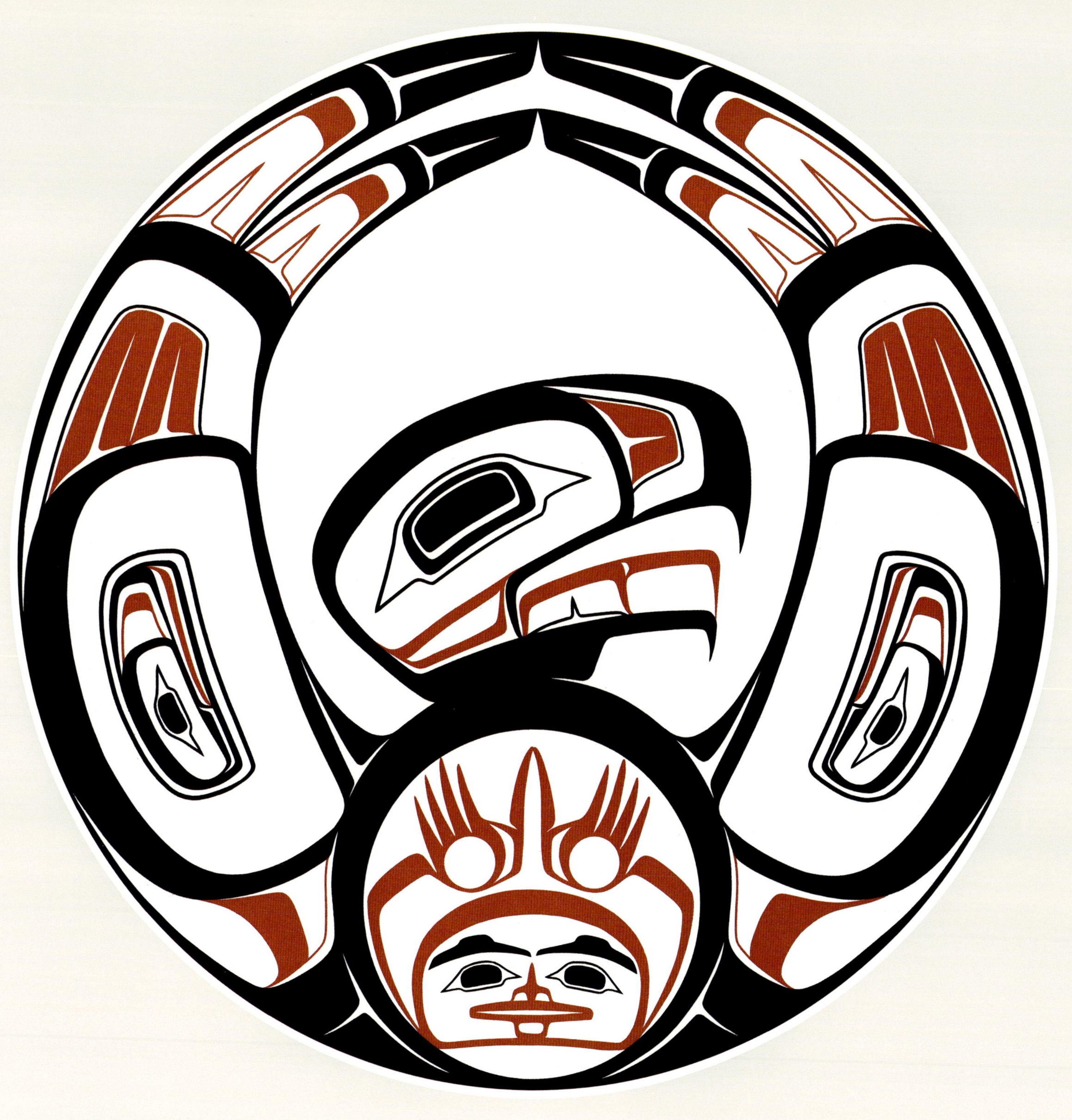

EAGLE DANCER

Being born into the Eagle Clan has caused me to design many eagles. Having lived on the coast all my life has also given me many opportunities to observe eagles in many different situations. These experiences include a pet that friends had when I was a boy in Kitkatla.

I had been working for years in a rigid and traditional Northwest Coast Indian style that required symmetry or static forms. When I did this piece, I wanted to capture some action and asymmetry. Eagles tend to hop as they spread their wings to fly away. This movement is often copied by Indian dancers. It was with this in mind that I created EAGLE DANCER.

(Released 1979)

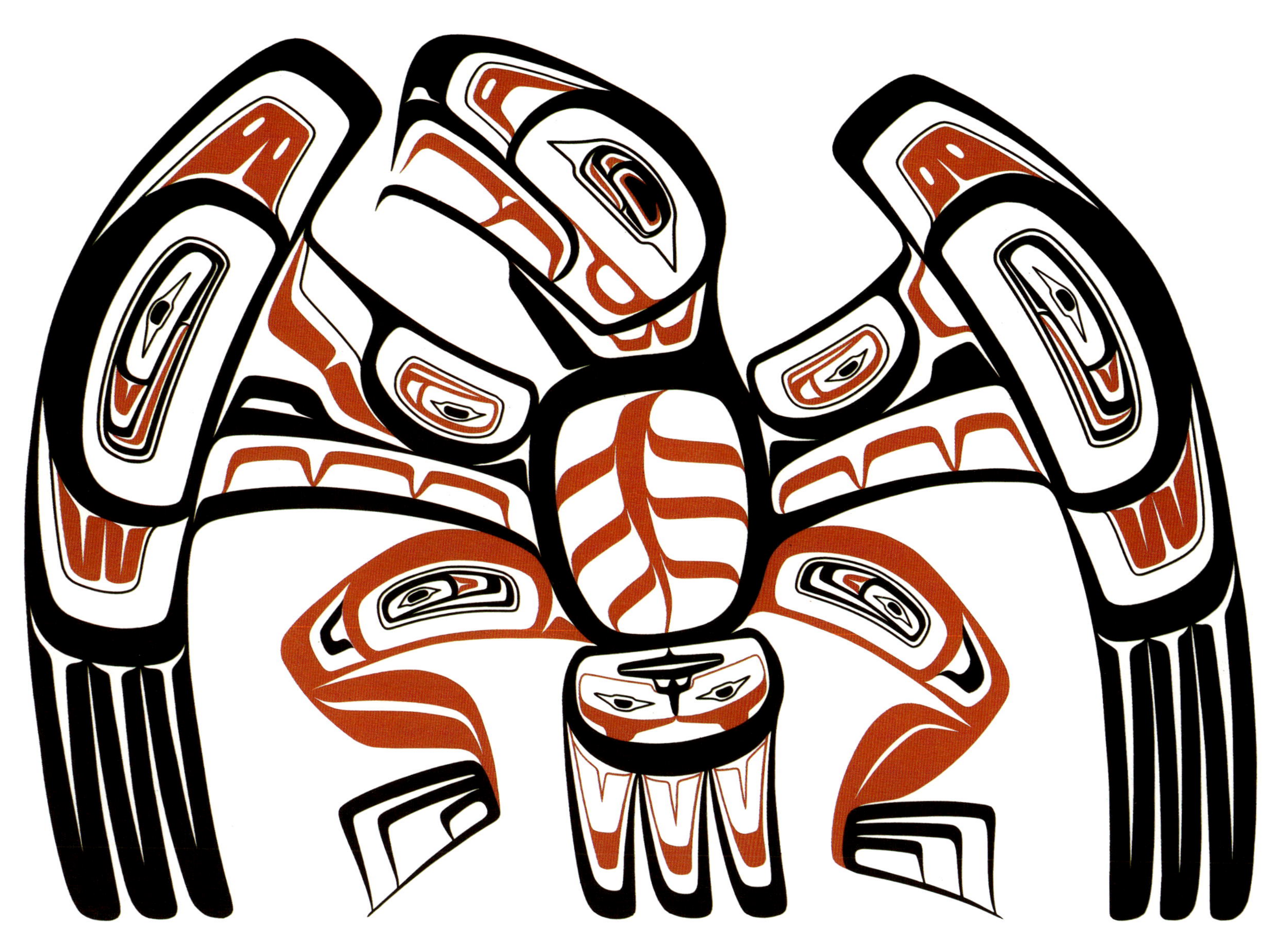

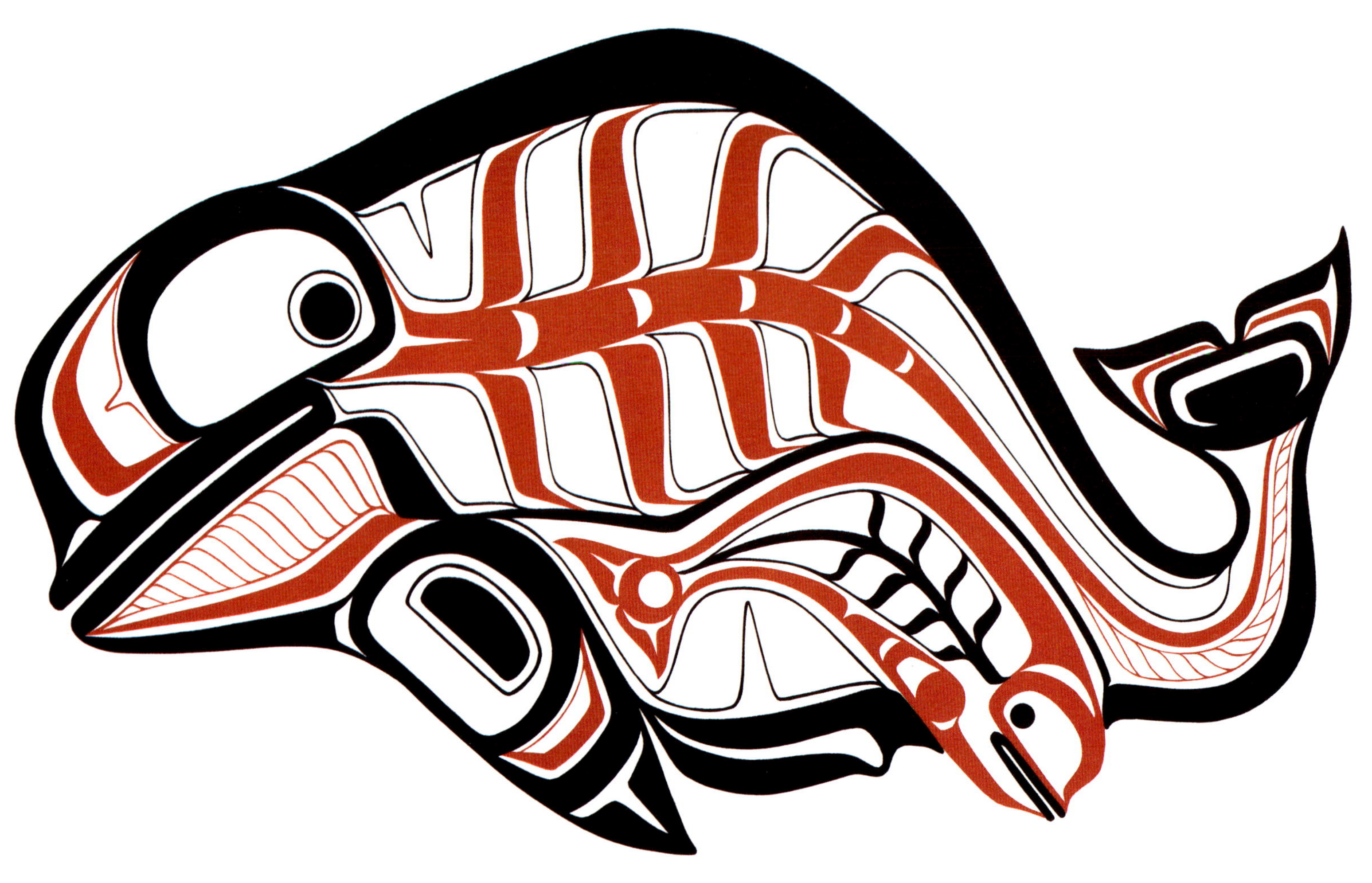

TUAQ—THE ONLY ONE

I have made many visits to the Vancouver Aquarium in Stanley Park to enjoy insights into that gigantic world beneath the ocean's surface. There have been many exciting events at the aquarium, not the least of which was the birth of a beluga whale!

It seems that a recent acquisition of a female was actually two whales, for the beluga whale called Cavna was pregnant. Cavna gave birth to a male baby, a first for aquariums. I remember the National Film Board recording the entire birth for the world to see.

And so it was that we had a young beluga male named Tuaq. It is an Inuit word meaning 'The Only One'.

Tuaq died that fall of 1977 and the world mourned. My love of whales and this unique event have moved me to paint TUAQ—THE ONLY ONE.

(Released September, 1977)

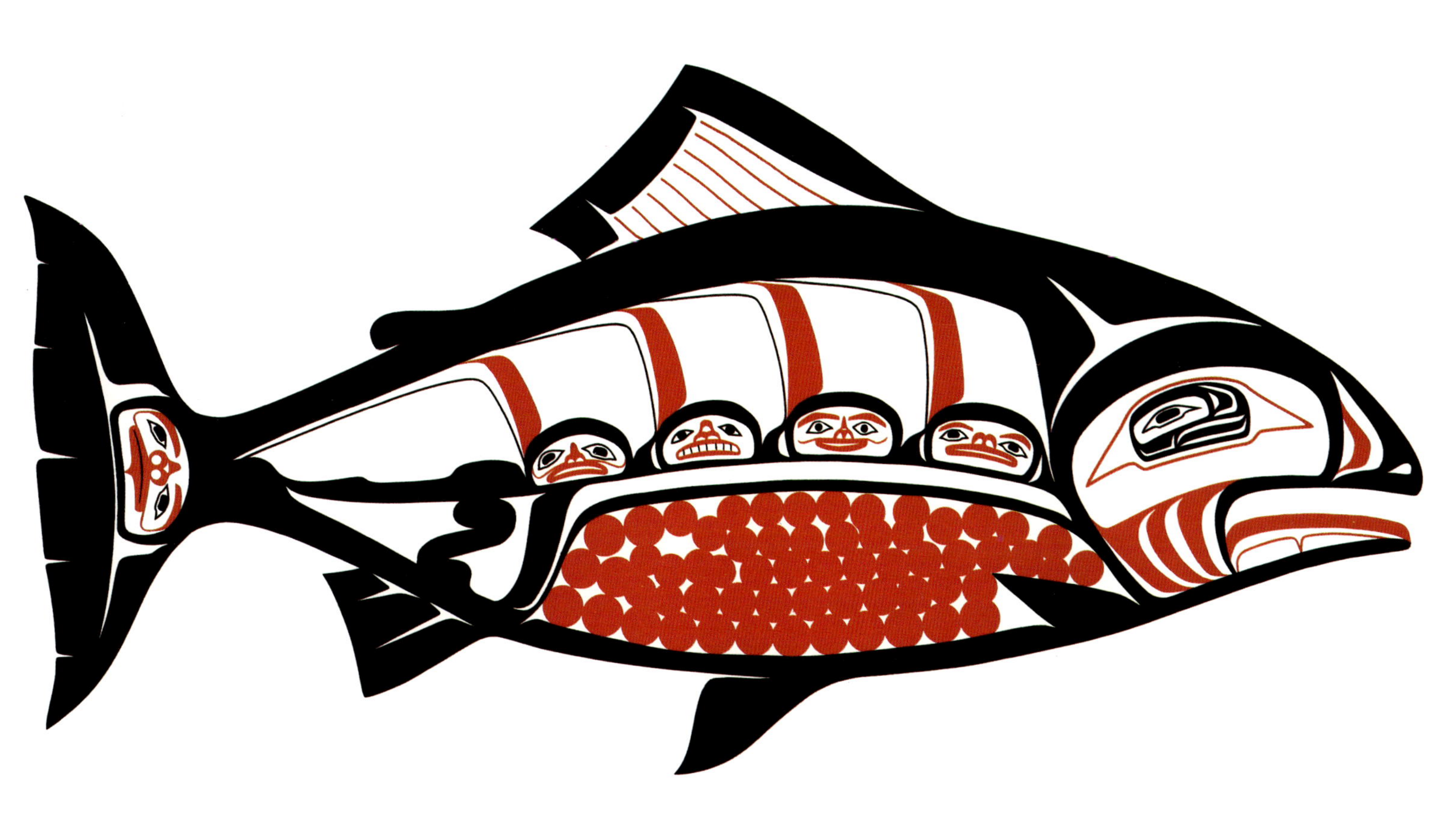

SPRING SALMON

After spending two years on the ocean following in the wake of my ancestors, it was natural for me to want to create in a painting, the largest of all salmon, the spring salmon. It was an eye opener for me to take a sabbatical and work as a commercial fisherman for that period of time. I especially enjoyed the summer I fished alongside my uncles and other fishermen from Kitkatla.

I realized, however, that my art could not be ignored forever, and that I should get back to what I did best.

SPRING SALMON, then, is representative of my lineage and of that experience. The four faces represent my great grandfather Arthur Amos and myself—from the head of the salmon to the tail. The face in the tail represents the generation that follows me. The red circles are roe which indicate that the salmon is female from which comes all future generations.

(Released 1979)

FULL MOON

The evening was one of those spell-binding ones during the autumnal equinox, with a full moon rising over the beach. I put down my brushes and gazed at the huge sphere. Giving in to a compelling urge to walk, I stepped out into the crisp night air that was filled with the sound of the gentle waves rolling onto the sandy beach at my feet.

I contemplated the whales returning to their winter home and the story I had heard about the moon being a woman who had won the heart of a young warrior. The scent of a beachwood fire on the night air turned me back to my paints and brushes.

When sleep finally calmed my soul in the early hours just before dawn, there on my table lay a painting of FULL MOON. In it, she smiled delightfully down upon the faint outline of a whale's tail, just before it slipped silently beneath the waves.

(Released 1979)

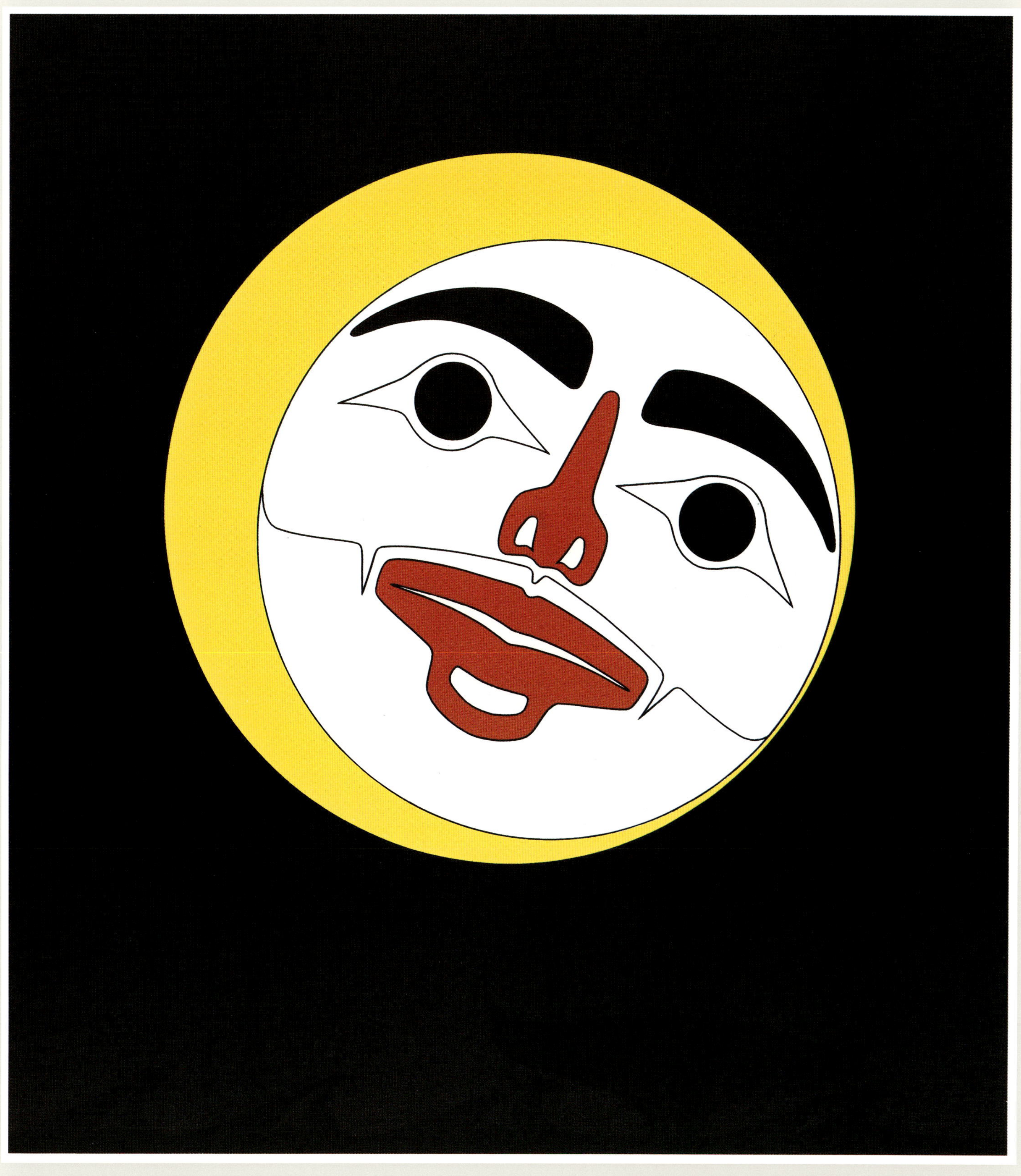

THE CREATION OF EVE

As an artist, I have an ever-ready eye for good works by other artists. There is one person in particular whose work I find fascinating—Albrecht Durer. I saw his rendition which illustrates the Biblical account of the Creation of Eve. It inspired me to create the same scene from the mind of someone who could only work with the traditional shapes and colours of Tsimshian art. I used the same method of representing the human body and its parts as I would a bird or a fish, or any other animal. I have portrayed Adam lying on the ground and Eve emerging from his rib cage. The spirit of God has been mentioned throughout the Bible as being represented by a dove, and so God is represented here as a bird hovering over THE CREATION OF EVE.

(Released February, 1977)

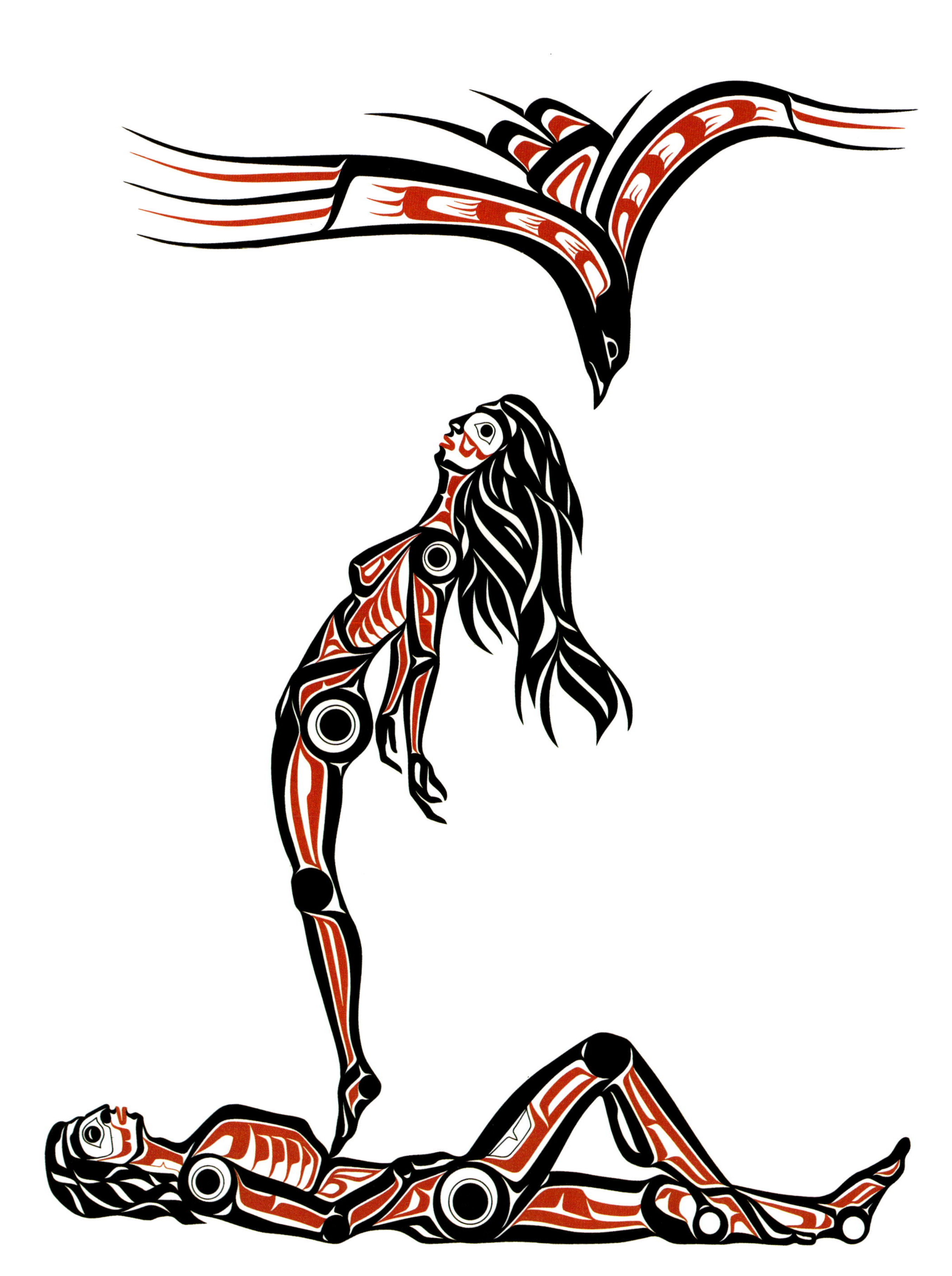

RAVEN DANCER

The inspiration to paint RAVEN DANCER came from close observation of Northwest Coast Indian dancers and dancers from the Pacific Ballet Theatre of Vancouver. It was truly a bicultural creation, unique to British Columbia.

For the Northwest Coast Indian artist, both the rhythm and movement of music and dance are intimately associated with two-dimensional design. There is a constant flow of movement reflected in the undulating formlines of all the art. The discipline of adherance to the traditional forms of this ancient art is reflected in the power of the performer as he readies himself for the first steps.

(Released September, 1982)

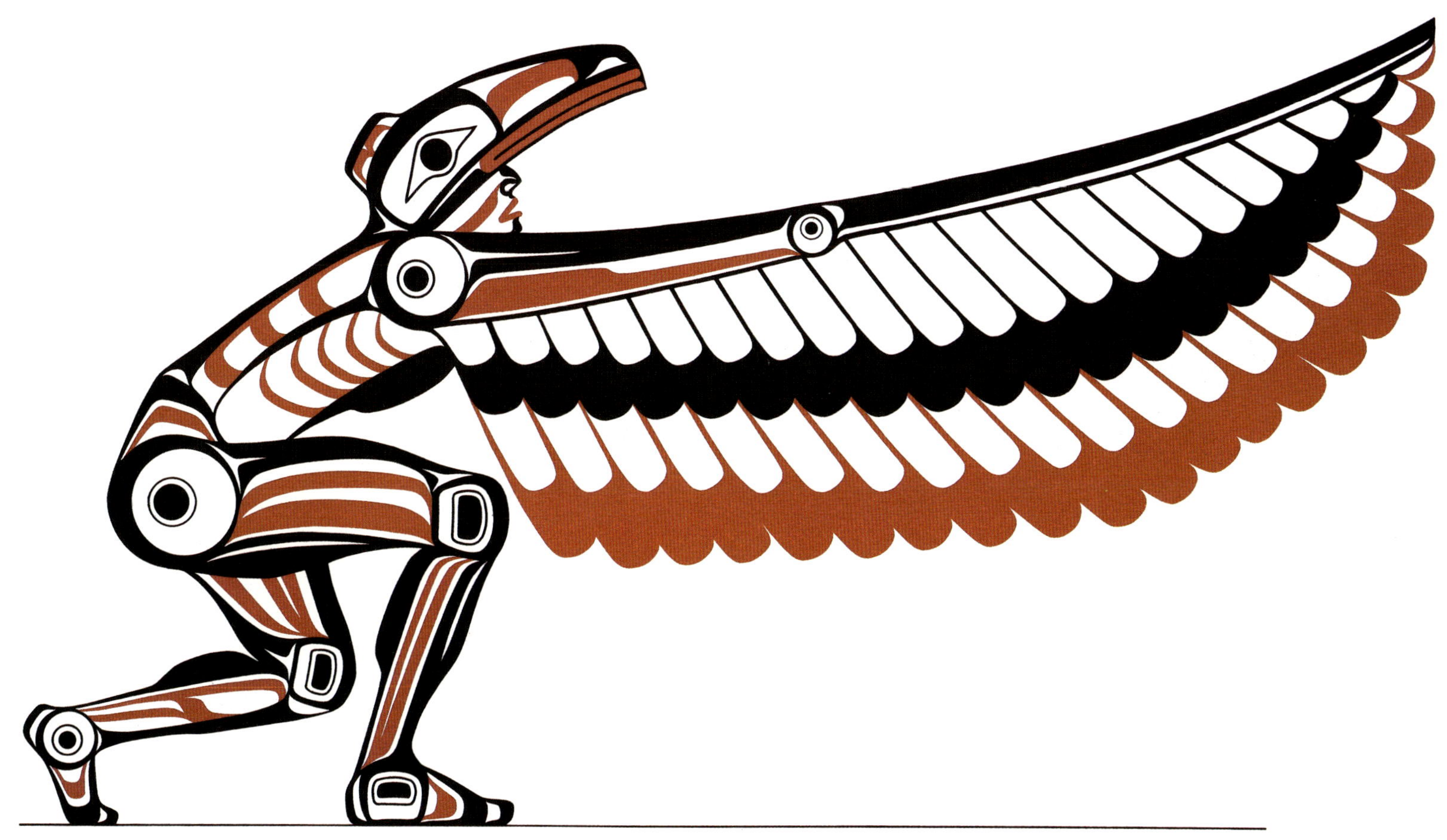

THE LOON

'The Loon's Necklace' is one of the first Tsimshian legends I have heard. It has been written and recorded by many different people in as many versions. Basically, it is about an old blind hunter whose sight is restored by a supernatural loon.

The loon dived under the water with the old man on his back. When they surfaced the old man's sight was restored.

Upon reaching the shore, the old man threw his shell necklace to the loon in appreciation. The necklace landed around the loon's neck, with some pieces breaking off and scattering over the loon's back. To this day, the loon proudly wears his friend's gift.

The beautiful haunting cry of THE LOON always brings to my mind the ancient legend of my people.

(Released November, 1982)

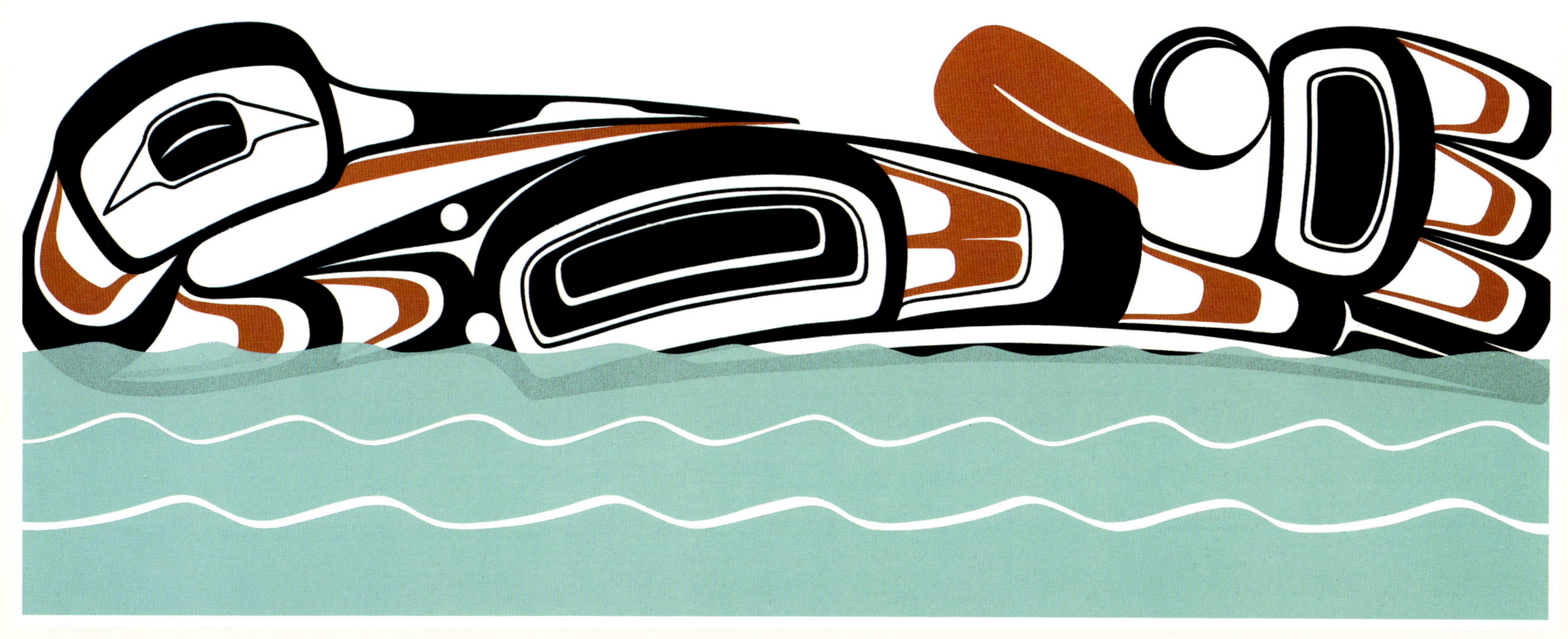

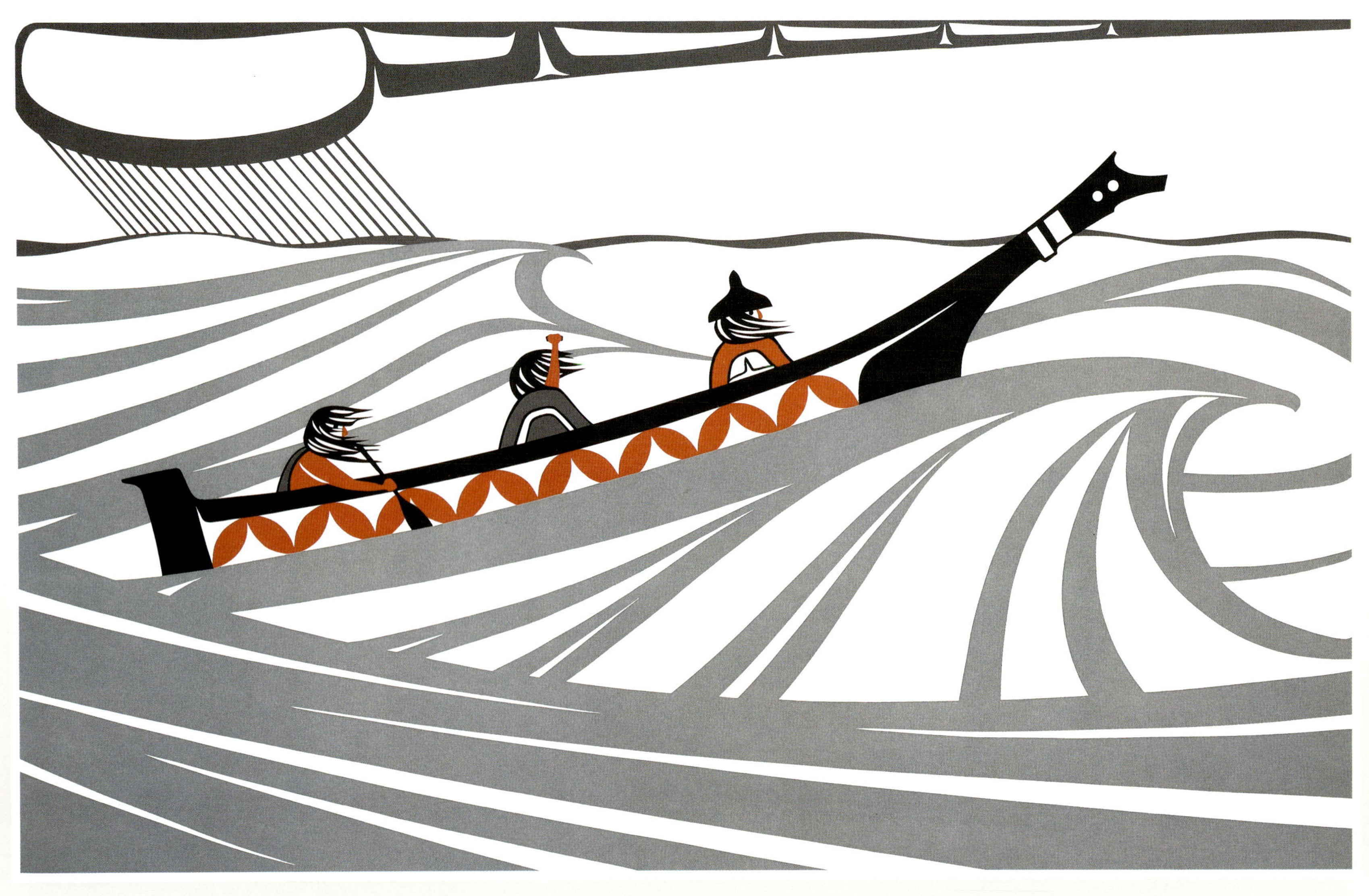

THE WESTCOASTERS

The Indians who live along the West Coast of Vancouver Island are direct descendants of a race of people who have occupied the land for thousands of years. These brave mariners navigated the open ocean of the North Pacific in hand-hewn, cedar canoes long before the arrival of the European. They knew intimately the perilous area of the West Coast referred to as 'The Graveyard of the Pacific'.

The original inhabitants of this coastline hunted the mammoth whales for centuries. Now the introduction of advanced technology has almost brought the whales to the verge of extinction.

I have lived and worked with the people on the West Coast for years and have come to respect them. THE WESTCOASTERS is a tribute to the courageous and indomitable spirit of the West Coast People.

(Released September, 1982)

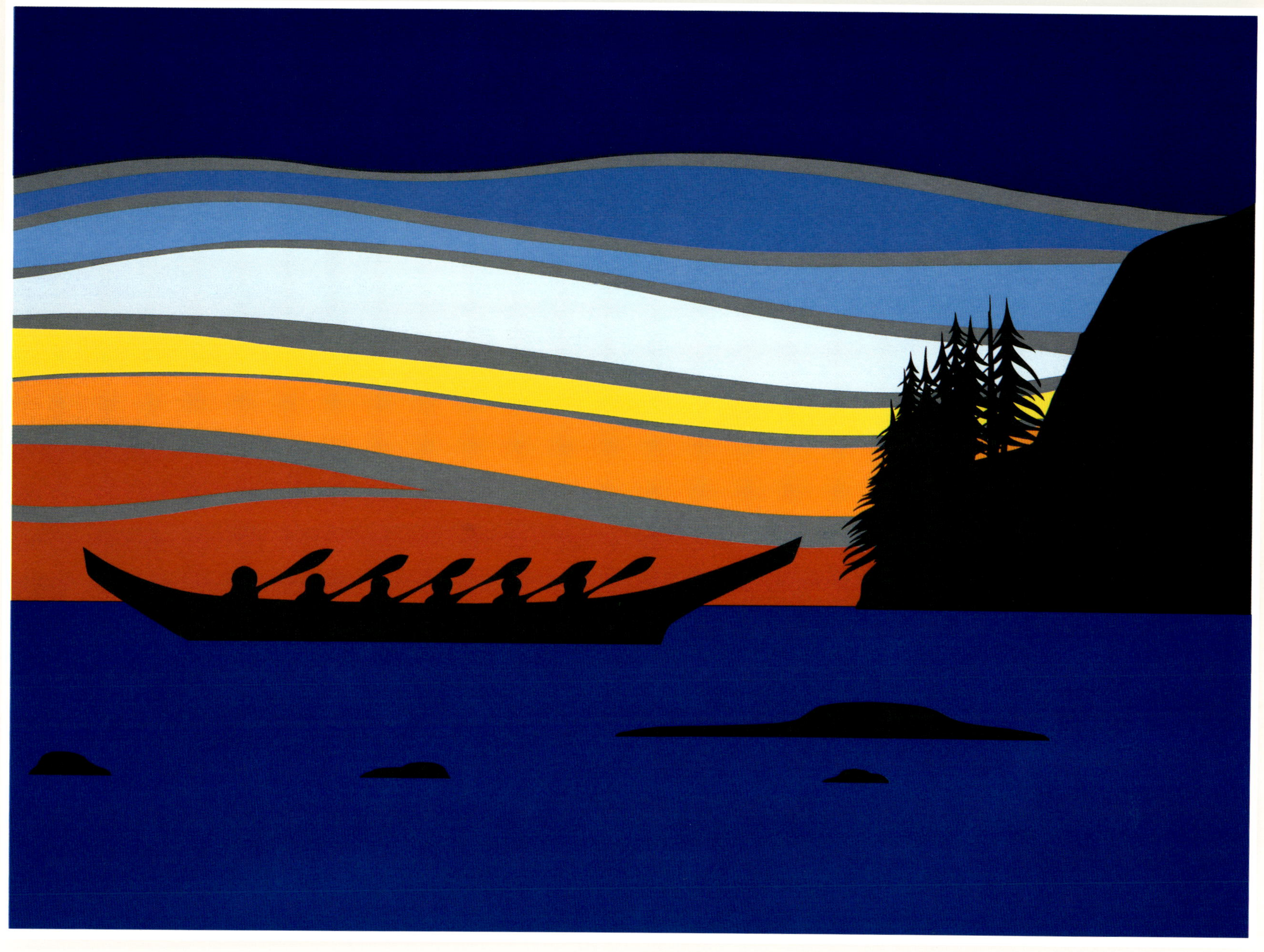

WESTCOAST SUNSET

I had the occasion to paddle a canoe from Prince Rupert to Kitkatla one summer, following a route that was used by my ancestors many times. I left the harbour at the wrong time, and had to face adverse tides at the mouth of the Skeena River and down the channel to the village. I wished at that time I could have learned something of the seamanship of my ancestors prior to the voyage. In time—about seventeen hours—myself and a friend finally arrived at the village just at sunset. It was this memory that inspired WESTCOAST SUNSET.

(Released 1982)

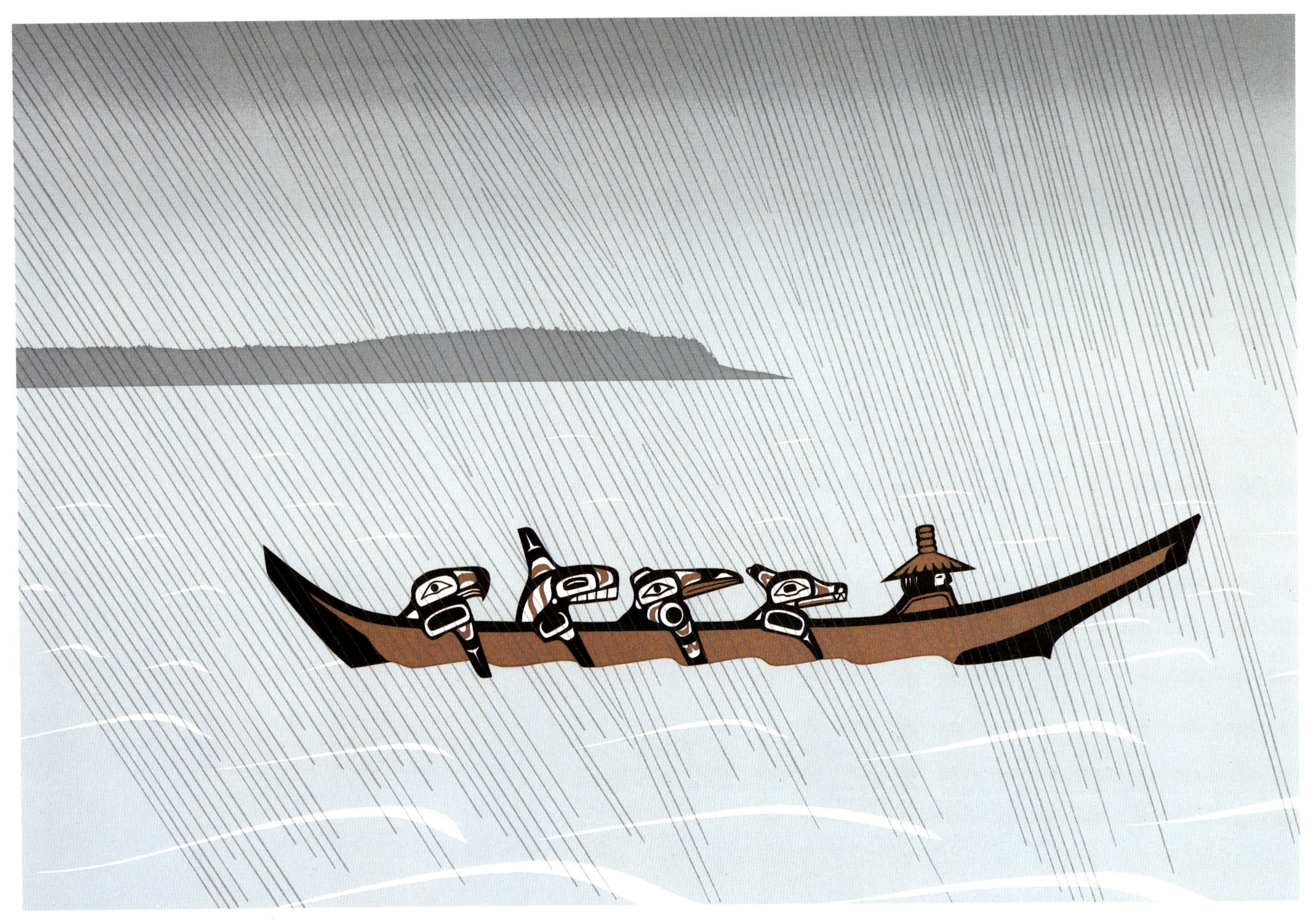

CHIEF'S DREAM

The Tsimshian canoe has inside it a chief and four supernatural chiefs. CHIEF'S DREAM is set on a stormcast, rainy autumn day. The landfall is the northern tip of Banks Island. The water is Principe Channel just south of Kitkatla. The figures in the canoe are the supernatural chiefs of the four tribes of the Tsimshian people of Kitkatla: The Eagle, Raven, Whale and the Wolf. The young chief dreams of going to a potlatch with supernatural chiefs powering his canoe towards Kitkatla.

(Released 1982)

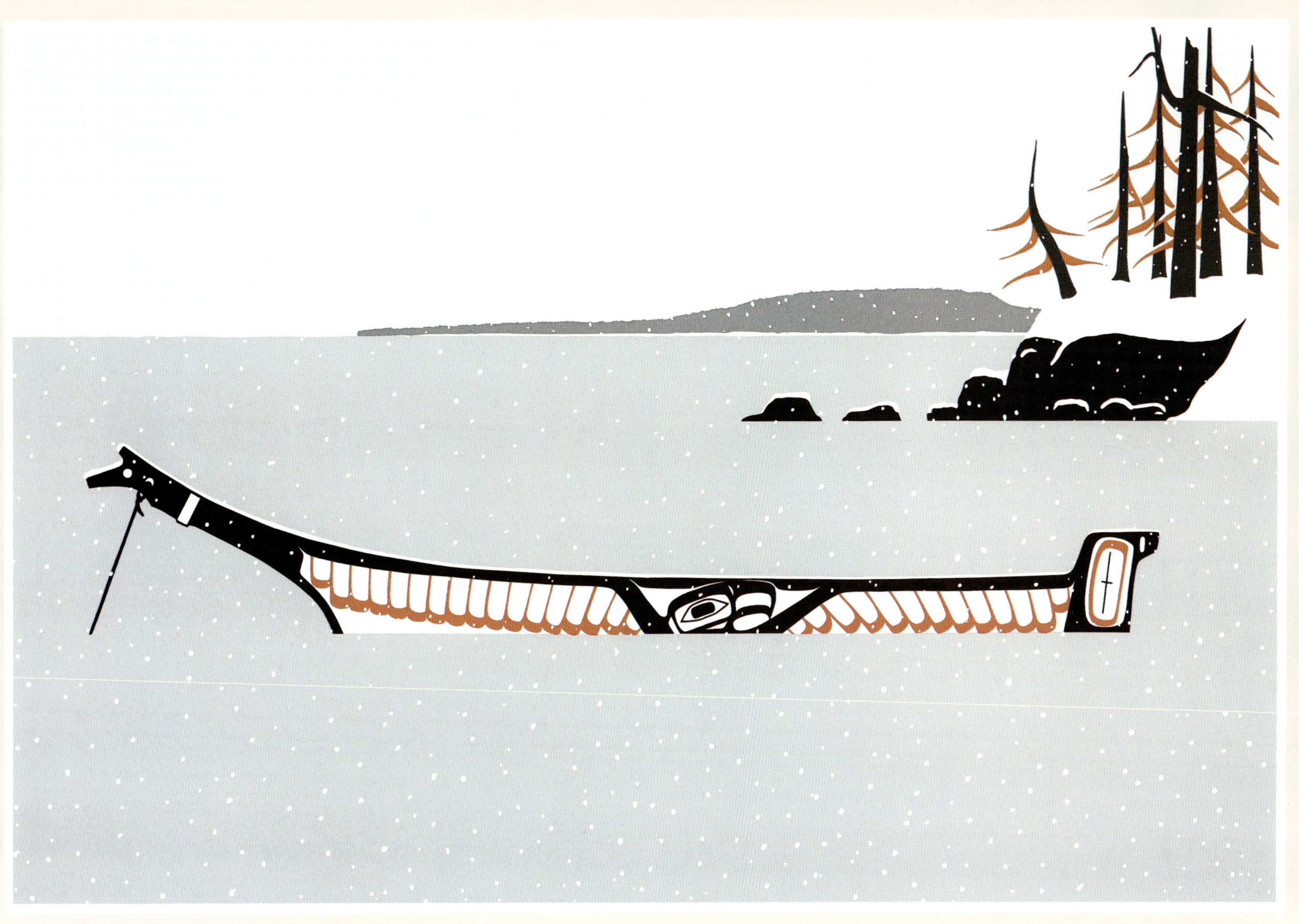

ELEGY

ELEGY—for a young man, an old man, and a way of life . . . The empty canoe at anchor is a sign of trouble and death.

This piece is a tribute to a very dear friend, Bill, to my grandfather, Henry Vickers, and to the passing of the old culture that used to exist on this coast.

(Released 1982)

CANADA GOOSE

The Canada Goose has inpsired generations of Northwest Coast Indian artists to recreate its image in many forms of wooden bowls, ladles, and other utilitarian art objects. This rendition of CANADA GOOSE in a circle is symbolic of the annual cycle the geese go through as they announce the changing of the seasons to the people of the Northwest Coast.

(Released May, 1983)

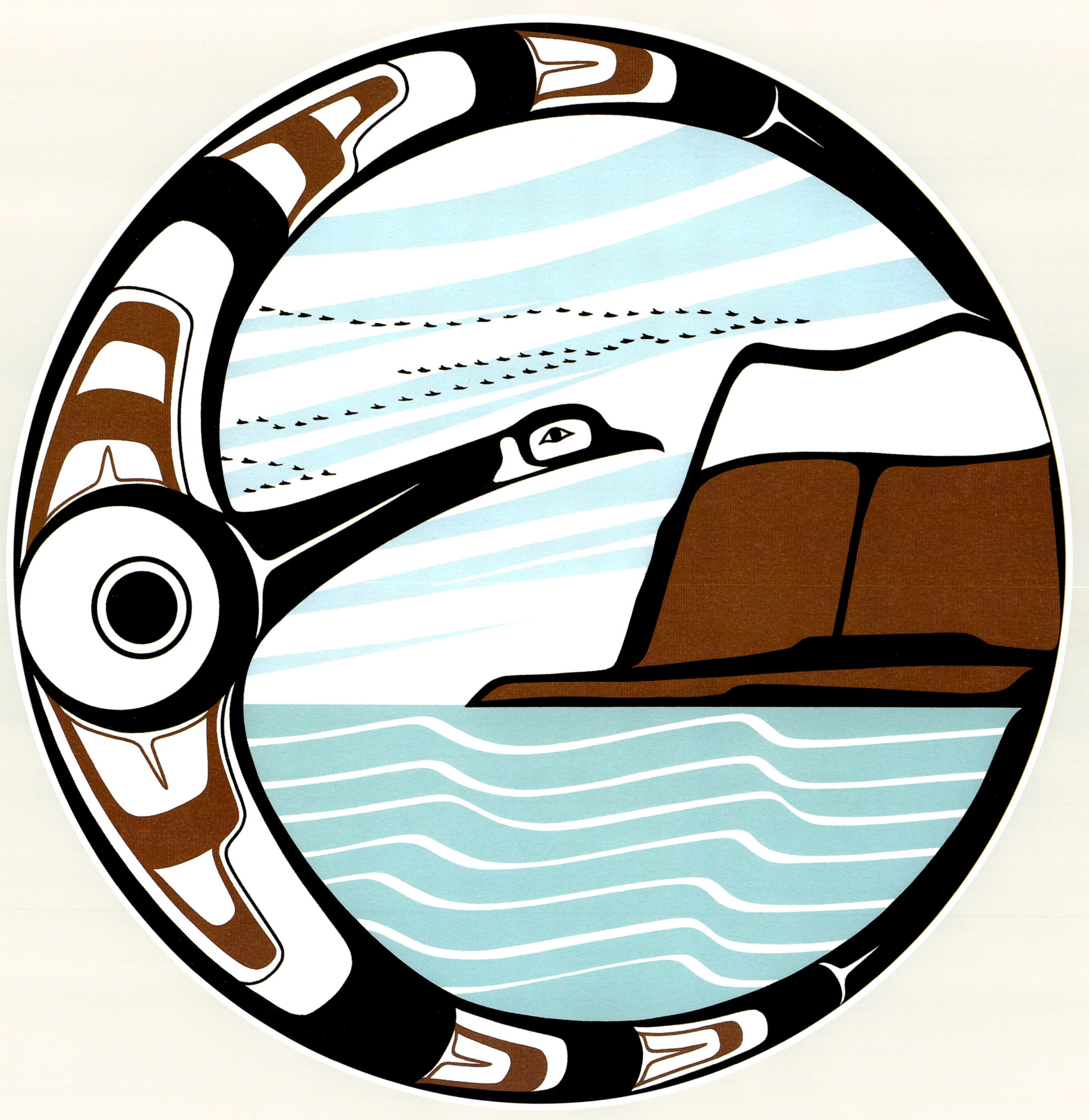

INDIAN SUMMER

Images of the past
and dreams of the future . . .

The totem is
whale
raven
eagle
and human
from the top to the bottom;
it represents family.

The longhouse is
eagle
with an eagle on each perlin.

The two whales in the ocean
are images from the past

and the entire scene is a dream
of a future home
somewhere
on the Northwest Coast.

(Released June, 1983)

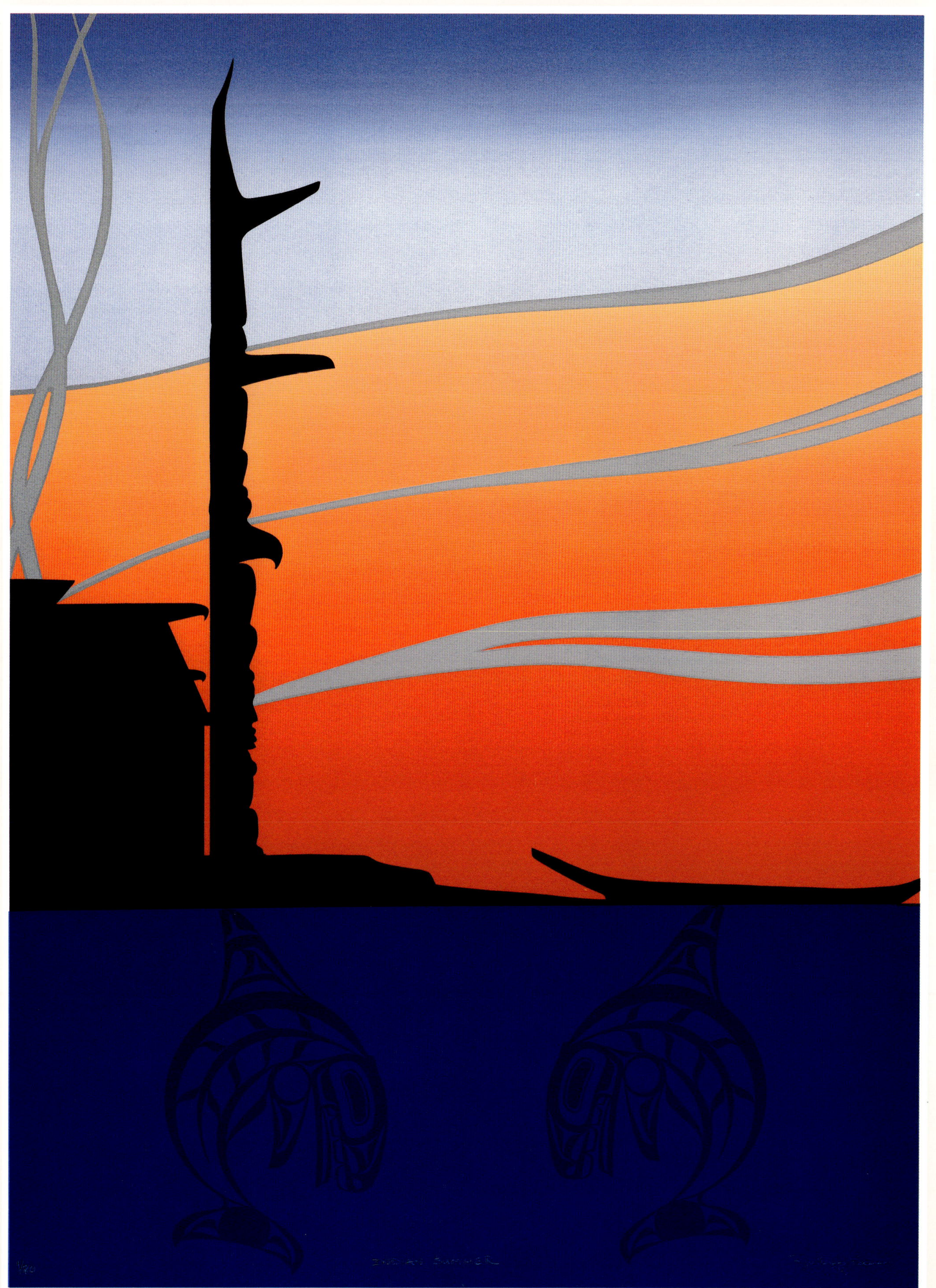
INDIAN SUMMER

PACIFIC SANDS

PACIFIC SANDS was commissioned by the owners of the resort, Pacific Sands. It was also lithographed as a poster to support the endeavours of the West Coast Whale Research Foundation.

Mostly, it is a tribute to the majestic grey whales which frequent the waters around Tofino on the West Coast of Vancouver Island. The whales come each year from April through to September and are always a welcome sight.

(Released August, 1983)

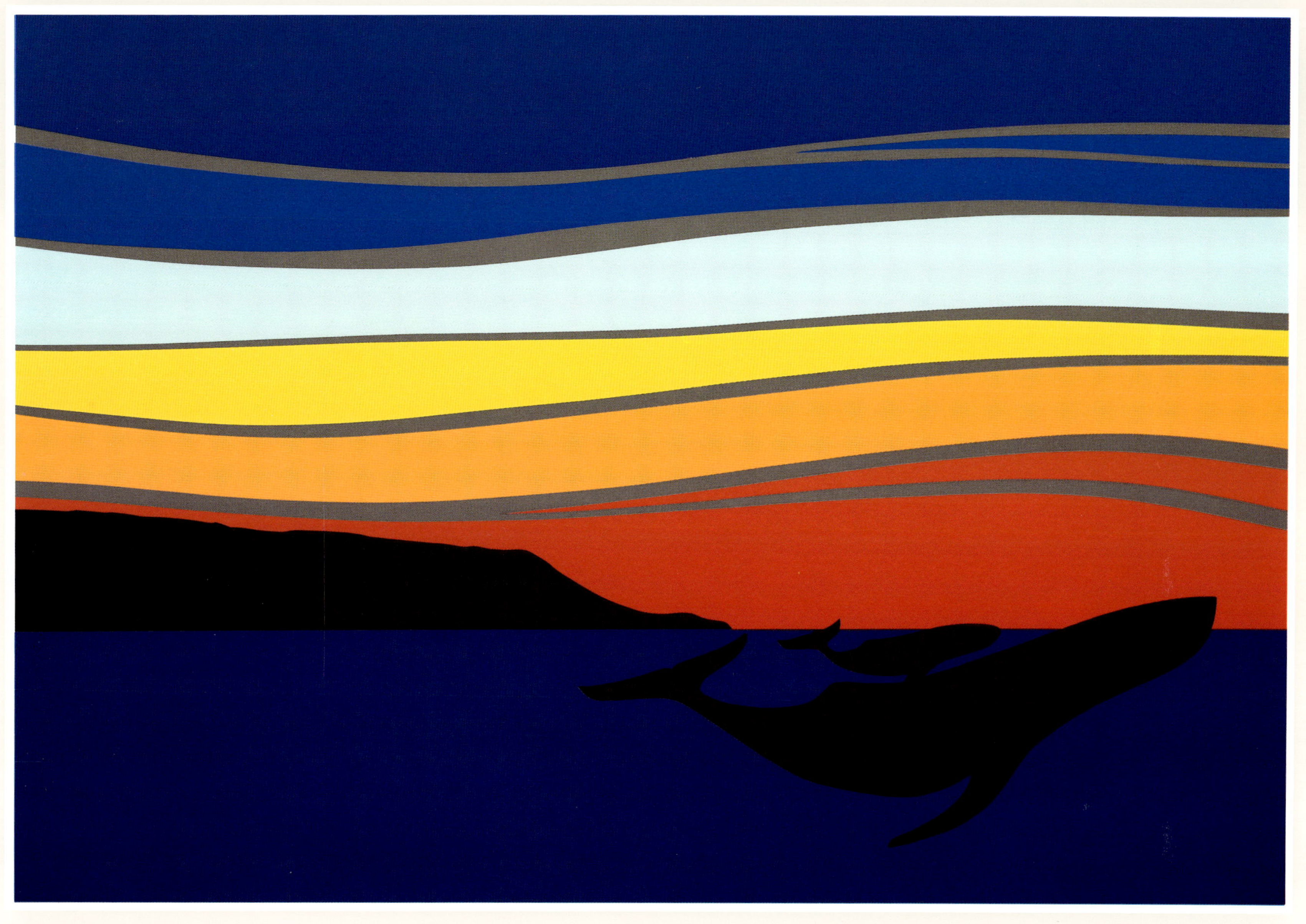

YA-A & TSI-I

YA-A and TSI-I are the Tsimshian words for grandfather and grandmother. The original idea and sketch for this work was done by my brother, Arthur Freeman Vickers. It is dedicated to our grandparents, Henry and Kathleen Vickers.

The campfire in the scene brings to mind the ancient custom of travelling to hereditary, summer fishing grounds to gather salmon for the winter season.

(Released September, 1983)

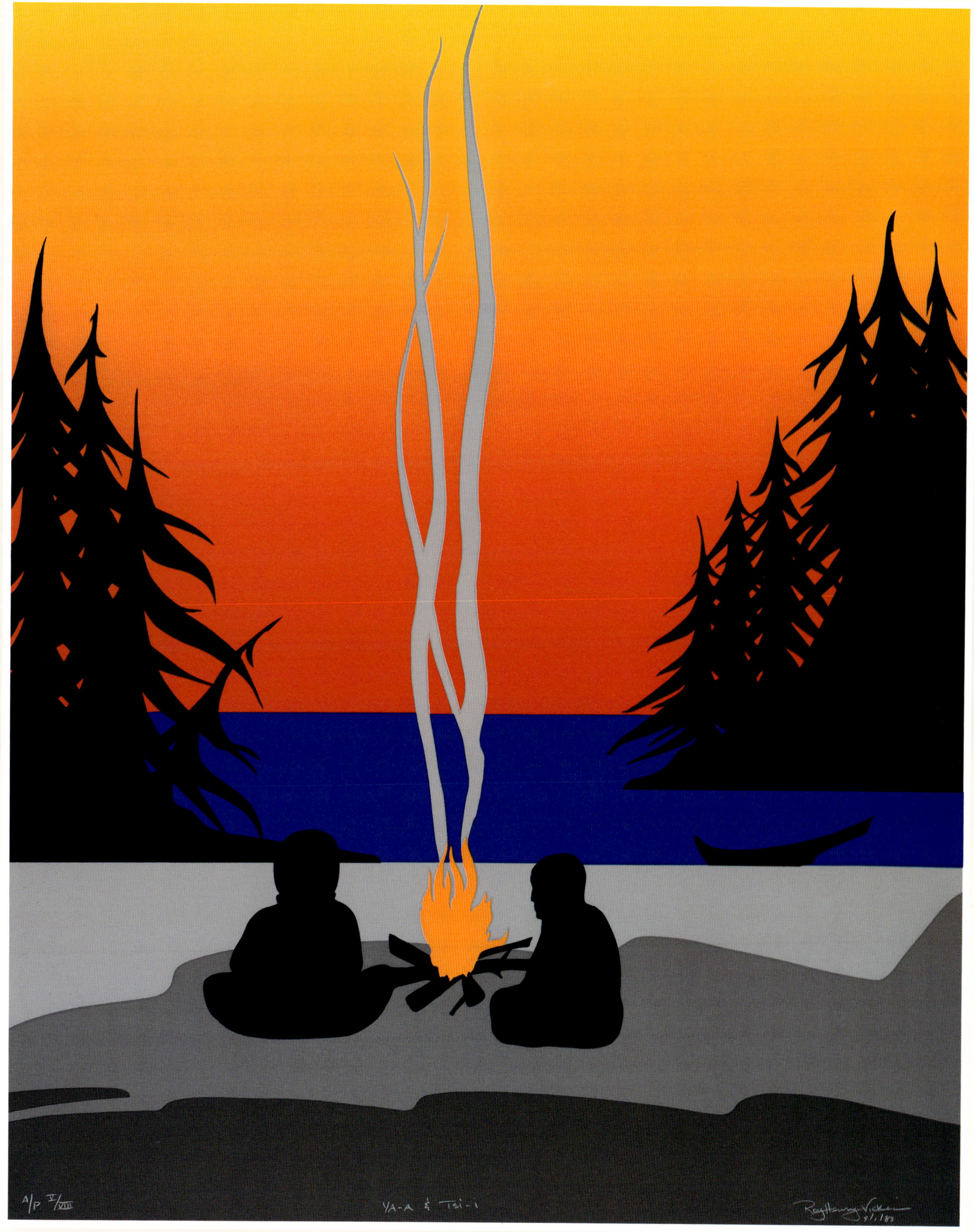
A/P V/VIII
YA-A & Tsi-i
Roy Henry Vickers

WESTCOAST WINTER

Kitkatla, one of the oldest continuously inhabited villages on the Northwest Coast dating back some five thousand years, and my childhood home, was the inspiration for WESTCOAST WINTER.

(Released December, 1983)

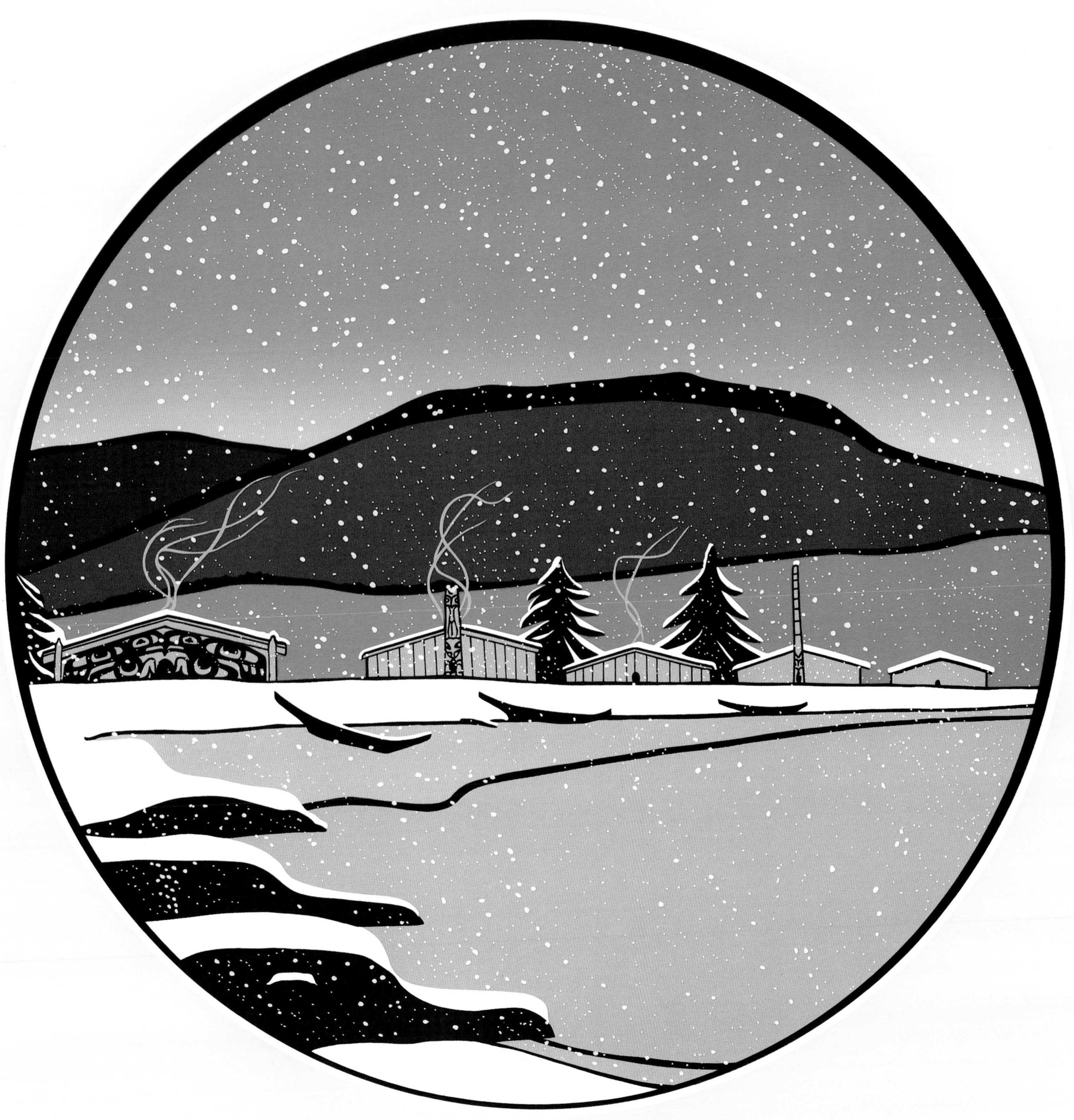

WINTER FIRES

The grey and magenta pastels of a winter sunset . . .
The salty sea air, and ever-present eagle and whale . . .
Woodsmoke from a cozy winter fire . . .
These were the inspirations for WINTER FIRES.

(Released January, 1984)

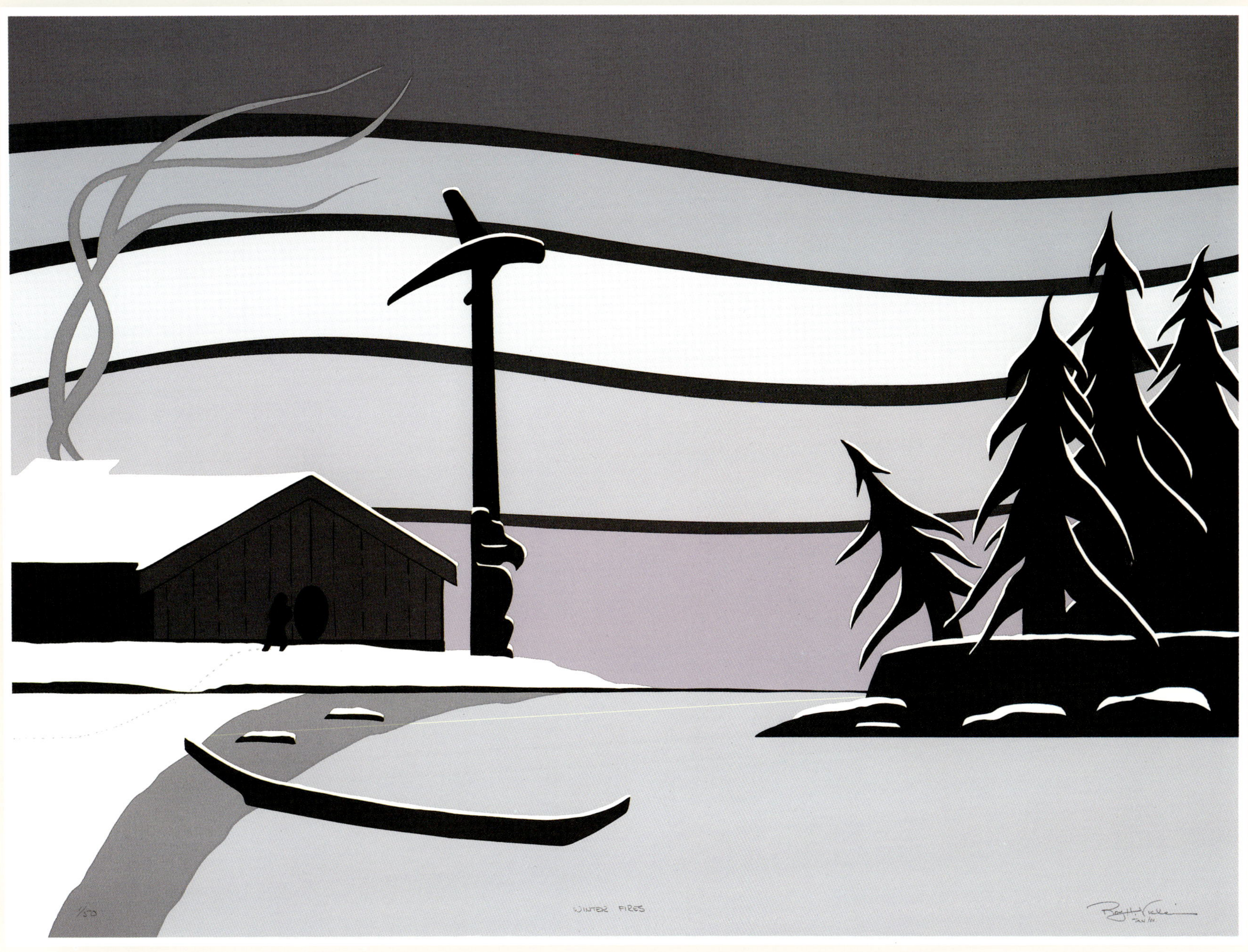
1/50
WINTER FIRES

MEARES ISLAND

MEARES ISLAND is a classic example of Northwest Coast beauty.

It is the home of the Clayoquots, a band of Indians who live at Opitsat, a village on the southwest corner of the island.

The eagle, bear, deer, otter, mink and many other species of birds and animals make Meares their home as well. The inter-tidal waters abound with scallops, abalone, oysters and sea urchin. The inlets and waterways support crab, geoduck, and salmon fisheries. Whale watching, sports fishing and cruising around Meares continue to satisfy the most discriminating of sightseers.

The provincial government decided to allow clear-cut logging on Meares. The effect of this type of logging on the island would have a long term detrimental effect on not only the beauty of the island, but more importantly, on the mariculture of the area.

There is a group of caring citizens known as the Friends of Clayoquot Sound, who gathered together to pressure the government to stop the logging of Meares. They succeeded in forcing a moratorium on the logging.

This limited edition print was sold by Eagle Dancer Enterprises with fifty percent of the proceeds going to the Friends of Clayoquot Sound to help in their struggle.

(Released February, 1984)

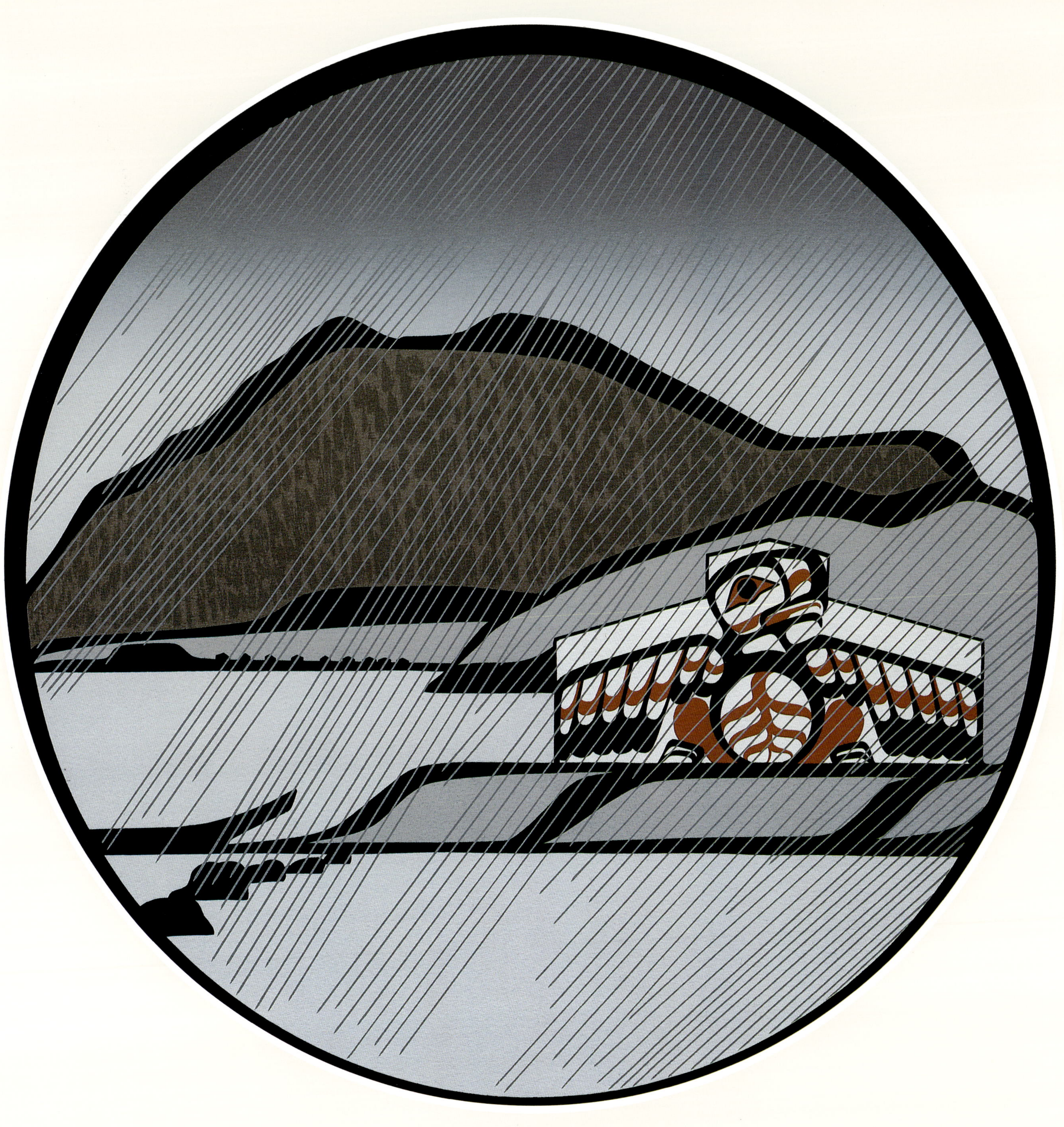

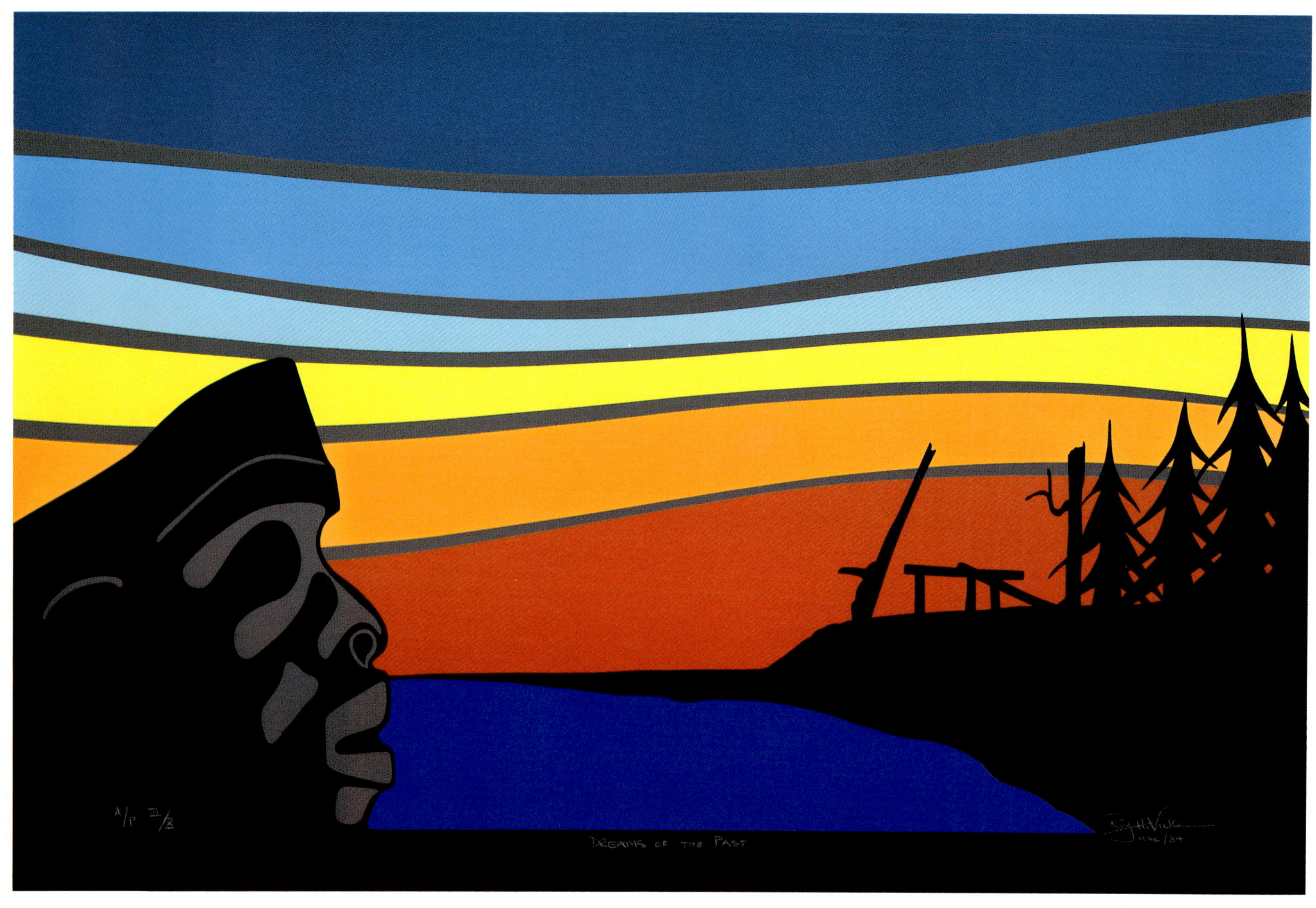

DREAMS OF THE PAST

DREAMS OF THE PAST was inspired by one of the 'Twin Masks' of the Tsimshian. The mask with no eyes or the unsighted mask makes one think of the sub-consciousness or the dream world.

I was prompted to reflect on the old culture of the Northwest Coast Indians, before contact with the whiteman. The culture that carried the people through centuries began to die upon contact with the whiteman and today no longer exists as it did. The stone mask created many centuries ago dreams of the past, and sees the once proud totem in decay, the ridge poles that held up the roof of a longhouse a skeleton of what was.

(Released March, 1984)

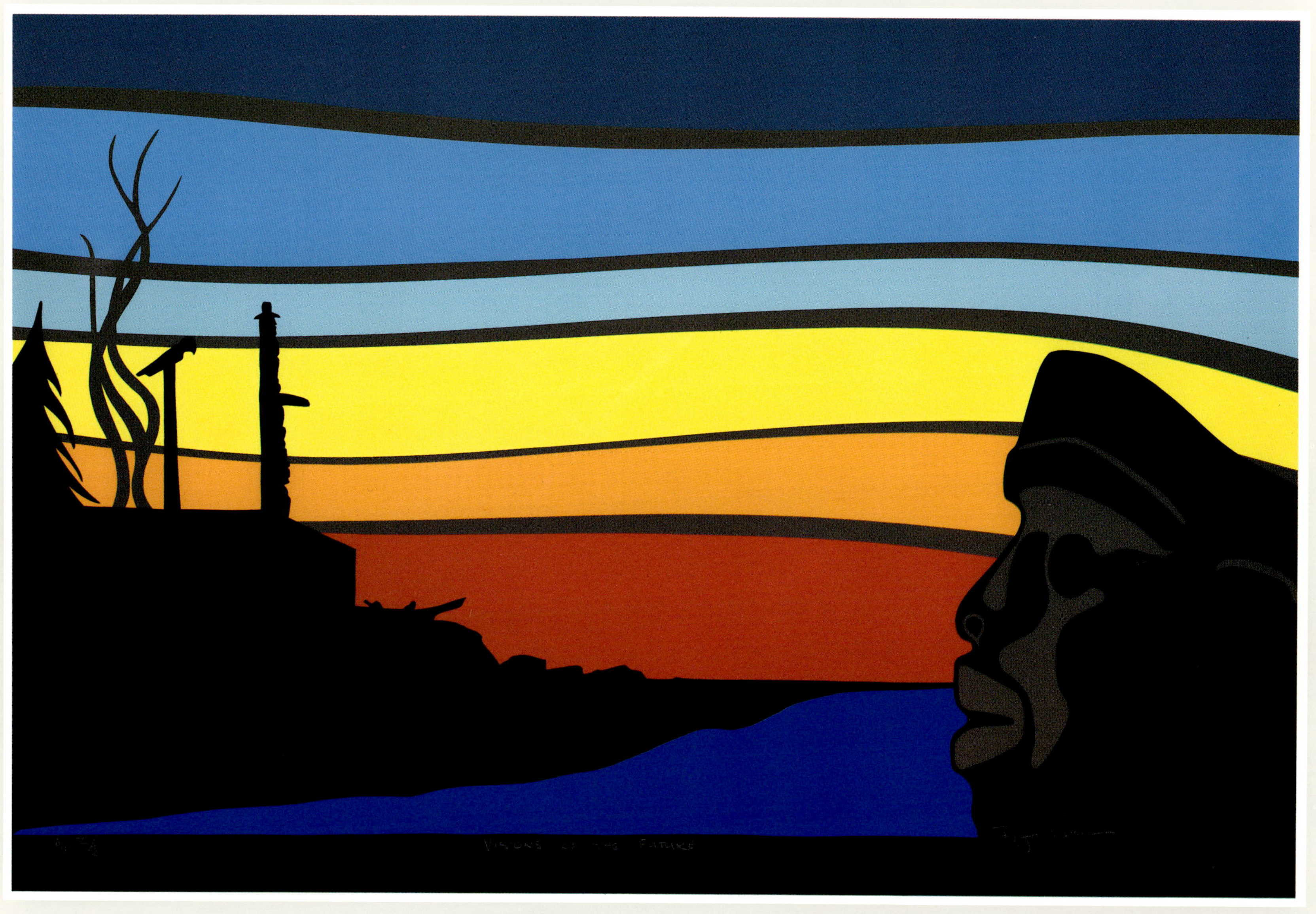

VISIONS OF THE FUTURE

VISIONS OF THE FUTURE was inspired by the 'Sighted Mask', a twin of the unsighted mask. The renaissance of the Northwest Coast Indian art of today is seen by the sighted twin that was created thousands of years ago.

Once again the cedar canoe is being carved, the longhouse is being erected, and a new totem is raised. The Indian artist of today creates, not only images from the past, but speaks to the world through images of today. A new language and modern technology facilitates a major contribution to Canadian art and culture based on a wealth of art and culture handed from generation to generation over centuries among the Indians of the Northwest Coast.

(Released March, 1984)

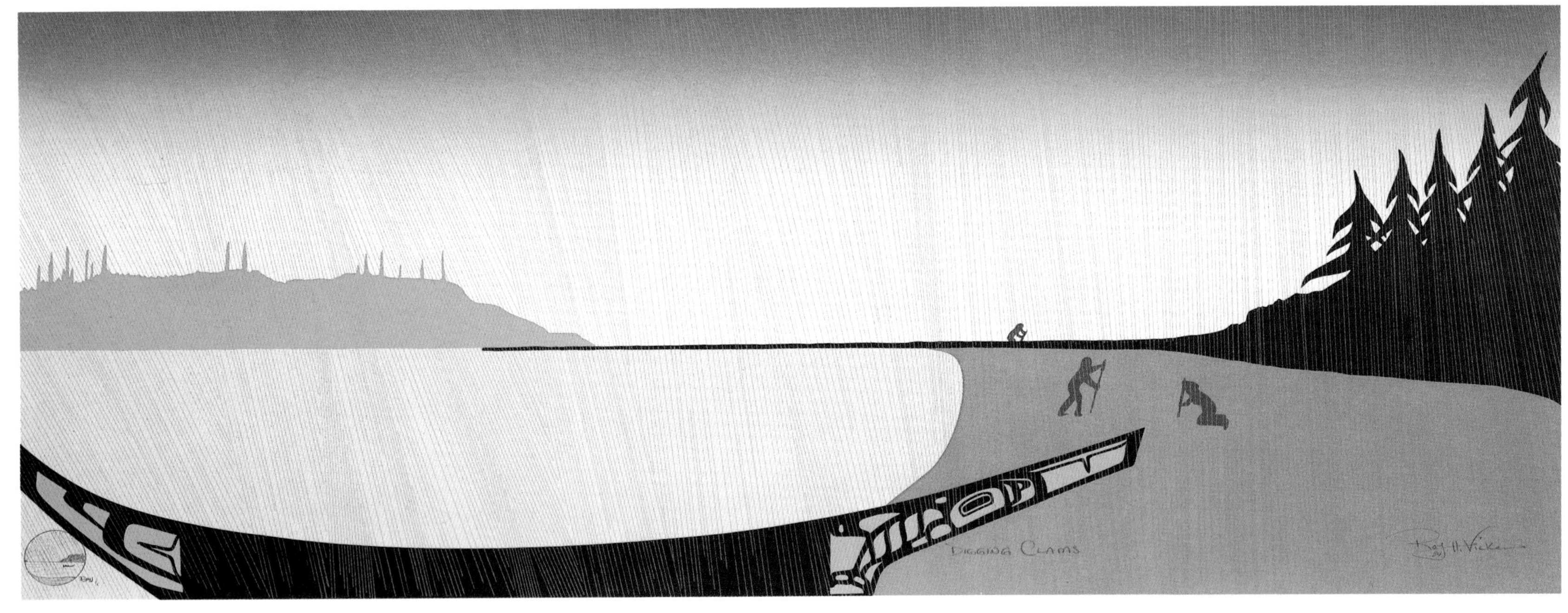

DIGGING CLAMS

Memories of clam digging go back to my early childhood. The earliest I remember earning a wage was at about seven years of age. Every winter the buyers from Prince Rupert would bring a barge out to the village of Kitkatla. Everyone went to the beach at low tide to dig clams, and sell them to the buyers. The weather was cold and wet, and sometimes snowy, so it was to your advantage to work hard and keep warm.

DIGGING CLAMS, the painting, was inspired by all of these thoughts. The painting, however, depicts clam diggers using digging sticks and not the twentieth-century forks of today. The canoe of old has been replaced by the speed boat with its outboard motor. However, each winter there are still hardy individuals who brave the elements to bring home the clams.

(Released July, 1984)

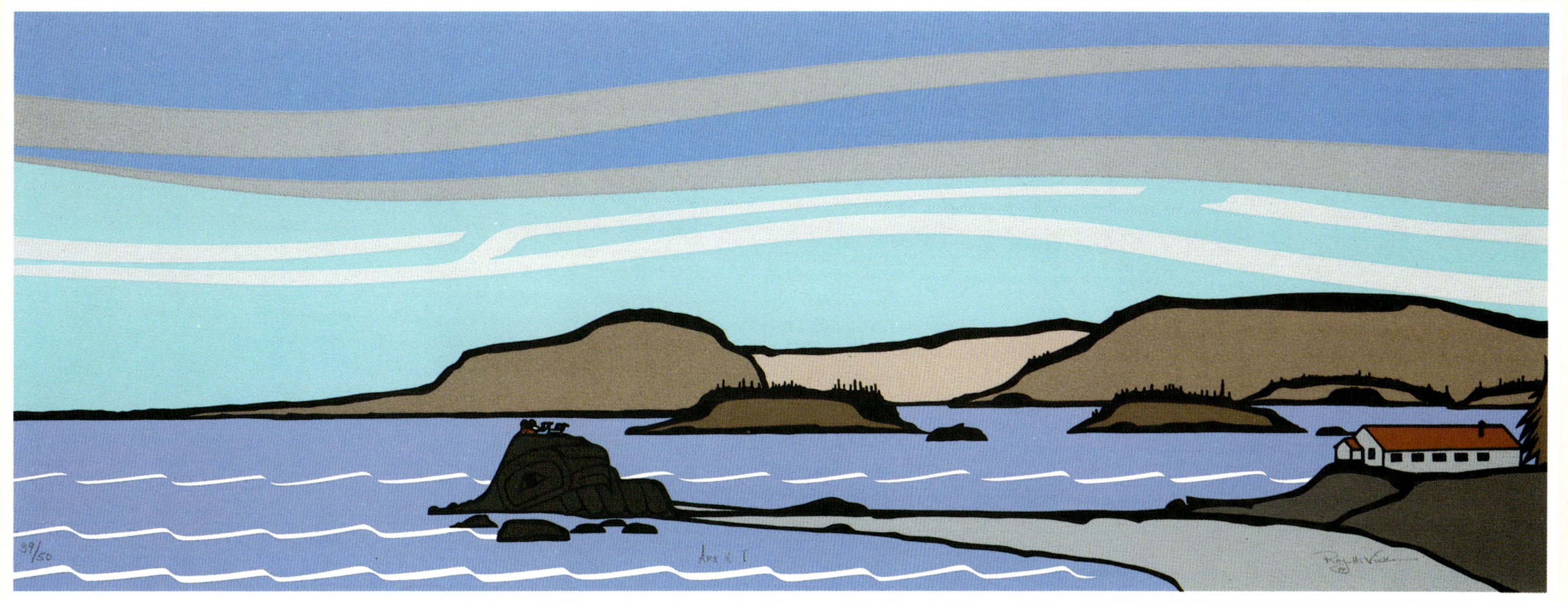

ART & I

Some of my earliest recollections of childhood are of my home village in Kitkatla, a small Indian Reserve on the North Coast of British Columbia. When we were children, we did not have the luxury of television or movies. We learned to occupy our time and entertain ourselves on the beach in front of the old school house that was our home.

Sometimes my brother Art and I would walk out on the point, climb 'Eagle Rock', and lie there, dreaming of the outside world and watching nature's theatre perform for our exclusive benefit. We saw the eagles fishing, or a clever raven break open a mussel shell and fly to the top of a tall fir tree to enjoy his meal. Other times we would make a game of finding shapes of birds, animals or fish in the clouds.

As I sit and recall those days, it seems they were full of so many things to do. Bedtime came much too soon. I don't seem to remember very many rainy days.

(Released May, 1984)

STEELHEAD

The very word brings to mind visions of the largest of its species ever seen by a human. For those of you who have never heard, the steelhead is the most exciting game fish that anyone could ever have on the end of their fishing line. Steelheading is usually pursued in some of the colder months on the West Coast.

This particular creation was strongly suggested to me by some of my fishing partners with whom I have spent many a happy hour seeking that elusive king of sportfish. STEELHEAD then, is dedicated to those I have fished with and to all those who sneak through the woods, trip over logs and windfalls, slide down riverbanks and fall into the icy waters of a mountain stream or river in a desperate search for this magnificent rival.

(Released July, 1984)

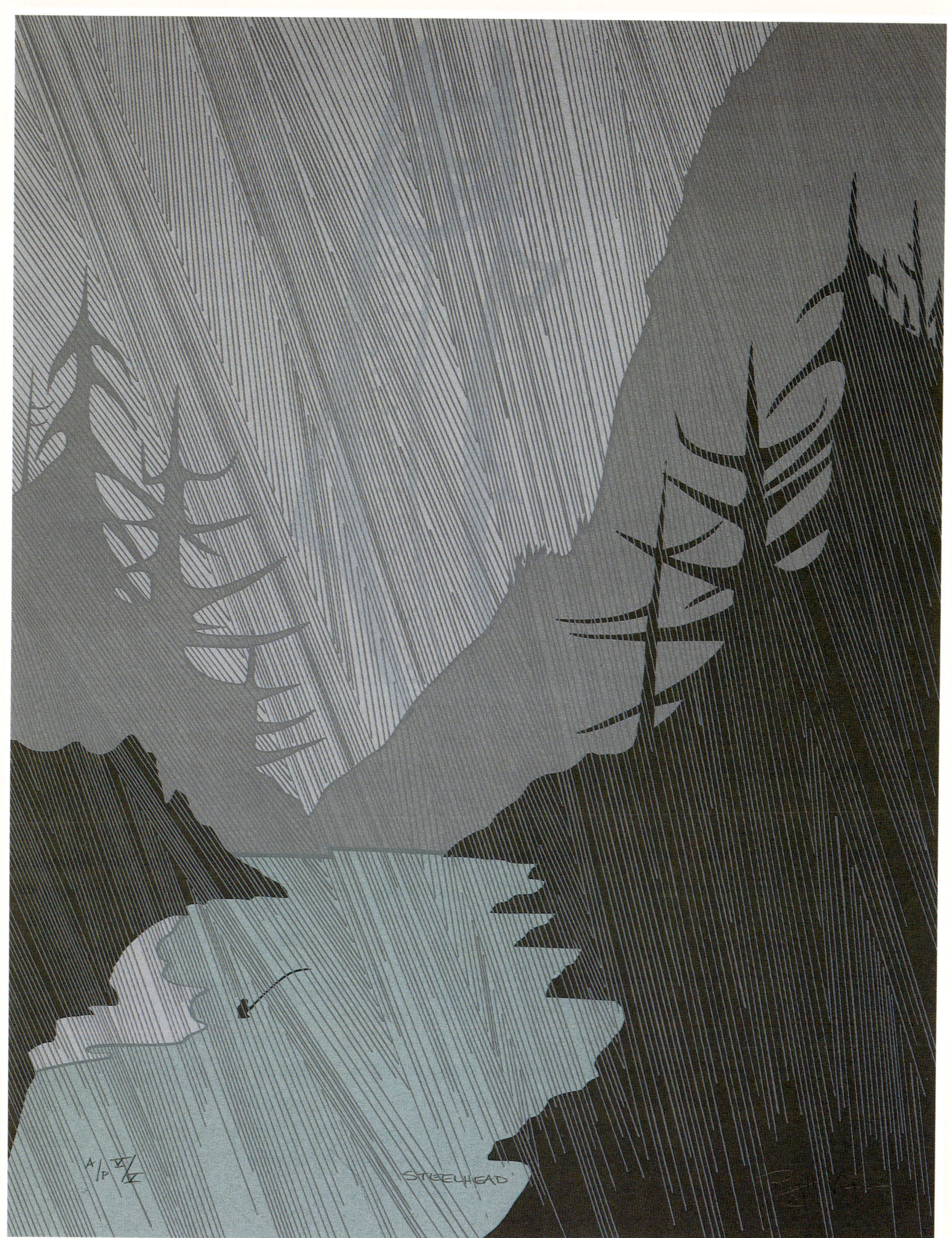
A/P V/V
STEELHEAD

CEDAR SNAGS

The eagle is in the moon. As the moon rises, he cannot see a tree to build his nest in . . . only CEDAR SNAGS—a legacy of man's injustice to his environment.

A first for my brother, Art and I. Art started the original painting for this print, and brought it to me so we could finish it together. It allowed us to voice a common concern regarding an issue that is becoming far too prevalent today.

(Released July, 1984)

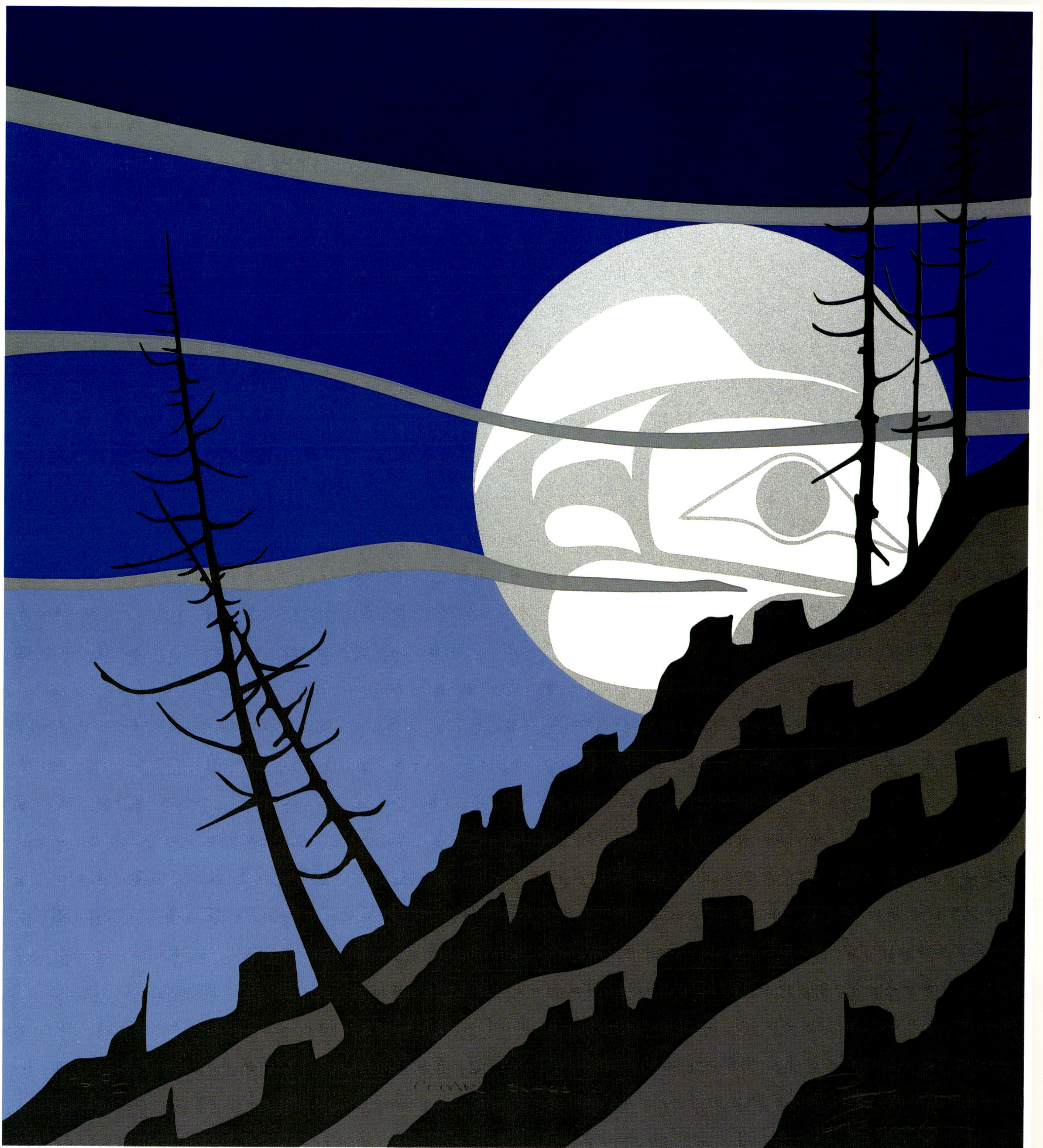
CEDAR

BIRD'S EYE VIEW

A lone eagle sits as a sentinel on Wilf Rock in Clayoquot Sound on the West Coast of Vancouver Island. This area is a favourite fishing spot for many 'westcoasters'.

I have seen grey whales, killer whales, sea lions and seals while angling for the big spring salmon that come by here each year.

I've jigged cod and fed them to the eagles not twenty minutes from my home.

These are the many things that come to one's mind to inspire a painting such as BIRD'S EYE VIEW.

(Released August, 1984)

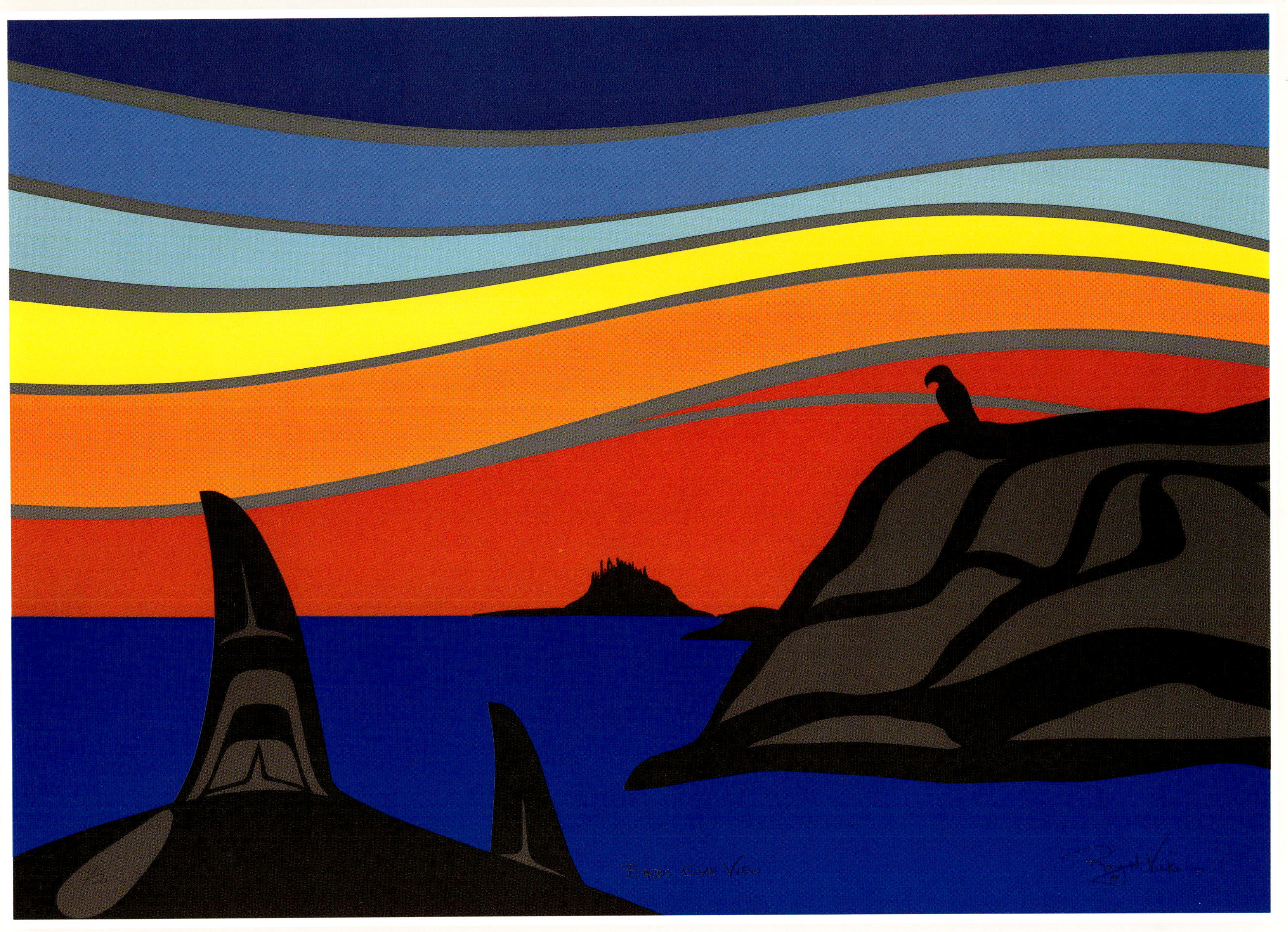
BIRD'S EYE VIEW

SEA LION ROCK

The sea lion is a common sight up and down the coast of British Columbia. My earliest recollection of a sea lion is from Kitkatla. When I was a child, my uncle found a sea lion pup abandoned and took it home to feed it. The pup grew to weigh about half a ton and used to parade up and down the streets, terrorizing the dogs. He was a beautiful big bull. In order to get rid of him, uncle Johnny had to take him on a three hour trip to Sea Lion Rock. He never did come back.

(Released August, 1984)

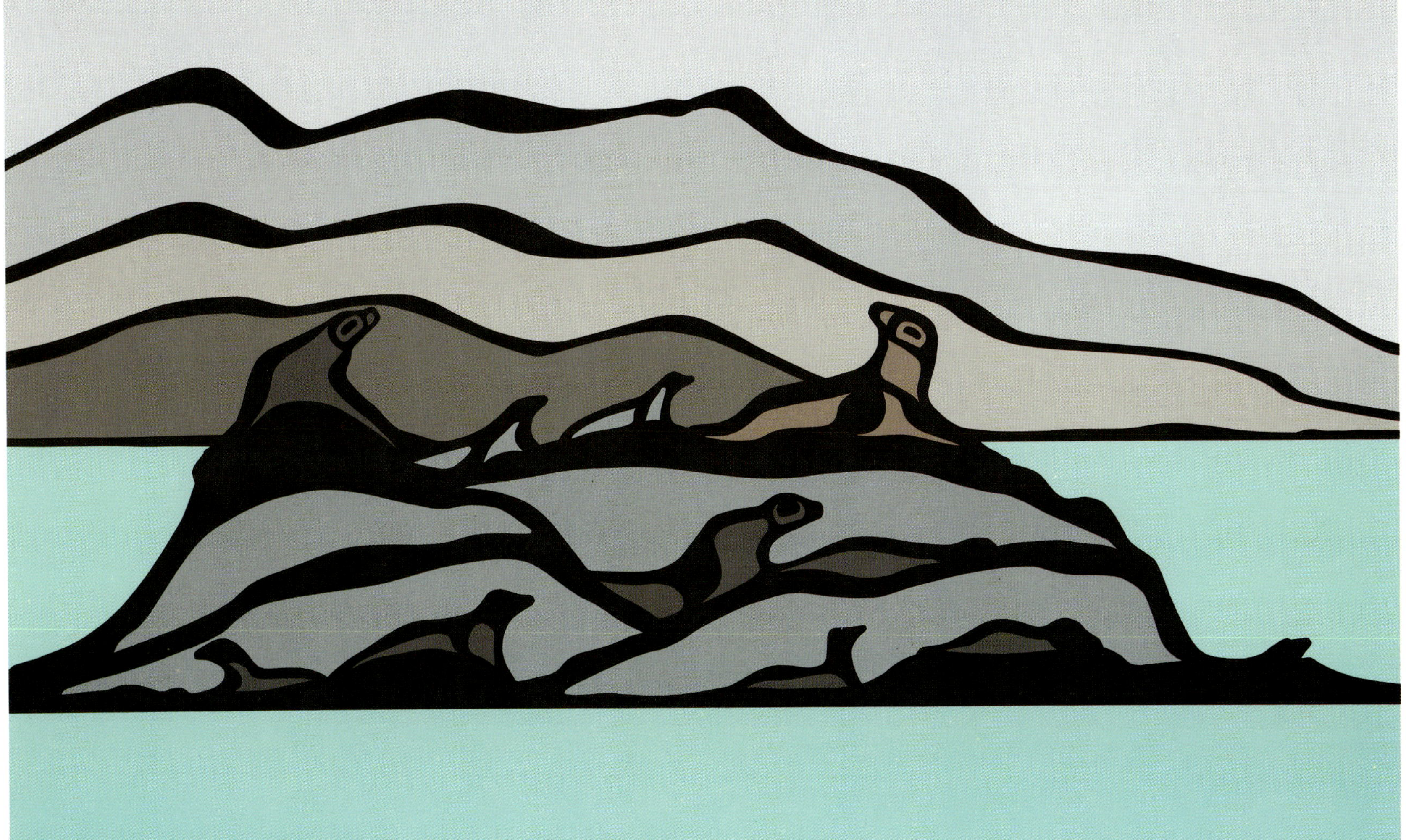
A/P 3/8
SEA LION ROCK

THE FISHERMAN

THE FISHERMAN was conceived from the idea of freedom. The actual painting was commissioned by Weigh West Marina. There was a period of time when I left my art and subjected myself to the rigorous pursuit of commercial fishing. It was good to get away from it all and work hard at the basic skills of survival.

It was equally wonderful to leave the pressures of chasing the elusive salmon to return and make a living from my world of art. The experience of fishing left me with thousands of inspiring ideas and not enough time left in this world to carry everything to fruition.

The eagle rising and transforming to a man represents the freedom to fish when I want to, and to work when I want to, and that can be a problem sometimes.

(Released August, 1984)

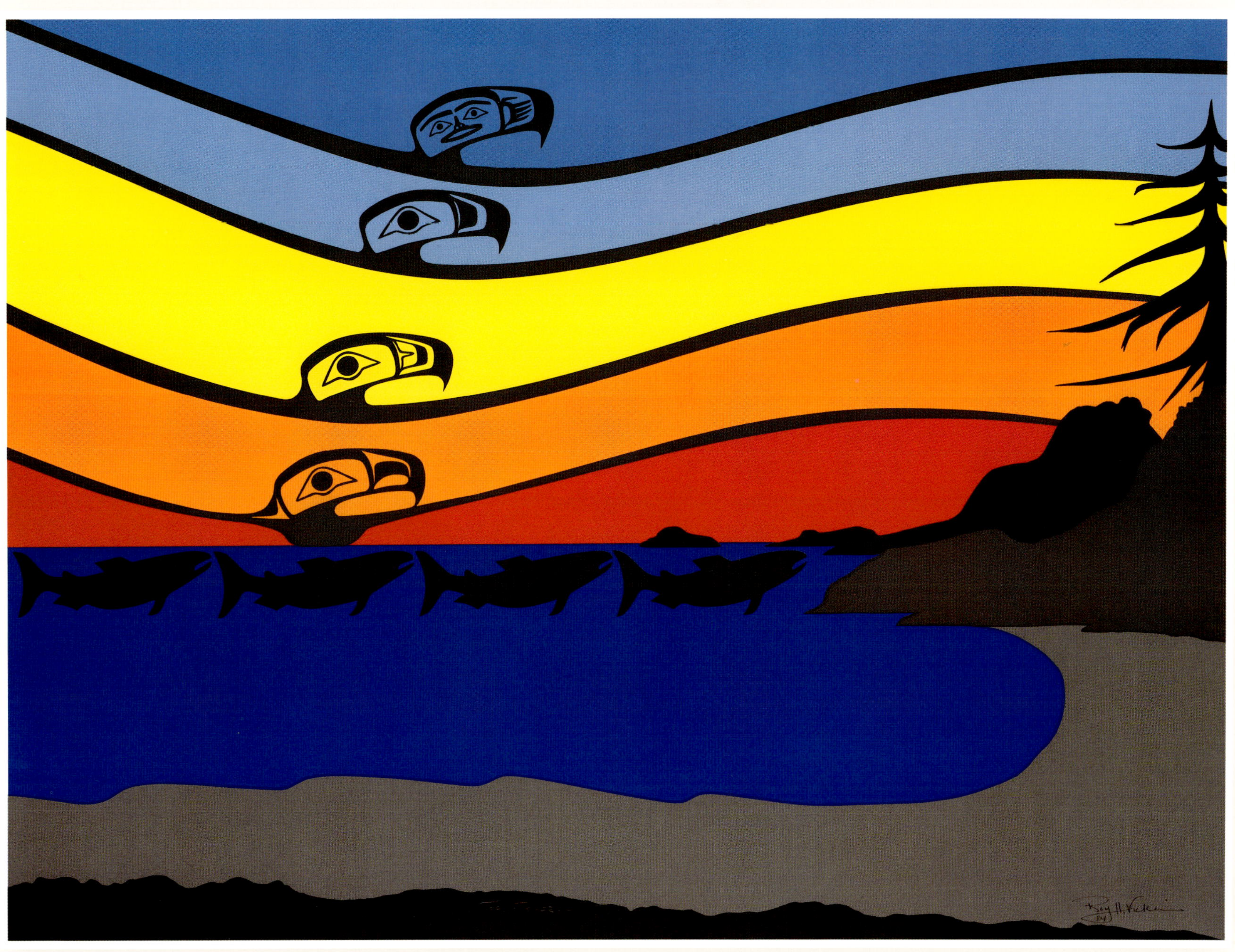

INDIAN ISLAND

The summer of 1984 will always hold a special place in my heart and mind.

Tofino and Clayoquot Sound had a very special visitor that came early in the summer and stayed until September. Most people called her 'Friendly.' She was a young grey whale about twenty feet long. Everyday she would come into Grice Bay with the high tide to feed in the shallow waters beside Indian Island.

Thousands of people came to see her and were thrilled by the sight of a grey whale at close quarters. We made many trips with friends on our boat to visit 'Friendly,' and were always excited, and somewhat in awe, of such a large creature who allowed us to come within a few feet of her. Friendly has left our waters to roam over the oceans, perhaps one day to return.

The painting, INDIAN ISLAND, was created in memory of a very special grey whale.

(Released October, 1984)

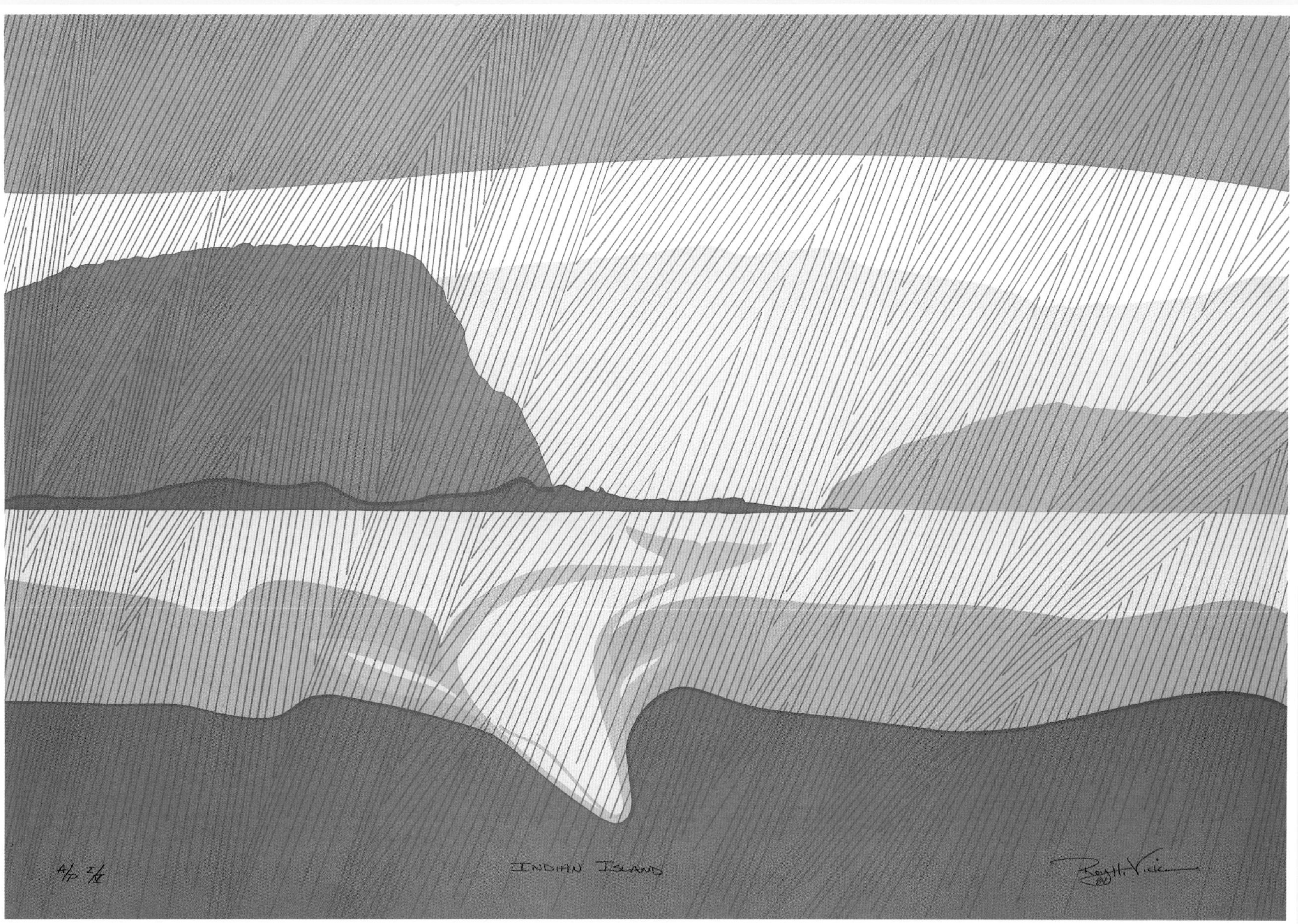
INDIAN ISLAND

A TIME PAST

Christmas seems to be
a time of remembering times
past. It seems fitting for me then,
to reflect on a time in history that goes
beyond my childhood—another era. I think
of a culture on the Northwest Coast that
has gone, and this saddens me, but not for
long. I realize the tremendous wealth that
comes to all of us through the art
of the Northwest Coast Indian
and it inspires me.

(Released December, 1984)

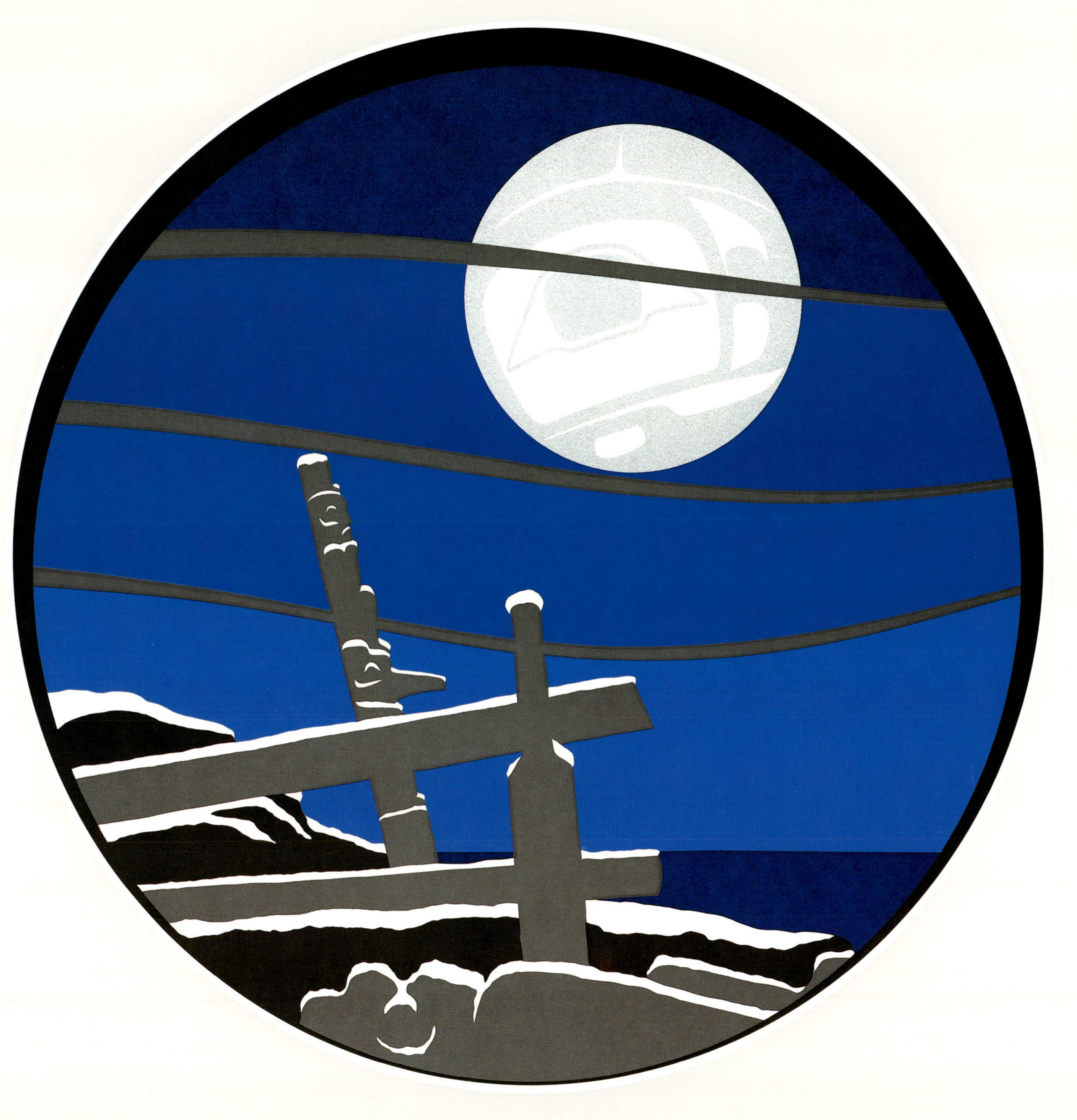

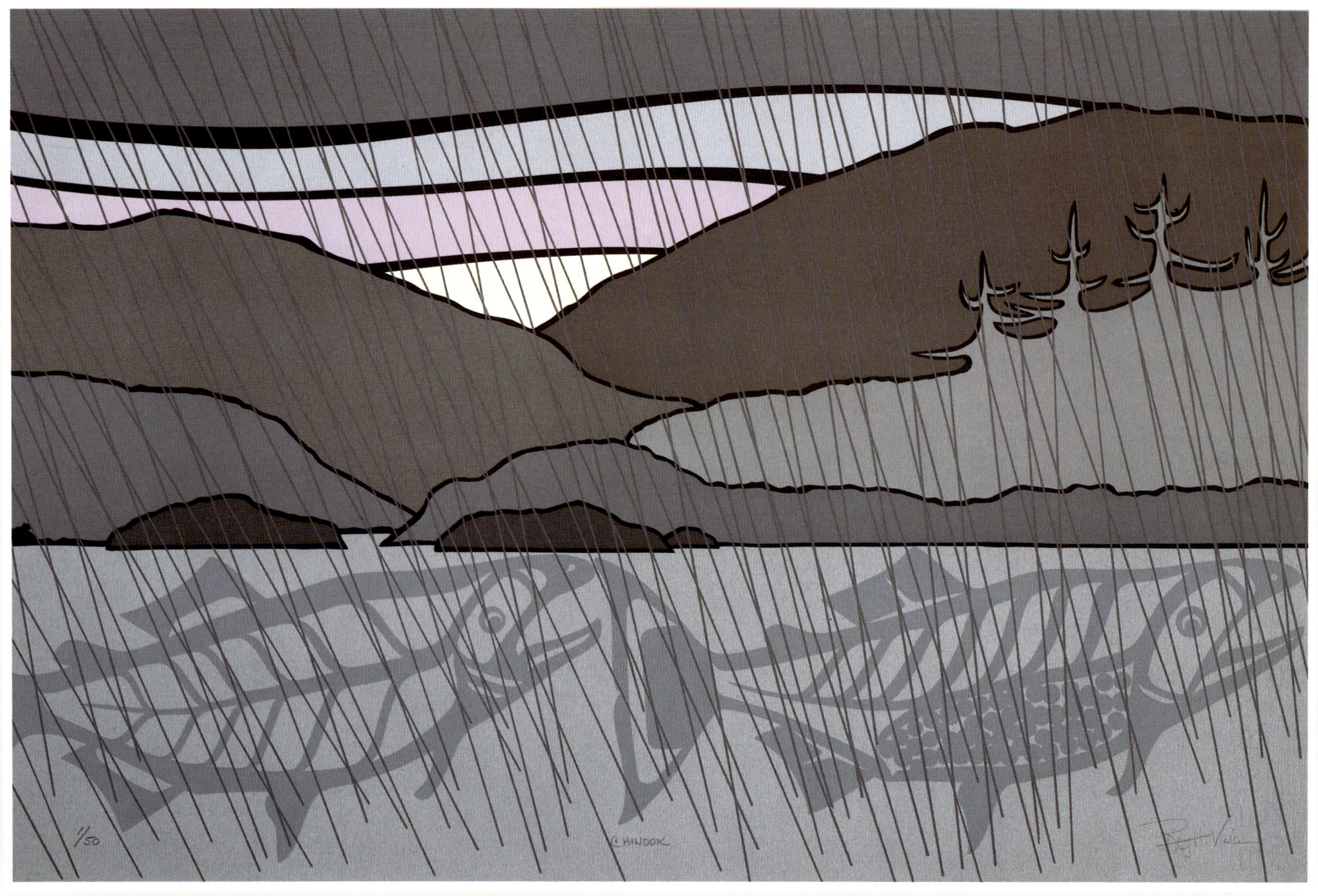

CHINOOK

Chinook—the very word starts the adrenalin flowing in the blood of every sportfisherman. I have spent many an hour in the rain, fog, and sometimes even in the sun, waiting for the king of salmon to select my particular lure.

After enduring the wet, southeast wind or the brisk westerly for two seasons, I was finally rewarded. I joined that small group of people who can claim membership in the Tyee Club. A tyee is any spring salmon (chinook) weighing over thirty pounds. I earned the honour by bringing in the largest chinook of my life, weighing in at thirty-five pounds. Such a special event should be the inspiration for a new creation, and so, with a great deal of emotion, I presented CHINOOK.

(Released November, 1984)

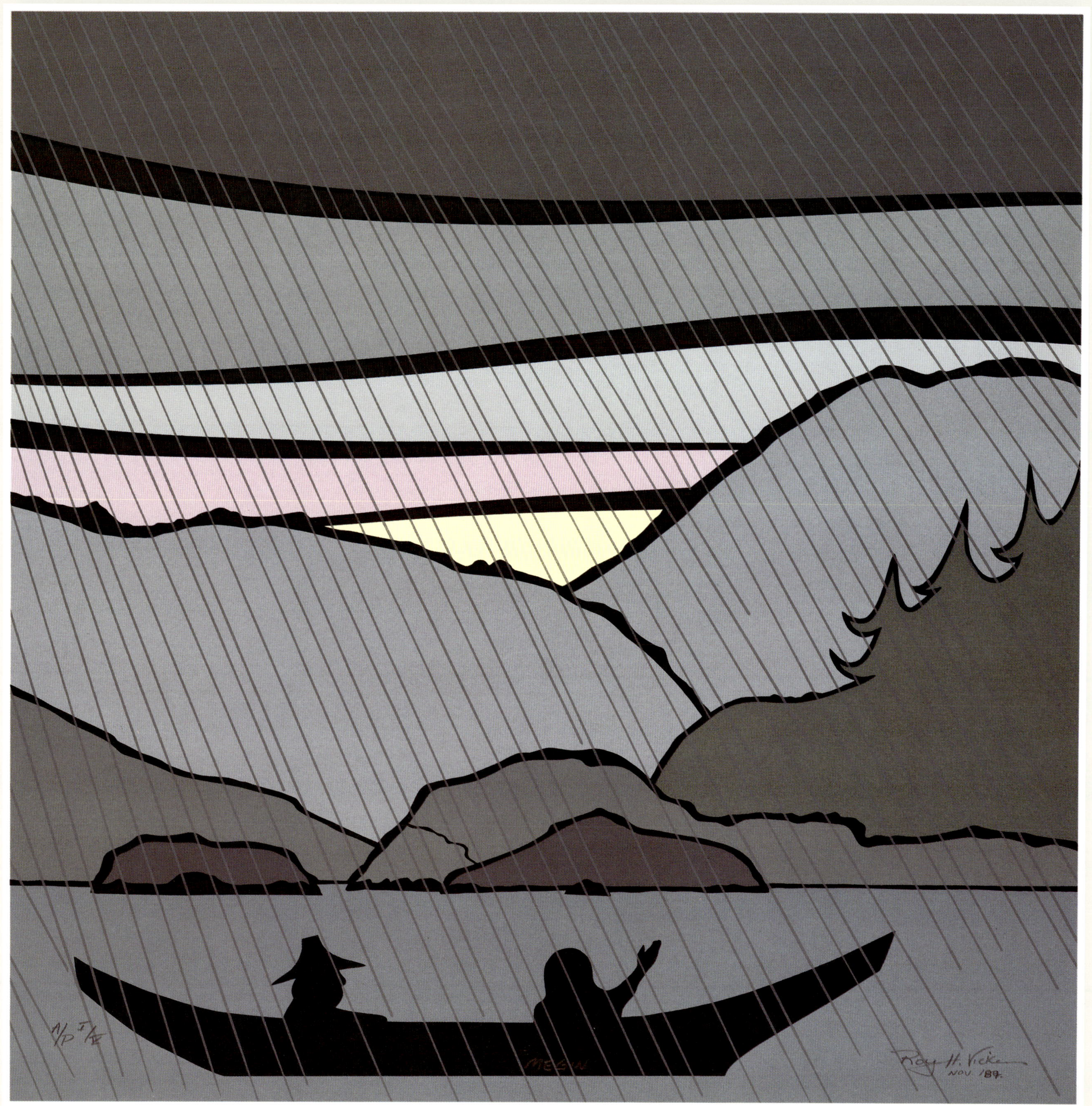

MEGIN

Dawn seemed slow to join us. The sound of rushing waters, accented by the cry of the gull, was a symphony to the drama of daylight, forcing night to release its grip on a brand new day. *(Released November, 1984)*

GOING TO THE POTLATCH

The landfall in this image is Friendly Cove on the West Coast of Vancouver Island. The lowlands of Hesquiat Peninsula are in the background. The season is winter, a time of feasting and potlatches on the Northwest Coast. I dream of what it must have been like for northern chiefs to be invited to attend a ceremony so far from home.

In this case, the occupants of the canoe are attending an important celebration on the West Coast of Vancouver Island and have travelled from the Tsimshian or Haida nations as indicated by the style of dress and the shape of the canoe. The chief who has extended the invite must be important, because this canoe has travelled hundreds of miles of difficult coastline.

Such was the way of life on the coast. Some things were most necessary, and all hardships were endured because you were GOING TO THE POTLATCH.

(Released December, 1984)

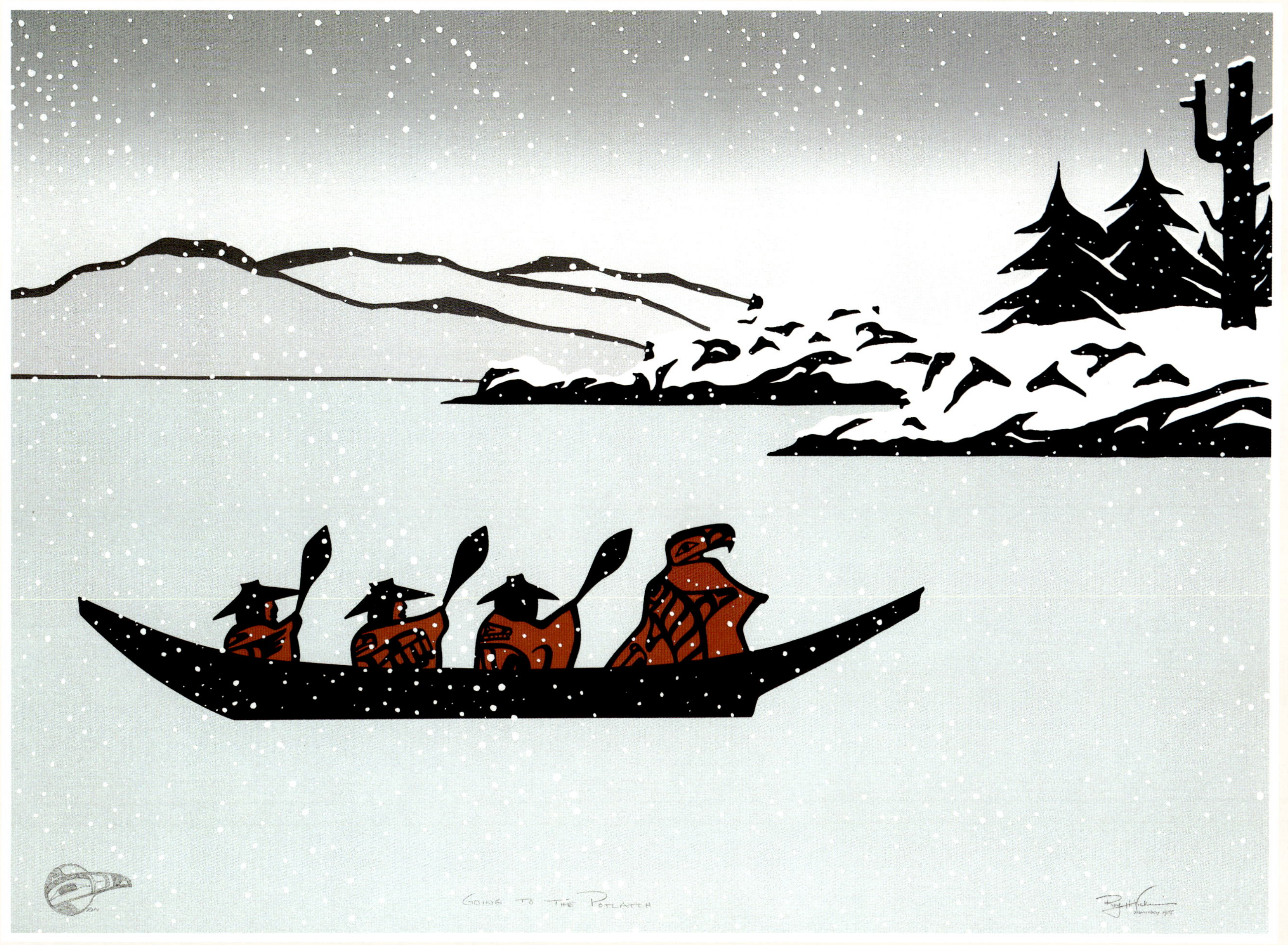
GOING TO THE POTLATCH

EASTER 1985

During the 1970's, I was struck by the message of Christianity and the culmination of religious celebrations that happen each Easter. I wanted to remind people that Easter was more than bunny rabbits and Easter egg hunts, and so I painted a number of renditions of the face of Christ.

The Easter of 1985 found me again wanting to create a work that would leave a lasting impression and provide the viewer with cause for meditation. I reworked an older painting, showing the face of Christ in red with a crown of thorns and the face of man in black. The basic thought behind this creation was that if we identify with Christ in his crucifixion and death, we also acknowledge his resurrection and everlasting life.

(Released 1985)

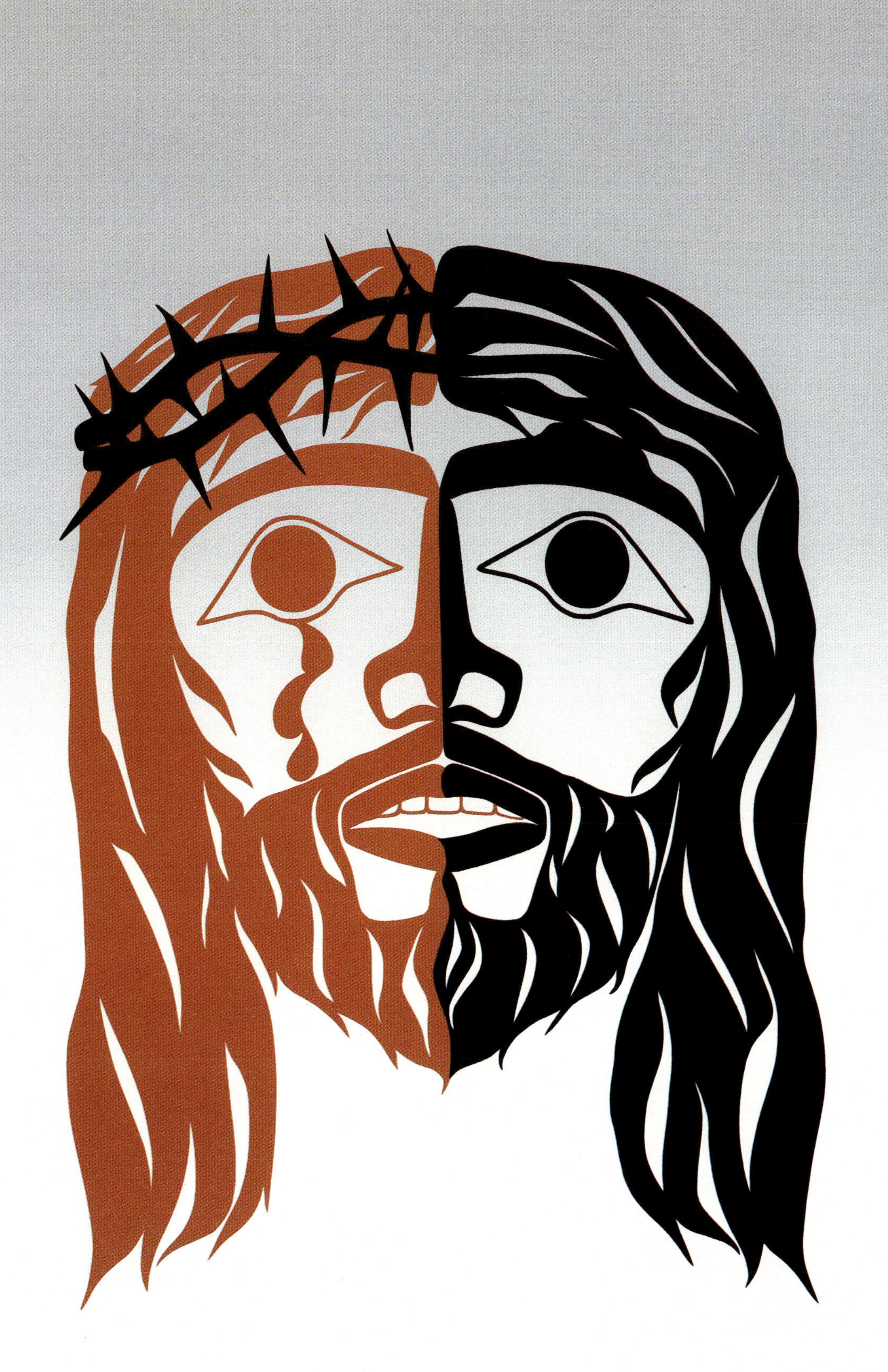

CYPRE RIVER

CYPRE RIVER, just north of Tofino where I live, has provided me with more hours of fishing pleasure than any other.

The first week in April I was fishing the Cypre when it began to snow heavily. The snowflakes seemed to blend into their reflections as they neared the river's surface and melted into the water. Around the calm, slow-moving water of the big pools, the silence was so immense you could actually hear the soft hiss of the flakes as they touched the earth.

It is experiences such as this that continue to inspire me and call me back to the beauty of nature.

(Released June, 1985)

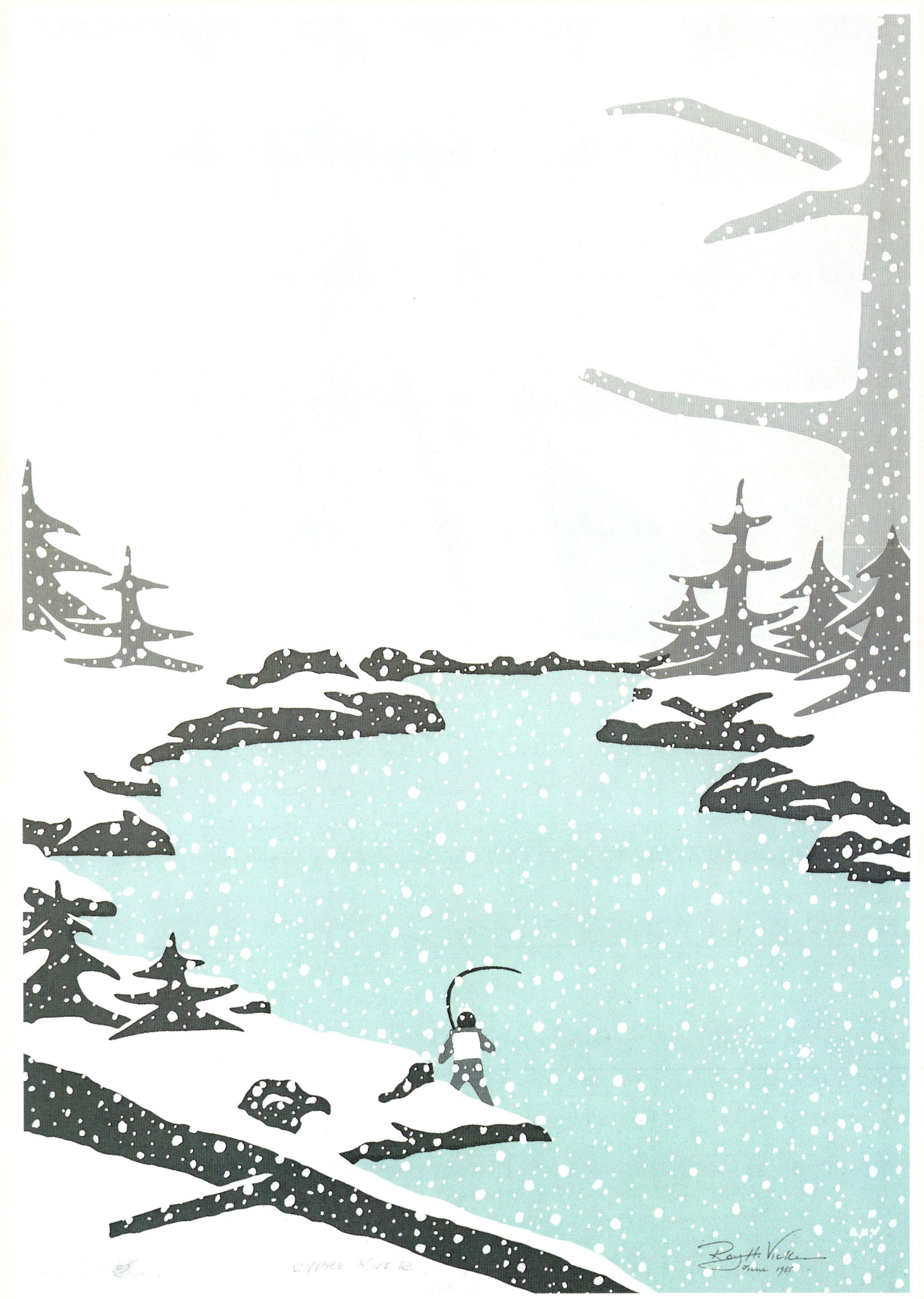
CYPRE RIVER
Roy H. Vickers
June 1985

LENNARD LIGHT

The lighthouse is a symbol of safety and protection, warning of danger. Lennard Light, situated on Lennard Island to guide mariners to the safe waters of Tofino Harbour, is one of the dominating landmarks in the area.

The whales swimming by Lennard Island in this painting are a tribute to 'Friendly.' Friendly is a young grey whale that frequented our waters for most of 1984, leaving in September never to return . . . or so I thought.

The following May I had the wonderful experience of seeing Friendly once again while I was out on a nature cruise with some friends. I have not seen the whale since that day, but who knows, perhaps I'll see it again . . . maybe in the ocean just off LENNARD LIGHT.

(Released July, 1985)

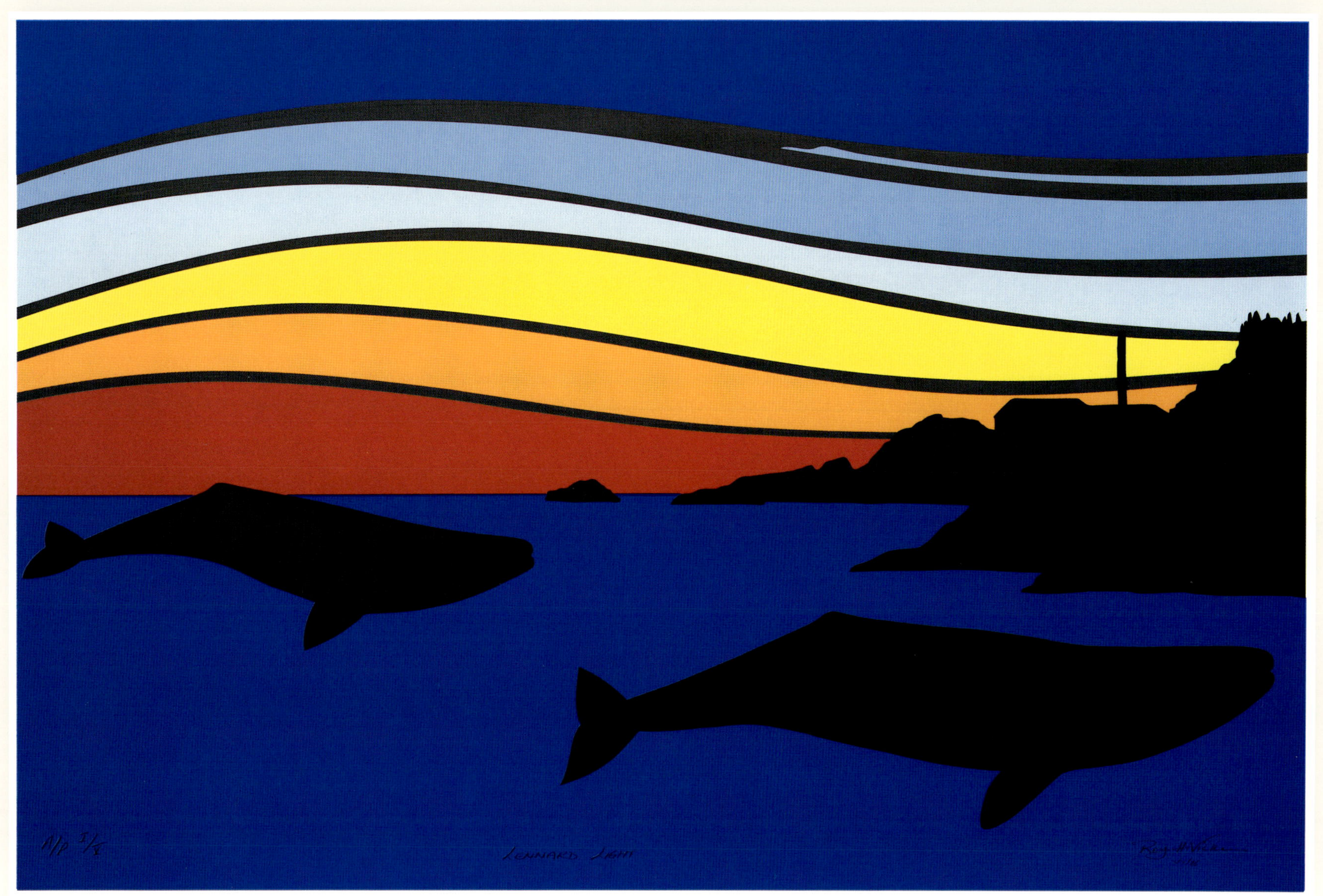
A/P I/X
LENNARD LIGHT

THE HUNTER

The eagle, a hunter and skilled catcher of fish, is a common sight on the Northwest Coast. One might think a person would get used to eagles if they saw them everyday, but I never tire of them.

Each year in our neck of the woods, you can see the eagles pair off in the spring, flying high in the sky as they go through their courtship rituals. In June, the eaglets hatch, usually one per nest.

It is during this time of the season that I enjoy one of my biggest thrills. At any opportunity, I am off on the ocean jigging cod, keeping the larger codfish for the frying pan and feeding the smaller ones to the eagles. It is possible to bring my boat in close to the huge cedars where they nest, stopping the motor and throwing the cod out in the water so an eagle can swoop down and snatch up the fish with its great talons. This is one of the most wonderful experiences a person can have, and it is also one of the few times in the year that the eagle does not have to be THE HUNTER.

(Released July, 1985)

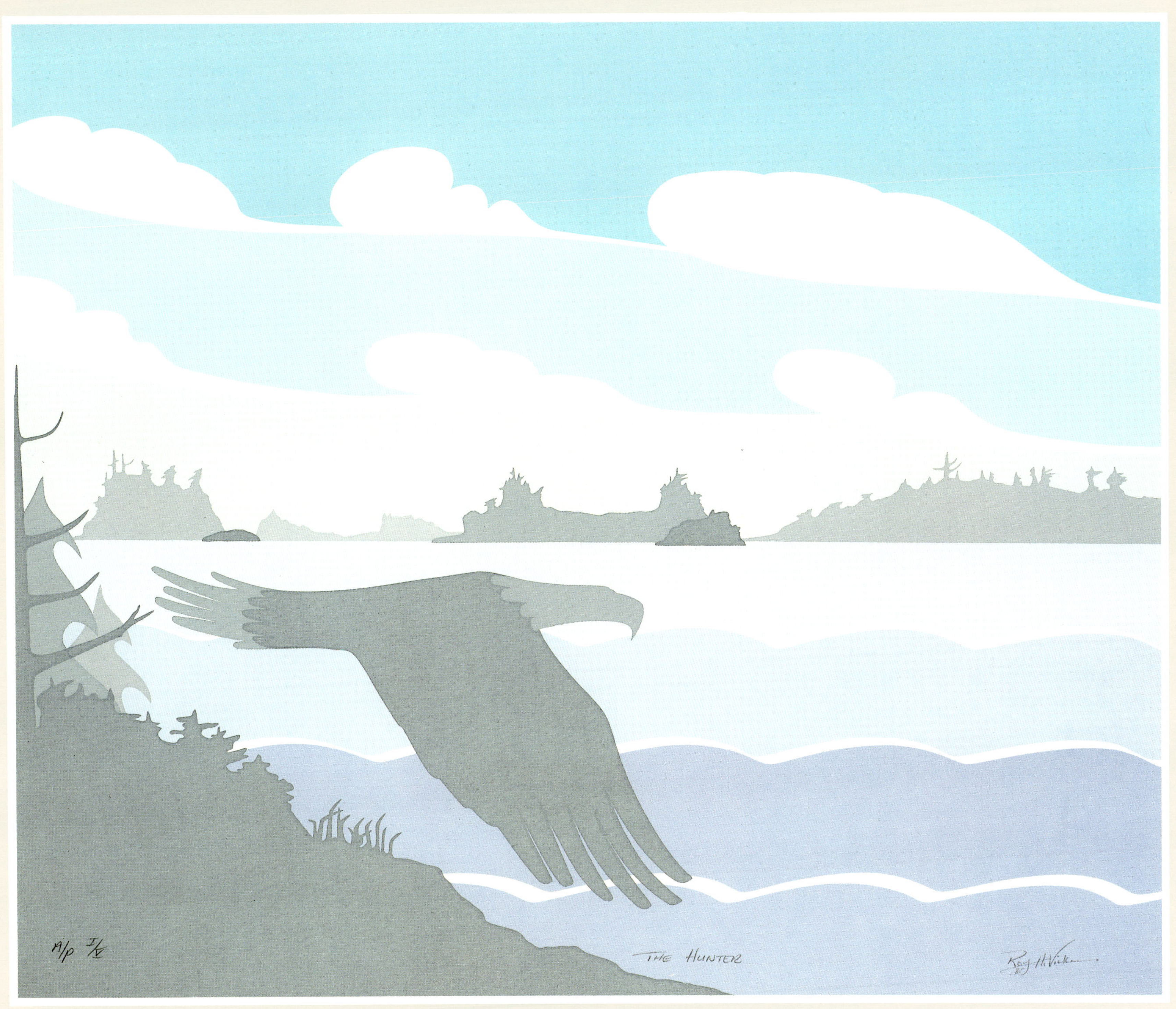
THE HUNTER

WHALER ISLETS

My first attraction to Whaler Islets was the beautiful, sandy beach that almost completely surrounds the larger of the two small islands. Later, I was drawn once again to the same islet by news of a beached whale. I thought it was an incredible coincidence that of all the islands the whale could have landed on, it happened upon Whaler Islet.

The islets are situated in the southwest portion of Clayquot Sound, and are a favourite stopping point for boaters who cruise these waters in the summer months. Some of the most beautiful sunsets I have ever seen were looking west to WHALER ISLETS and the open Pacific Ocean beyond.

(Released August, 1985)

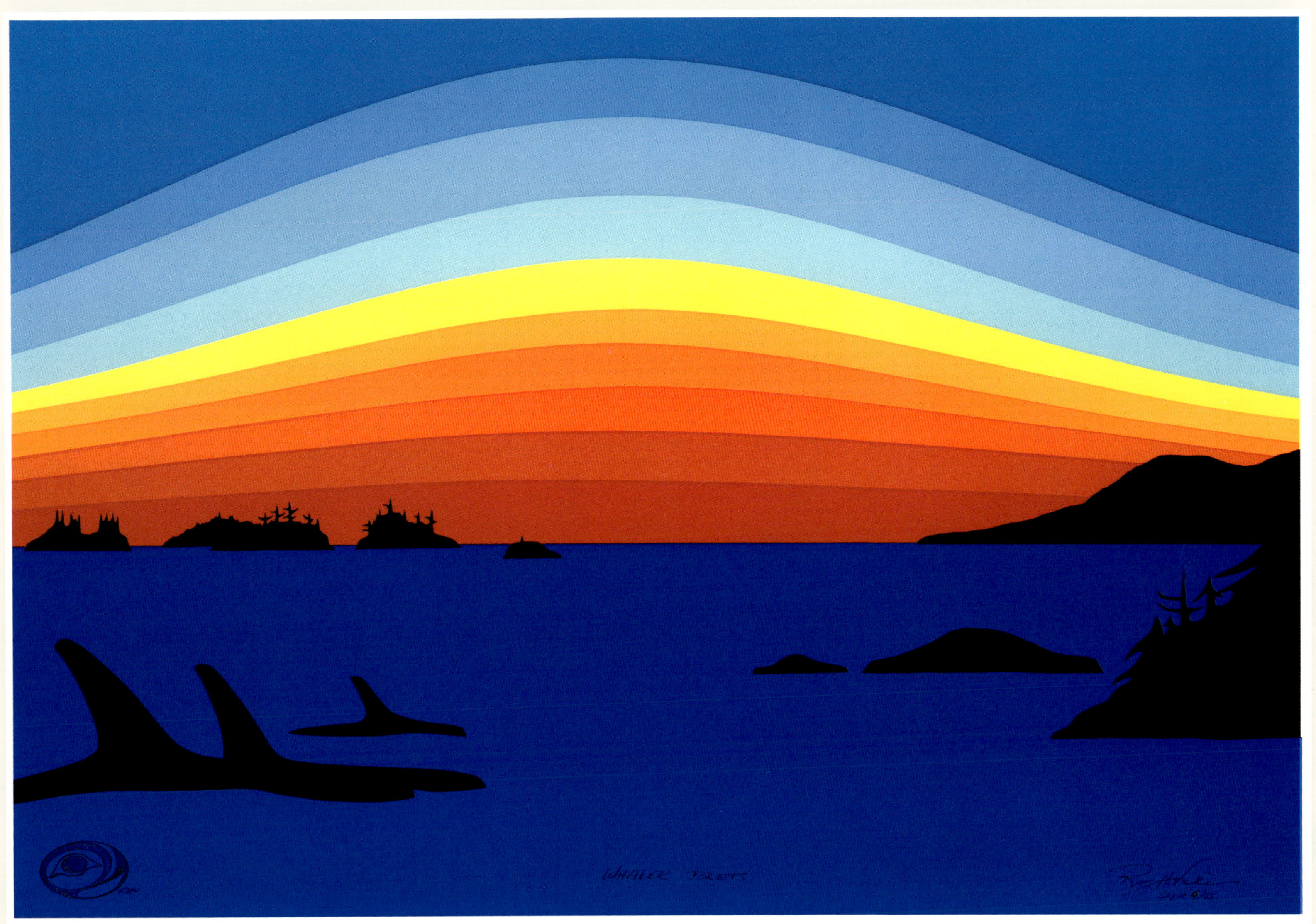
WHALER ISLETS

EAGLE'S MOON

A beautiful evening, basking in the afterglow of a West Coast sunset.

The moon has risen in the deep blue sky to the east, casting shadows on the beach and dancing moonbeams on the surf.

You know there could be no more perfection to an evening . . .

Just then, you gaze back at the moon to notice an eagle has landed in the uppermost branches of a tree, as if to come and share the magic. From that moment on, you will always remember the evening as the 'Eagle's Moon'.

I imagined a friend of mine captivated by this experience when he took the photograph that inspired EAGLE'S MOON.

It is just such a moment that forever calls one back to Vancouver Island's West Coast.

(Released August, 1985)

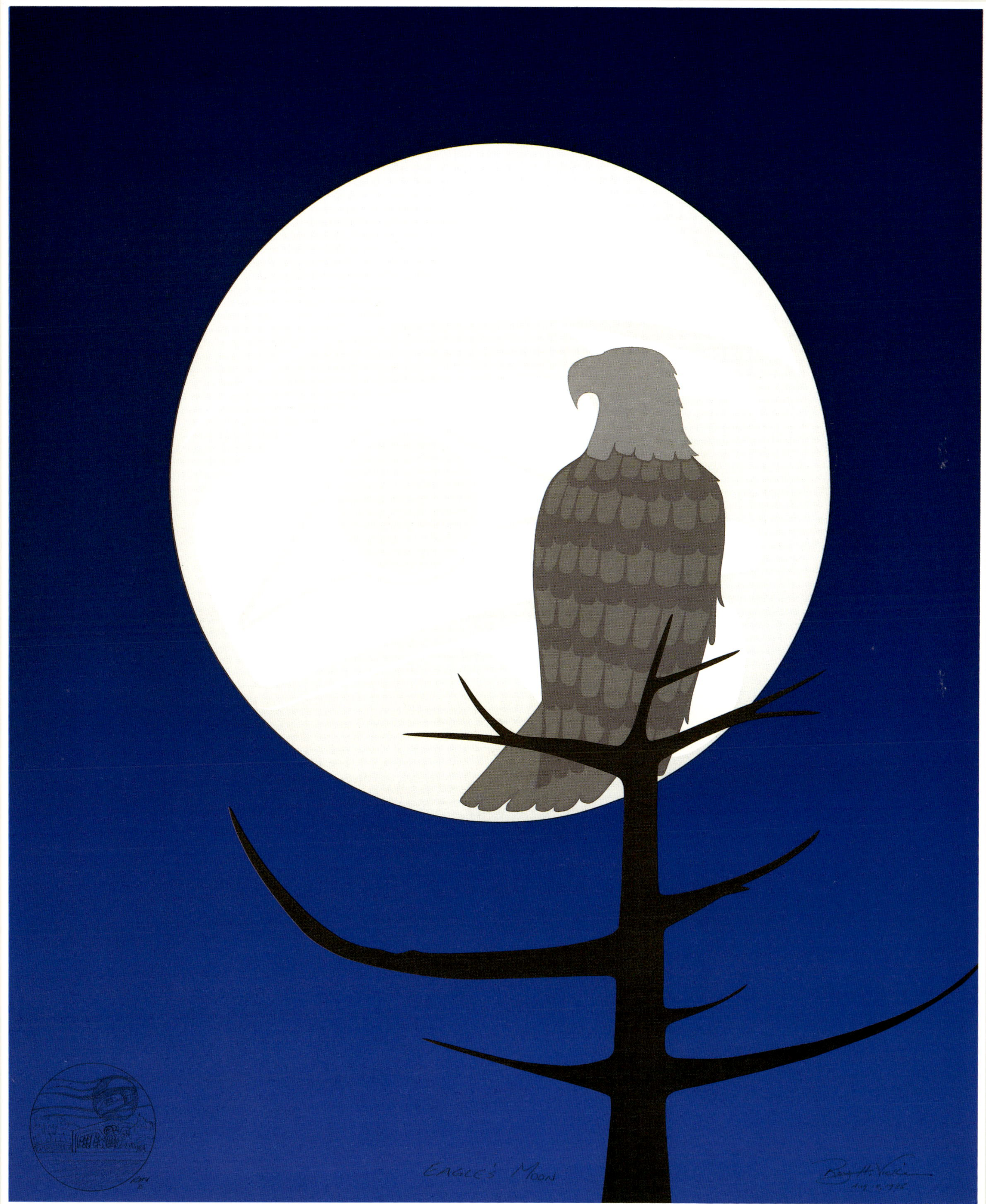
EAGLE'S MOON

COWICHAN

This work was commissioned by Hill's Cowichan Stores. Mrs. Francis Hill has been a great source of encouragement to me since the beginning of my career as an artist. When this commission from Hill's Stores came to me, it was natural to think of the first canoe races I saw when I came to Victoria.

The memory that came to mind was a Cowichan war canoe racing through the waters of Mill Bay or Brentwood Bay as the Indian paddlers chanted for timing in their strokes, the sun setting in the west. This was the inspiration for COWICHAN.

(Released August, 1985)

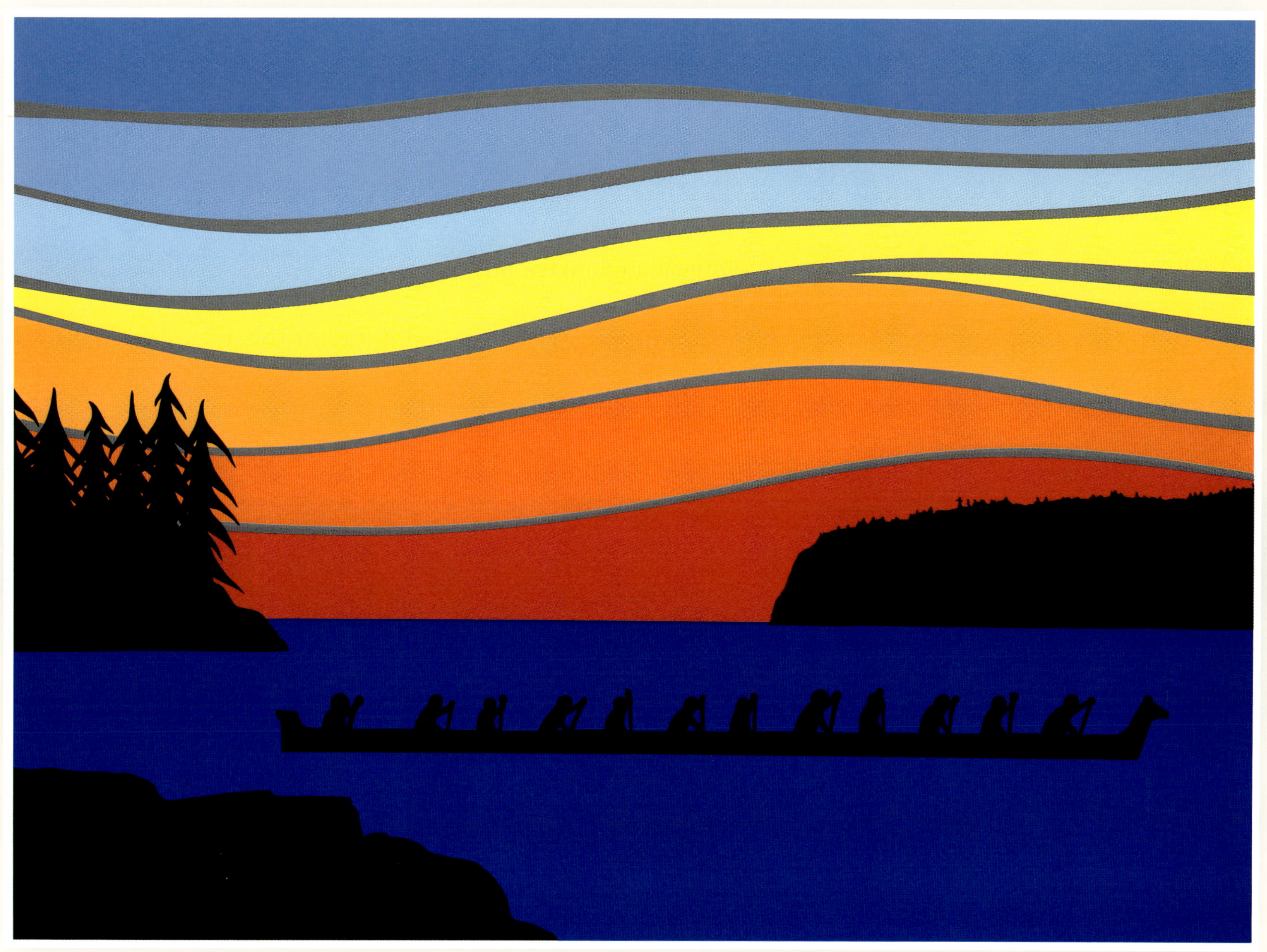

MEGIN LAKE

In the summer of 1984, I completed a painting titled MEGIN, named after the river that flows from Megin Lake into Shelter Inlet just north of Tofino.

I have made numerous trips into Megin Lake with fishing buddies and it is always a thrill. The trip to Megin Lake includes a float plane ride, landing on the lake, and then canoeing down to the ocean to be picked up by plane.

It is with cherished memories of the pristine beauty of our coast and the thrill of catching the 'big one' that I have created MEGIN LAKE.

(Released November, 1985)

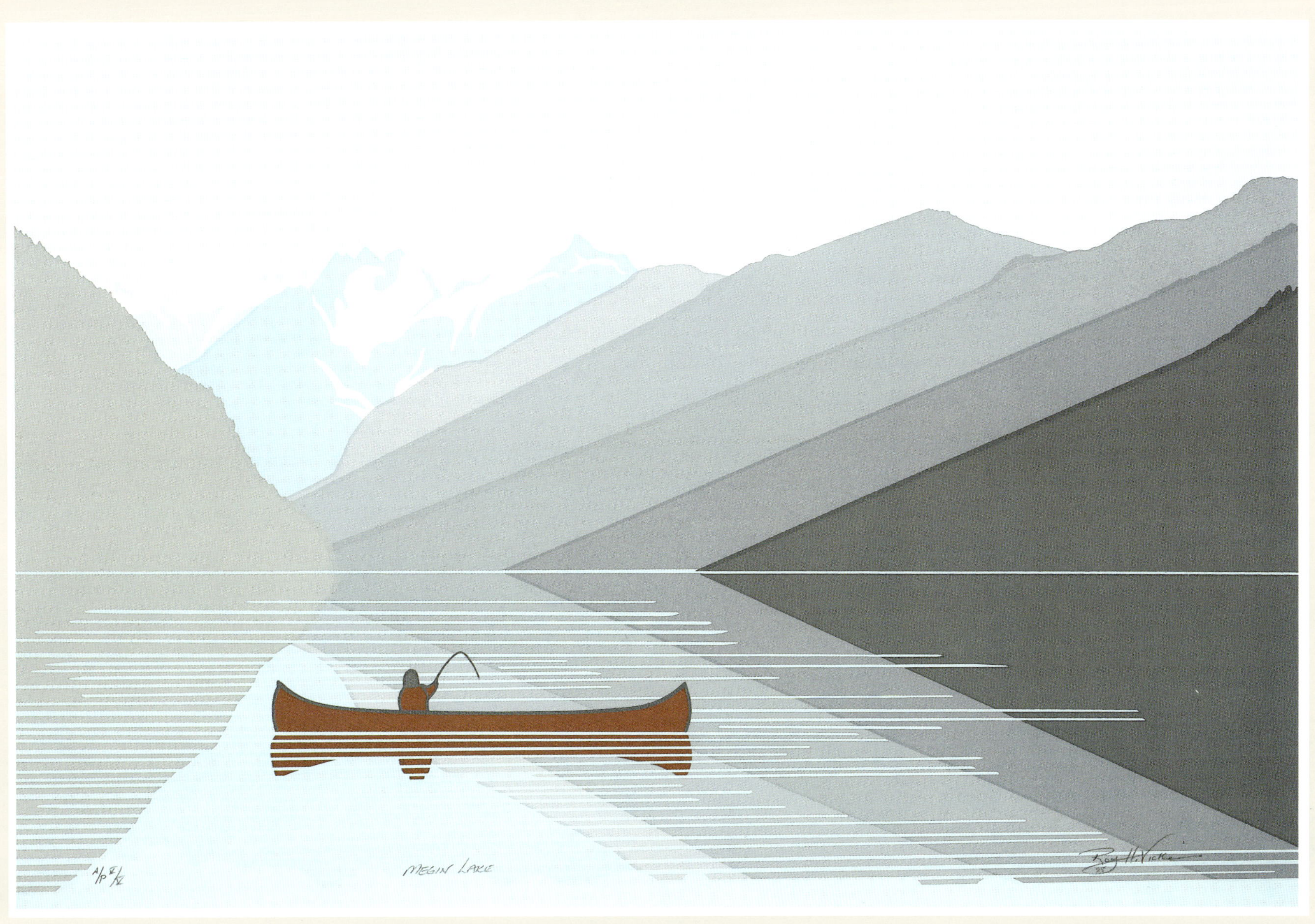
MEGIN LAKE

AN OLD EAGLE

On a visit to the ancient village site of Ninstints, I came upon an old eagle totem pole that had seen better days. Easily a lifetime of years of wind and rain and sun had left their marks on this stately old pole. The beak had long since decayed and fallen from the bird's face. The remains of the old eagle were silvery grey with deep, weathered lines in the grain of the wood. The pole was standing at a great angle that hinted at its descent, to be reunited with the womb of Mother Earth. A desire to capture the demise of this once tall and proud sculpture overcame me. The result of my efforts was AN OLD EAGLE.

(Released October, 1985)

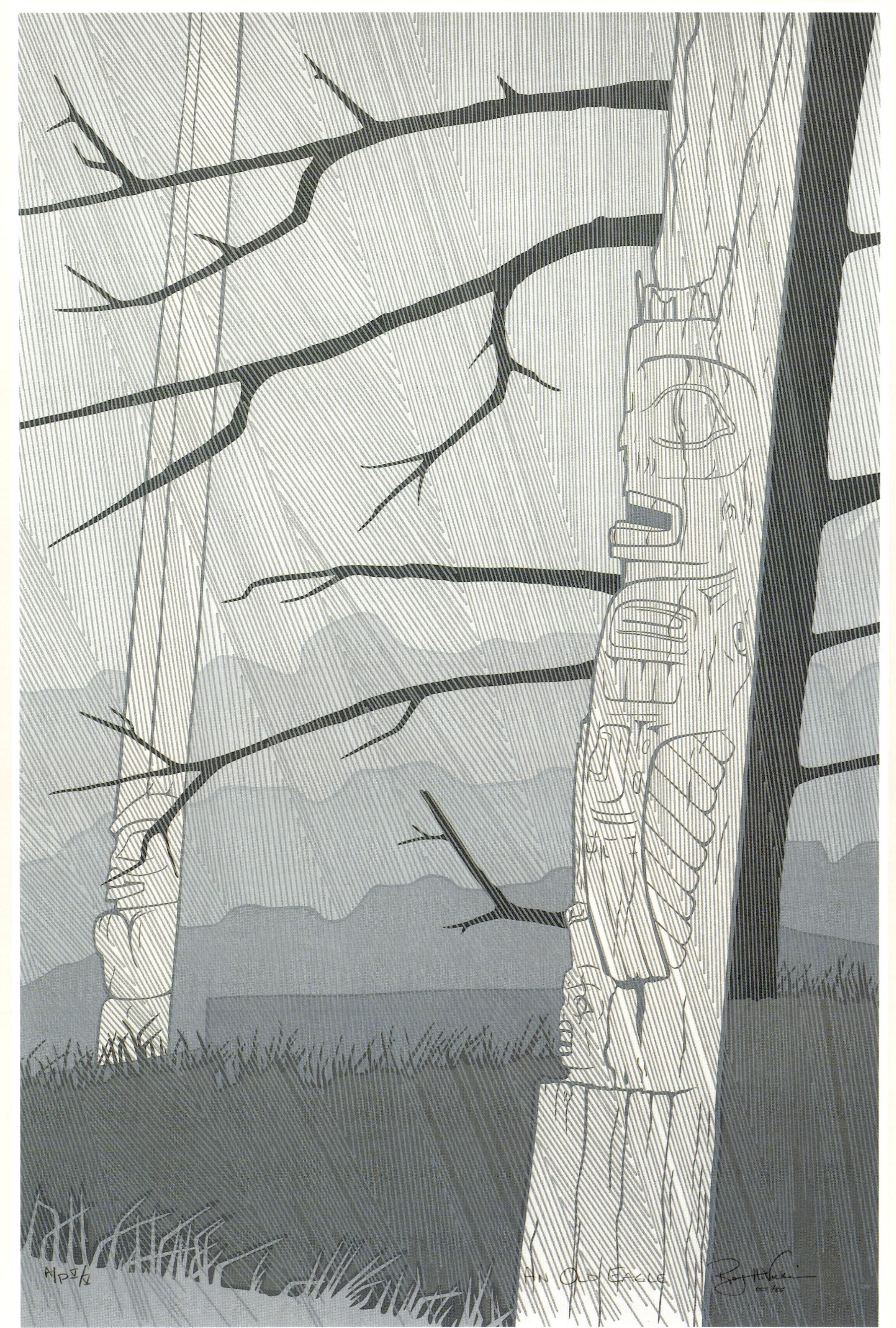
A/P V/X
An Old Eagle
Oct /88

THE OLD BULL

A cruise with friends to Sea Lion Rock on a beautiful summer day is always an exciting experience and an inspiration. The particular day that inspired this rendition of THE OLD BULL, we were out enjoying a lazy afternoon. As we approached the rock, the sea lions began a scramble to the safety of the ocean. That is all except one—The Old Bull. This bull sea lion was easily distinguishable because he was the only light brown bull in the herd. King of his domain, he sat there quite dignified, and then let out a roar of disapproval as he returned our gaze. The cormorants in the background seemed to take courage from the old bull and also remained there, much to our pleasure.

(Released February, 1986)

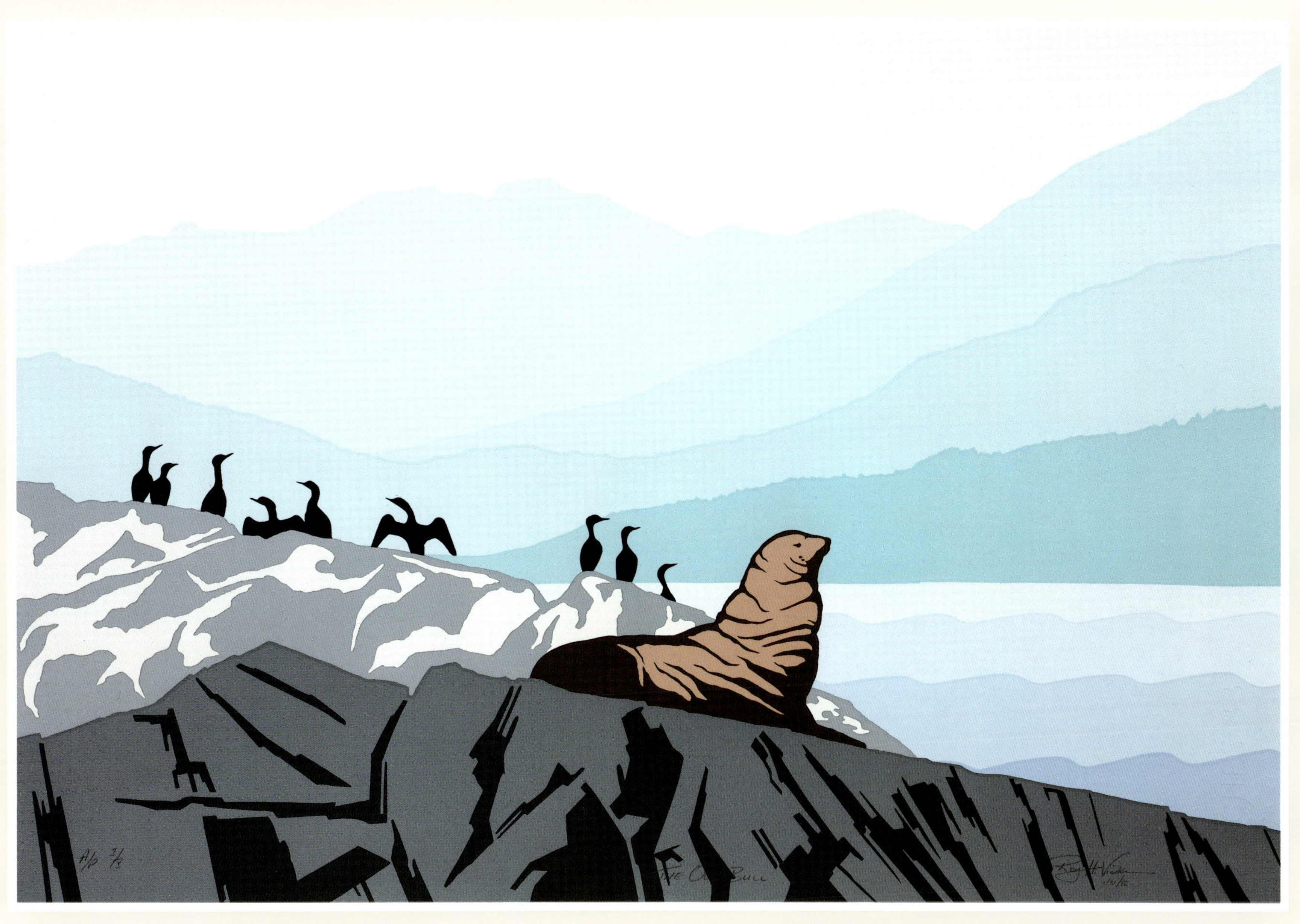

MORNING GLORY

This is another fishing story, inspired in part by a fly-tying kit I received for Christmas.

Over the winter, my friend Ed taught me the fine art of tying my own flies. This got me dreaming of catching a steelhead fish on my own hand-tied fly.

I set out on a fishing trip with Ed to fulfill this dream and simultaneously gather inspiration for a new painting. The painting and edition of prints were to be framed and matted in such a way as to display a mounted fly tied by me personally.

As luck would have it, I didn't catch a steelhead. Ed did, albeit not on a fly, but there was my inspiration anyway!

When the painting was completed, Ed and I stopped in at the Stamp River Angler in Port Alberni to discuss with Ken, the owner, a suitable fly pattern to compliment the artwork. A unanimous choice was MORNING GLORY. Hence, the title of a new painting and edition of prints.

(Released May, 1986)

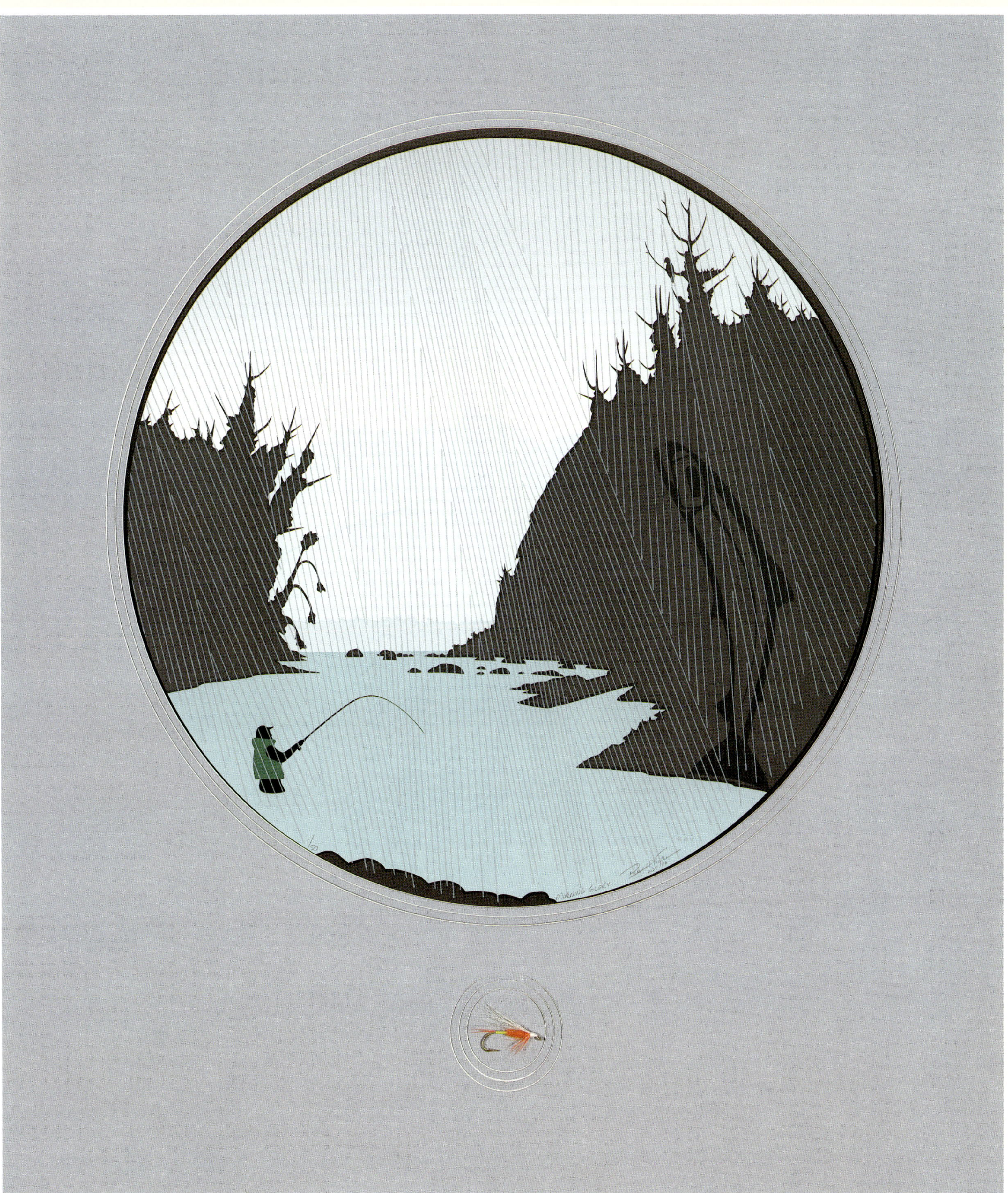
MORNING GLORY

PORTHOLES TO THE PAST

Many times throughout each year, I find it necessary to reflect on the past. It always seems to give a better understanding of the present and an ability to think more clearly regarding the future. As the years go by, I find myself treasuring the knowledge of my heritage and wanting to share it with as many people as I can before my life is over. Often I have looked at old village sites from the deck of a boat and wondered what people thought when the first ships came within view of those ancient lands.

The theme of 'Portholes to the Past' developed slowly over three years. Choosing five villages was very difficult. It was with a degree of nostalgia and a great deal of pride that I presented SKEDANS, NINSTINTS, BELLA BELLA, KITKATLA, KINGCOME—the 'PORTHOLES TO THE PAST.'

(Released October, 1986)

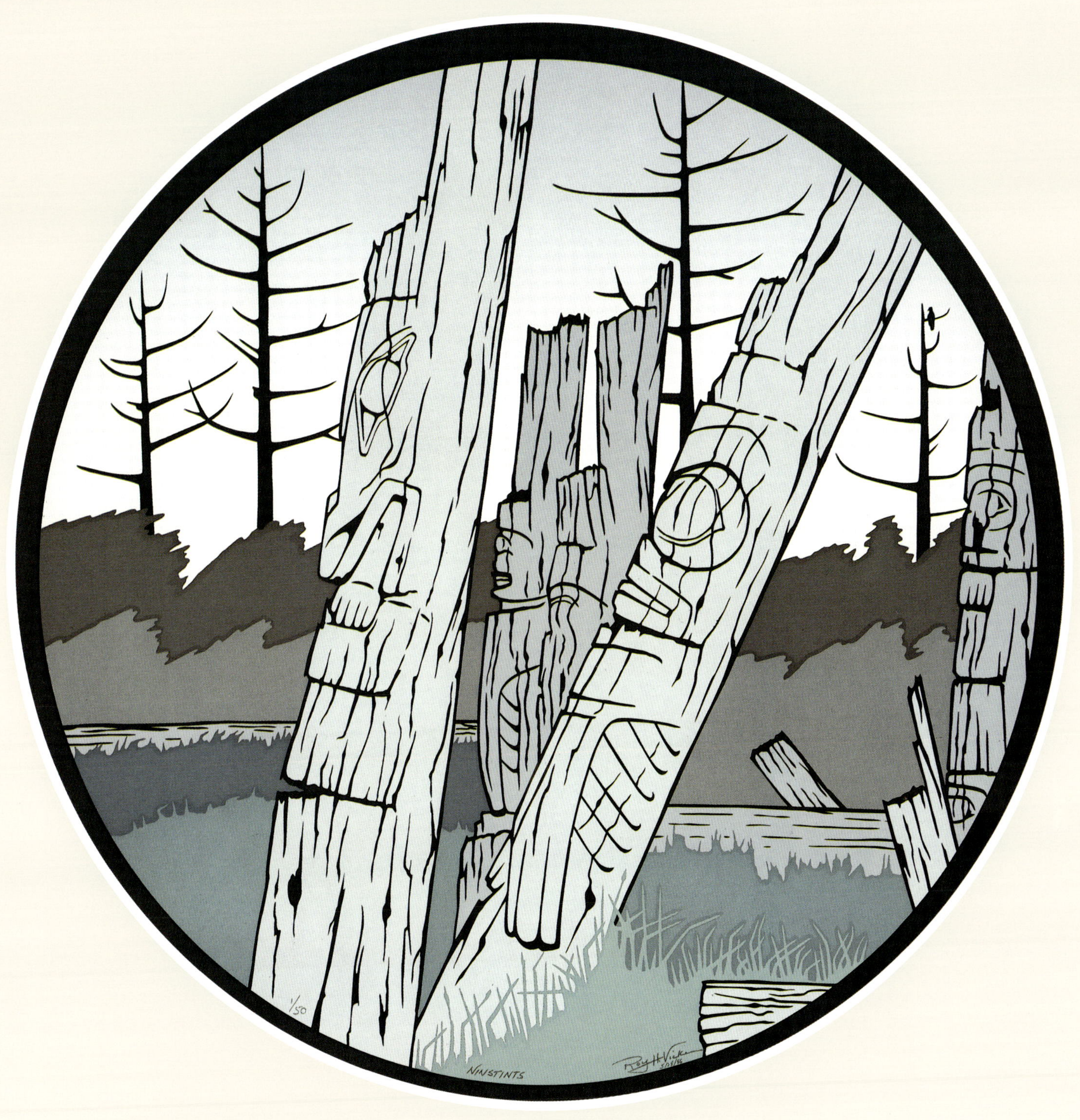

NINSTINTS

NINSTINTS, now a world heritage site, was my first choice as a subject for 'Portholes to the Past'. Its remoteness and famous stand of old, weathered, silver totems long interested me. On my visit to Ninstints, I felt as though I was stepping into a cathedral. I was overcome by a feeling of awe and sadness. As I sat amidst the remnants of the village, I was impressed and inspired by the power and majesty of what remained.

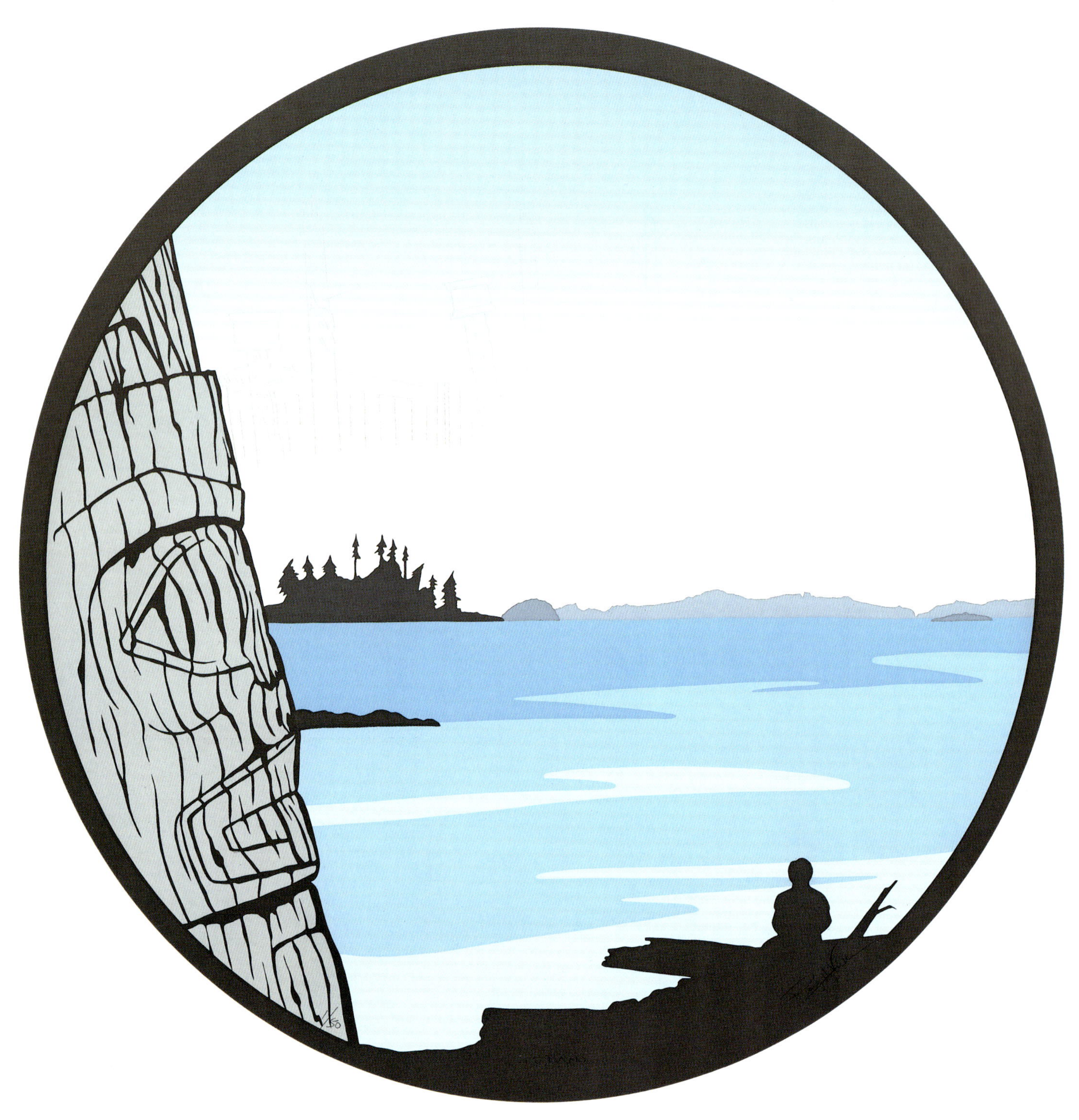

SKEDANS

Situated on a little bay on Louise Island, south of Sandspit in the Queen Charlottes, is a beautiful village site—Skedans. My first introduction to Skedans was in the early 1970's when I met John Smyly at the British Columbia Provincial Museum. On my numerous visits to the museum, I used to stop in and visit with John, who was carving the entire village and poles of Skedans in miniature. The model village is now a permanent display in the museum. At that time I had no idea that one day I would create a painting called SKEDANS.

I finally arrived at the old site in October, 1985 and most of those grand, beautiful totems were lying on the ground in varying states of decay—slowly returning to the earth. I found myself overcome with emotions. I sat in the autumn sunshine gazing upon the same seascape as the villagers once had, dreaming and envisioning the ancient village as it once must have been.

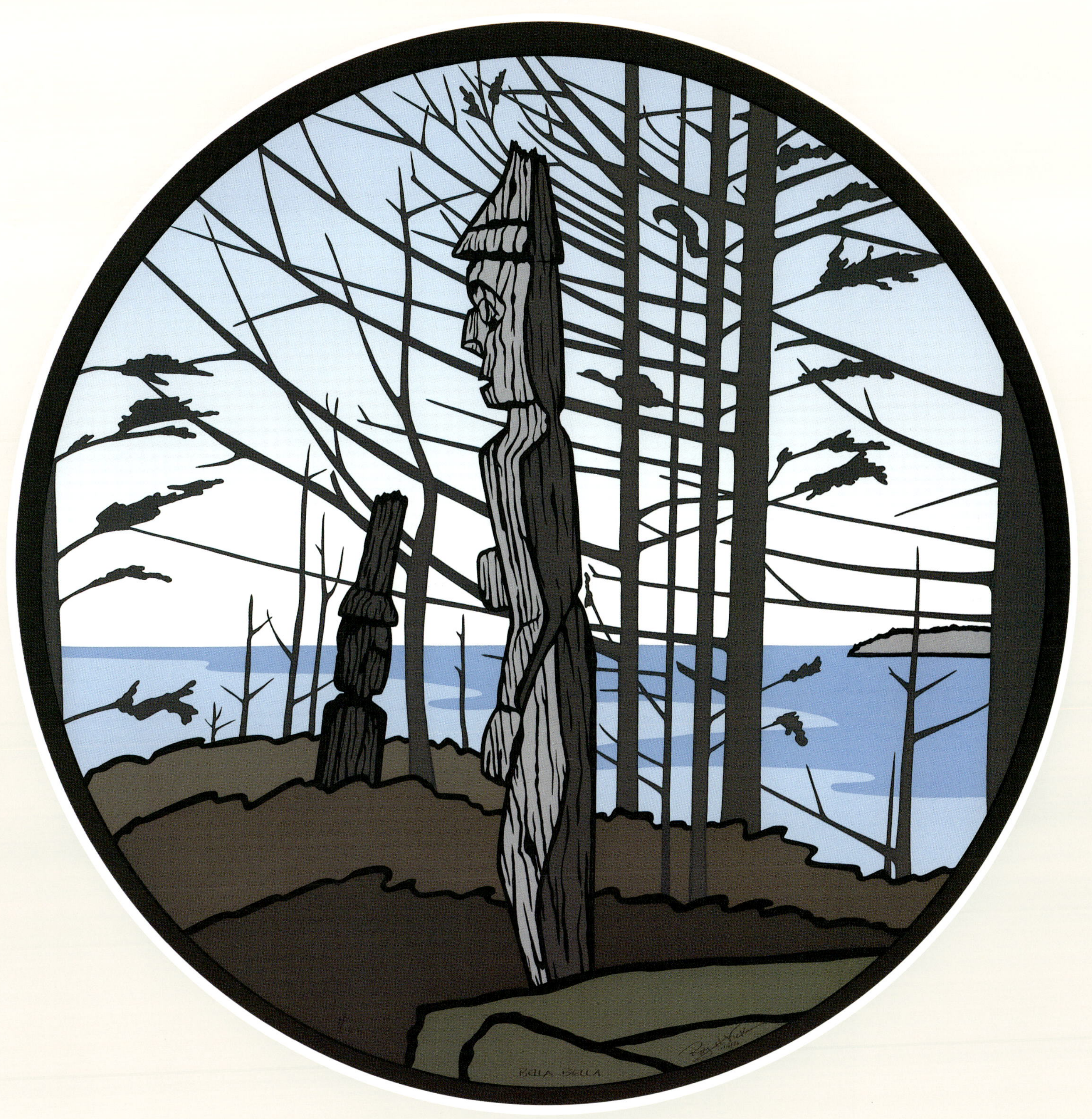

BELLA BELLA

BELLA BELLA, the home of my grandfather, Henry Vickers, was an obvious choice for the 'porthole series', because the Vickers' name comes from this area. On my visit to Bella Bella, I was taken by a friend to an old grave site high on a bluff overlooking the open ocean. Not much seems to be known about the two lone sentinels here, except that someone of importance drowned at this ancient fishing ground, and the two poles were carved and erected at the site.

Bella Bella is situated on Campbell Island about midway up the famous inside passage to Prince Rupert.

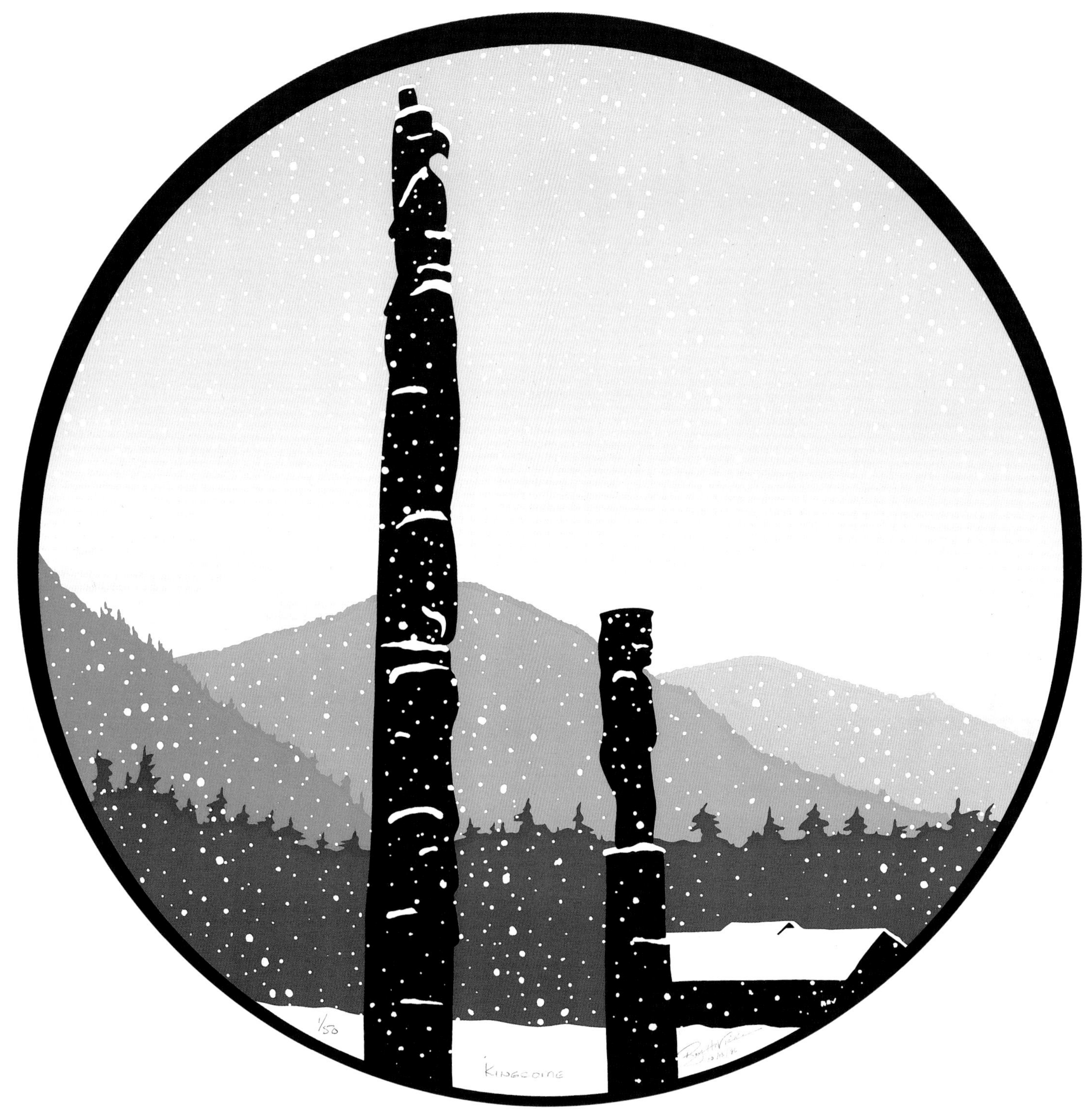

KINGCOME

I had difficulty with 'Mamalilicoola', which was to have been the fifth and final 'porthole'. The inspiration just would not come to me.

On my flight to Kitkatla, however, the pilot suggested the possibility of a stop at Kingcome Village, at the head of Kingcome Inlet. He knew of an old longhouse and a few poles. The result was a memorable visit to a beautiful little village on a warm, late, summer afternoon.

The two totems in KINGCOME stand on the path that leads to one of the oldest longhouses to still stand on our beautiful West Coast.

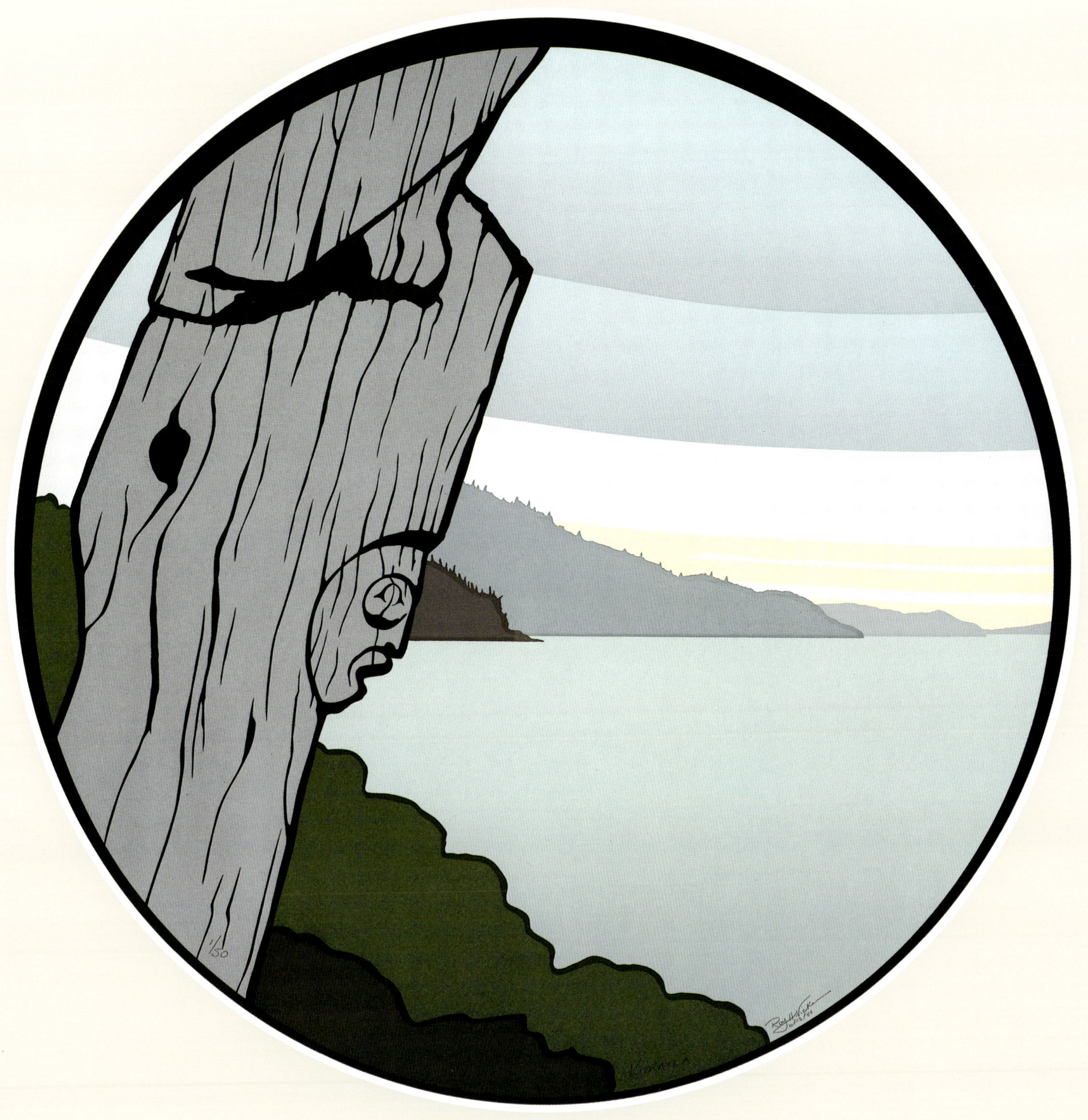

KITKATLA

KITKATLA, the home of my childhood, was a natural choice for one of the 'portholes'. In 1983, I had created a piece called 'Westcoast Winter', which was to be the inspiration and the forerunner of this series.

In the summer, I returned to the village of my youth to photograph the two totems that were left standing. I soon discovered upon my arrival that one of the poles had fallen, and the one remaining was in a state of decay. In the pole that is left, there is a face gazing out from the wood as if caught continually meditating on the past.

SUMMER SOLSTICE

It was the last day of spring and already the evening air hinted of summer. We were finishing a round of golf at the Long Beach Golf Course. The smell of fresh mown grass and the song of a Robertson's thrush whistled above the crashing surf in the distance, all reminders that summer was upon us. It seemed that the full moon appeared suddenly behind the gigantic cedar snag. It was another of those magic moments that one experiences on the West Coast.

(Released July, 1986)

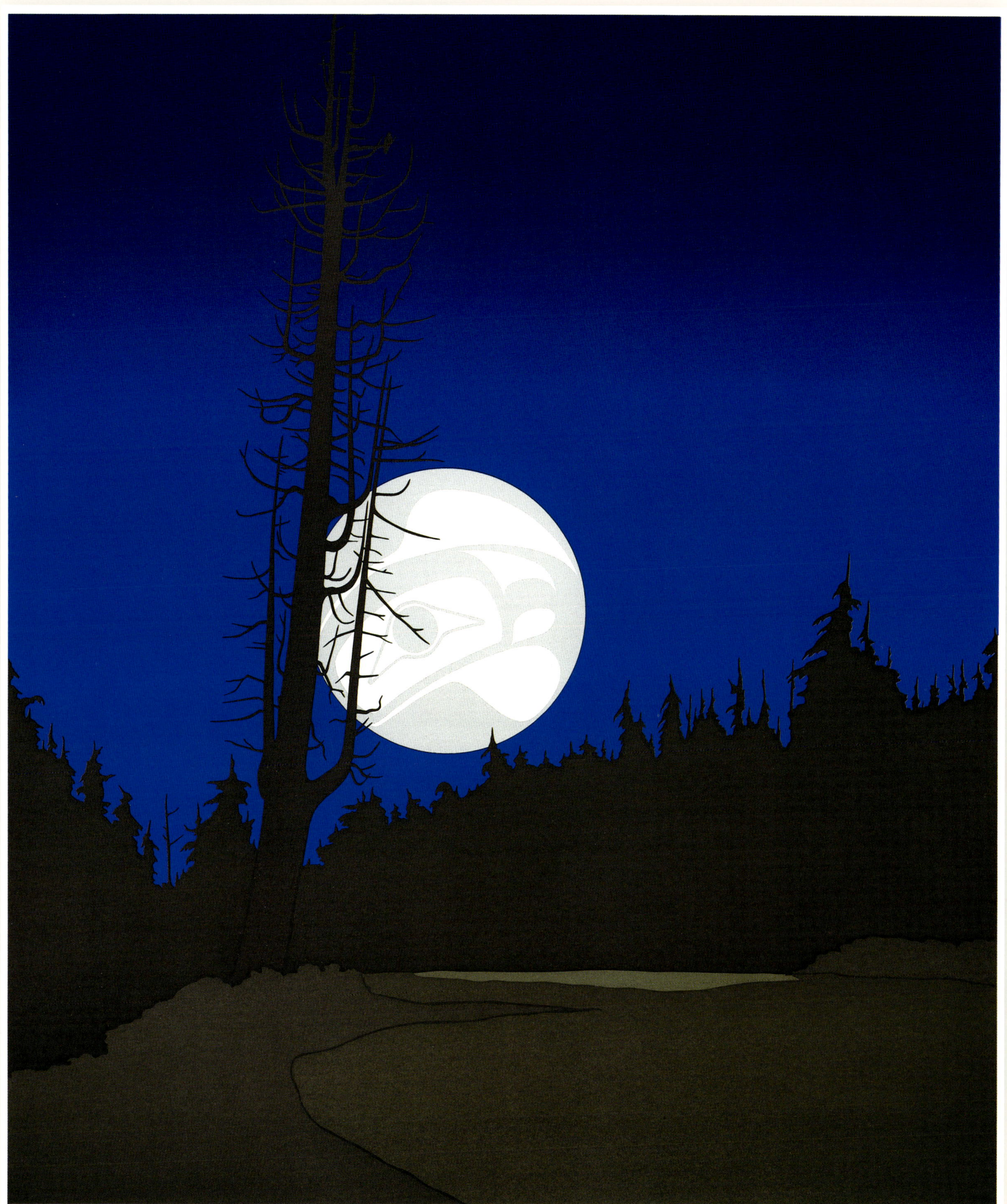

OLD TOWN

I was working on a very important series of images called 'Portholes to the Past' which required a visit to Bella Bella, the home of my grandfather Henry Vickers. During this visit, I spent some time in the cultural centre and was assisted by friends in understanding a bit of the history of this village that was so important to me.

I realized that many villages at the time of white or European contact evolved from smaller villages scattered over hundreds of square miles, with Bella Bella being an example. Today Bella Bella is one of the largest Indian reservations in British Columbia.

The intrigue for me in this learning experience was that Bella Bella never used to exist on its present site, but was a few miles south in a quiet bay. The old site is simply referred to today as OLD TOWN.

(Released August, 1986)

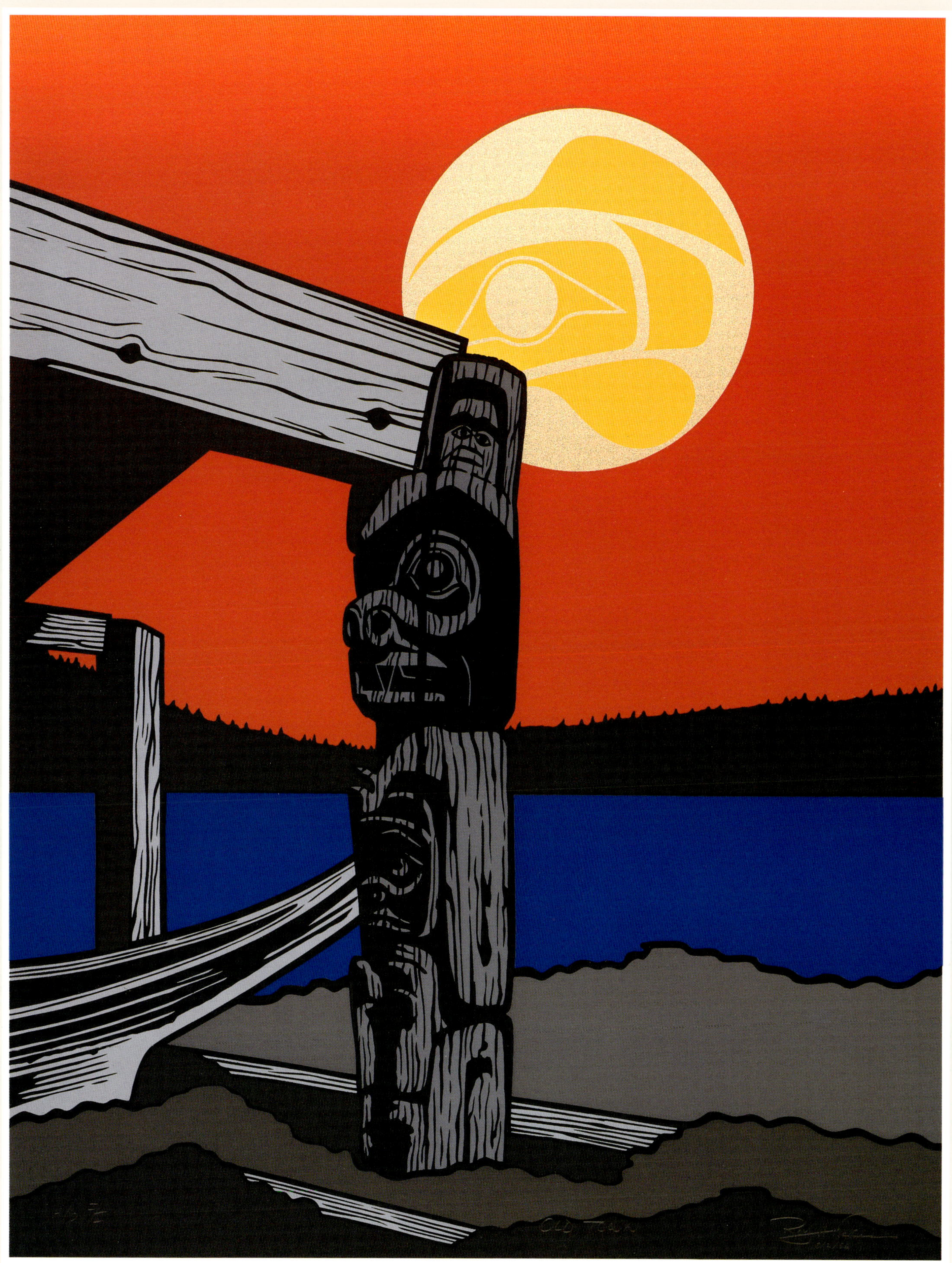
OLD TOWN

SKEENA CROSSING

Each time that I return to this picturesque village on the banks of the Skeena River, countless memories and emotions flood my mind and soul.

One of my most memorable recollections is as a child of five on my first visit to the interior of the province from my home in the village of Kitkatla. SKEENA CROSSING, with its snow-covered earth, trees with no leaves, horses and the wonderful smell of birchwood from a cozy fireplace, was a contrast with Kitkatla and its coastal rains, evergreen trees, eagles, whales and cedarwood fires.

I have travelled to many places during the ensuing years and it is always a pleasure to return to the Skeena River and the warmth of birchwood fires, particularly when it's snowing and sixteen below outside.

(Released December, 1986)

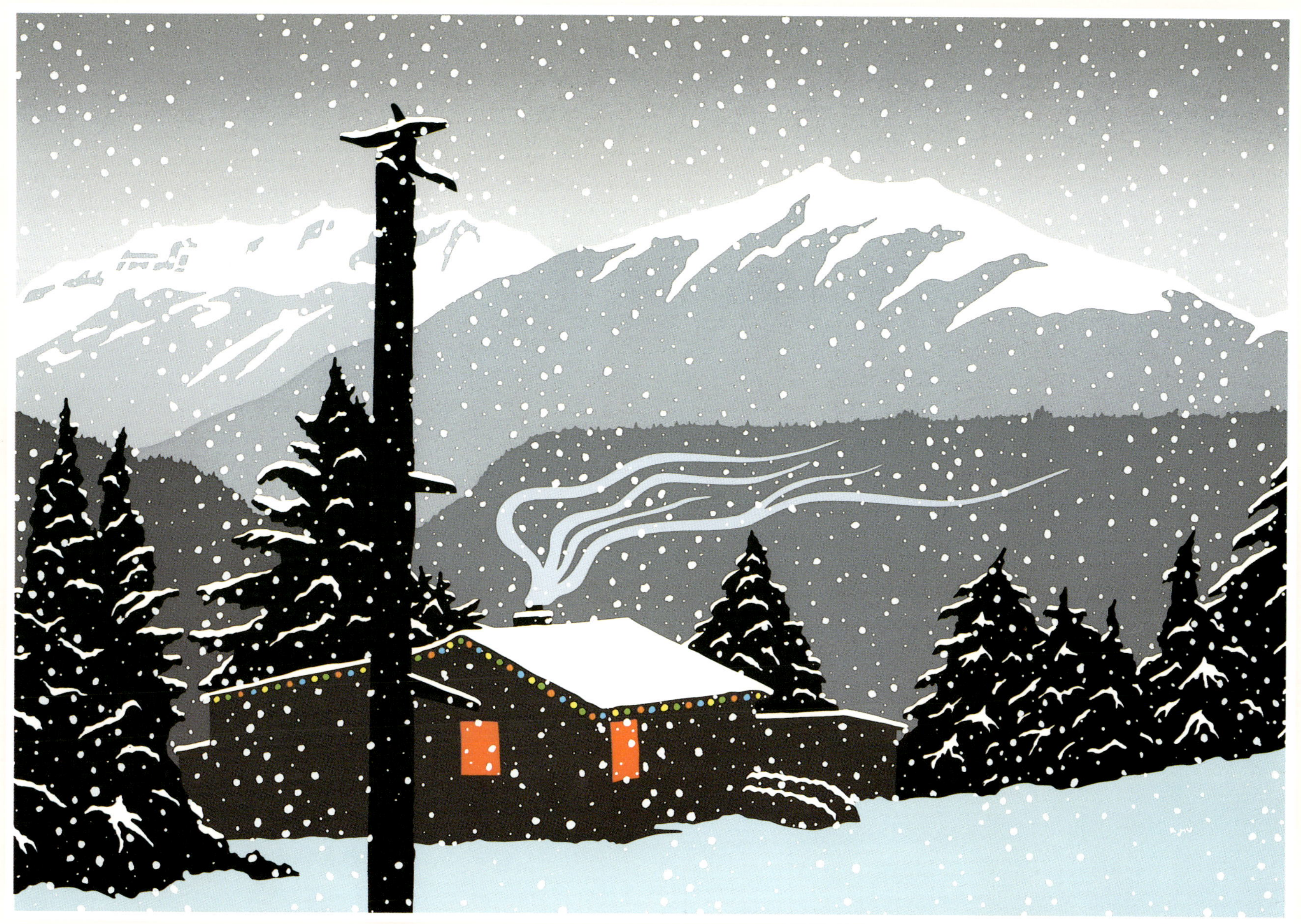

ICY RIVER

Any reason for travelling to a river with fishing rod in hand is an excellent reason.

There was a memorable experience responsible for inspiring this creation called ICY RIVER. I was working with a camera crew putting together footage to be used in a short documentary on myself and my work. Given my love of fishing, we had no choice but to venture out on a cool, wet, late September day and attempt to film the exhilaration and excitement of catching our wonderful, coastal cutthroat trout.

The trip was a success, as it usually is for anyone who likes to fish the West Coast. The feast was a special treat as we tasted the fruits of our labour. We all realized the rare experience we had shared as we sat in the warmth of the cabin and swapped tales of our trip to ICY RIVER.

(Released December, 1986)

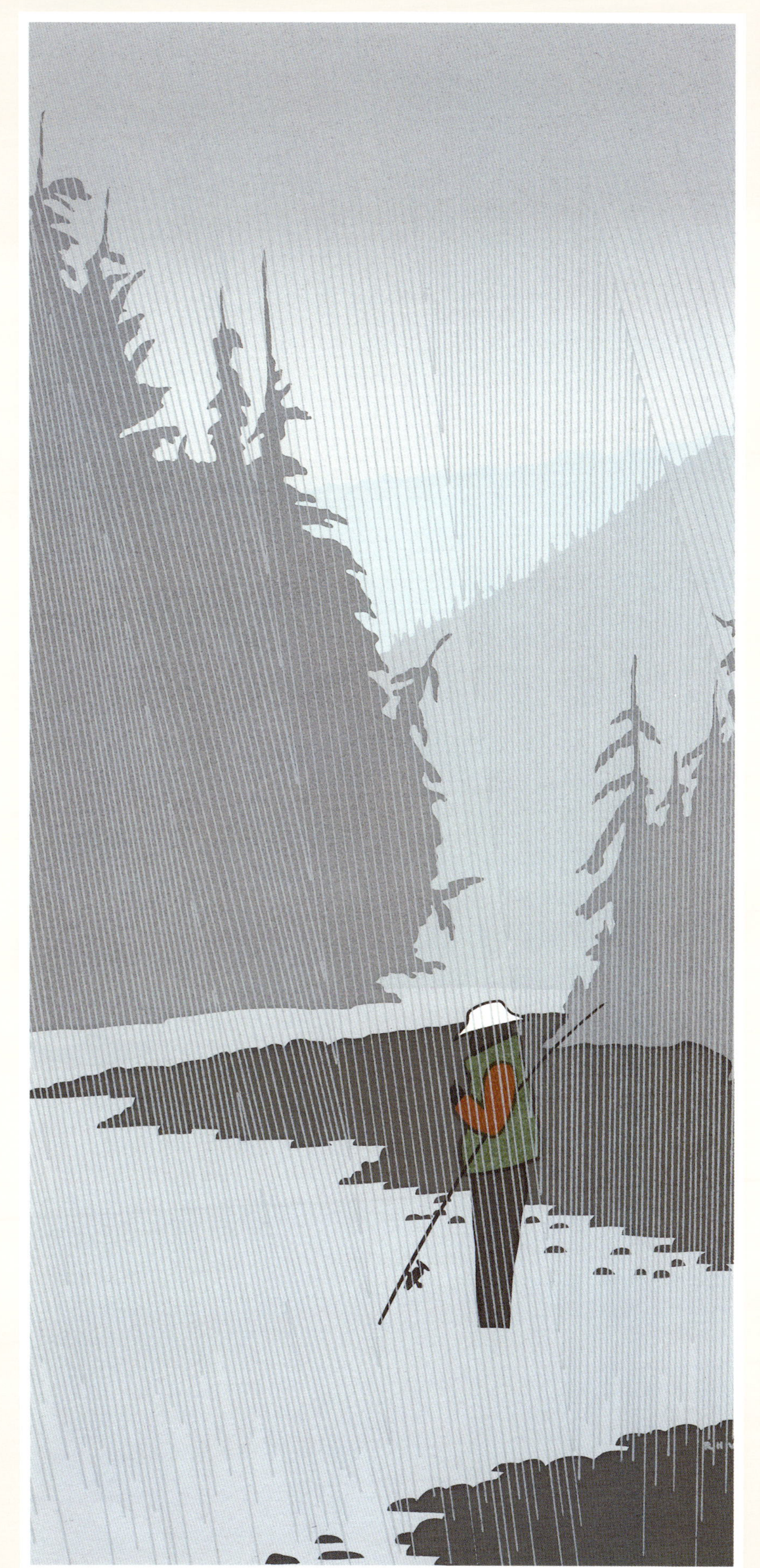

GROUP OF SEVEN

I have finally answered a personal calling, a beckoning to my beginnings. These are the places of some of my earliest and fondest memories and indeed the very roots of my heritage.

My artistic experience has taken me from the basics of traditional West Coast Indian design to a much more contemporary presentation of my work. I have found however, in the GROUP OF SEVEN, a means of expressing my past in a contemporary form of art, yet incorporating the traditional style within the content of each piece.

In the fall of 1986, I travelled to Prince Rupert and then on up the Skeena River. I was not merely in search of subject matter to paint. I was looking for the old memories. I was wanting to experience those places that had seemed so big, so vibrant and so very real to me as a child.

I was accompanied on my excursion by two friends who assisted in photographing the area and the trip itself. They served a further purpose in allowing me to verbalize my thoughts, feelings and emotions.

All of our senses were touched. We saw the majesty of Roche de Boule mountain outside of Hazelton, the towering poles of Kispiox and the enduring serenity and security of the long houses of Ksan. Ksan, the school of West Coast Indian Art where I spent so many hours learning the traditional art and honing my awakening skills.

We heard the roar of the mighty Skeena as it shouldered its way through Four Mile Canyon, and we stood in the stately silence of the poles at Kitwanga. My childhood memories had not failed me. It is now as it was then.

I reached yet further to rekindle those distant thoughts from my past. The feel of the rough grain of the aging poles and the cold winds tingling on my face urged me to express my thoughts and feelings in terms of wood, grey skies and snow. Those sensations that I felt, I have attempted to translate in my painting of the entire GROUP OF SEVEN.

The warmth and the traditional taste of smoked salmon shared at lunch in a native home at Kitwancool stirred even more memories and emotions. The cold, clear water of a mountain stream numbing my mouth as we drank, sealed the memory forever within me. It was as though that stream of my childhood had been trickling from those hills all of this time just so I could share it with my friends. It was a constant, a touchstone of my journey to the past.

The drama of a moonrise behind the pole at Kitsegeukla, otherwise known as Skeena Crossing, was a reaffirmation of my kinship with the artists of the Northwest Coast.

All of these stimulated senses, confirmed by the aroma of distant wood stoves and clean, cold air urged me on. More than ever I felt a compulsion, a driving urge, to put my emotions into paintings of the area as I had remembered it.

I trust that you too can feel in some small way what I felt then and now. If you can, then you too can understand the magnetic urges that I felt in travelling to the Skeena River. Never again will I have to rely soley on memory to sense my past, for I have preserved those sensations, emotions and moods, both for myself and for you in my GROUP OF SEVEN.

(Released April, 1987)

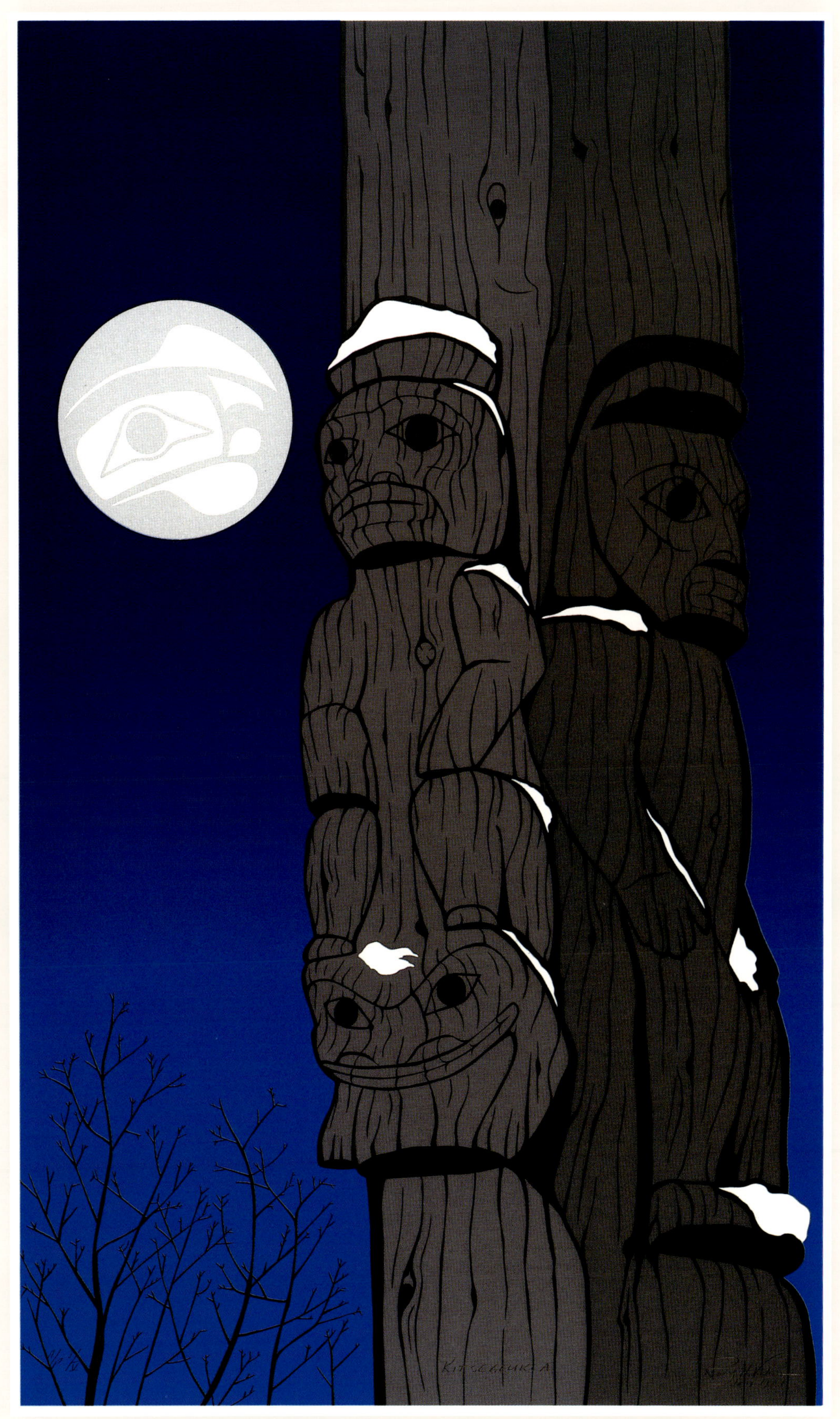

KITSEGUEKLA

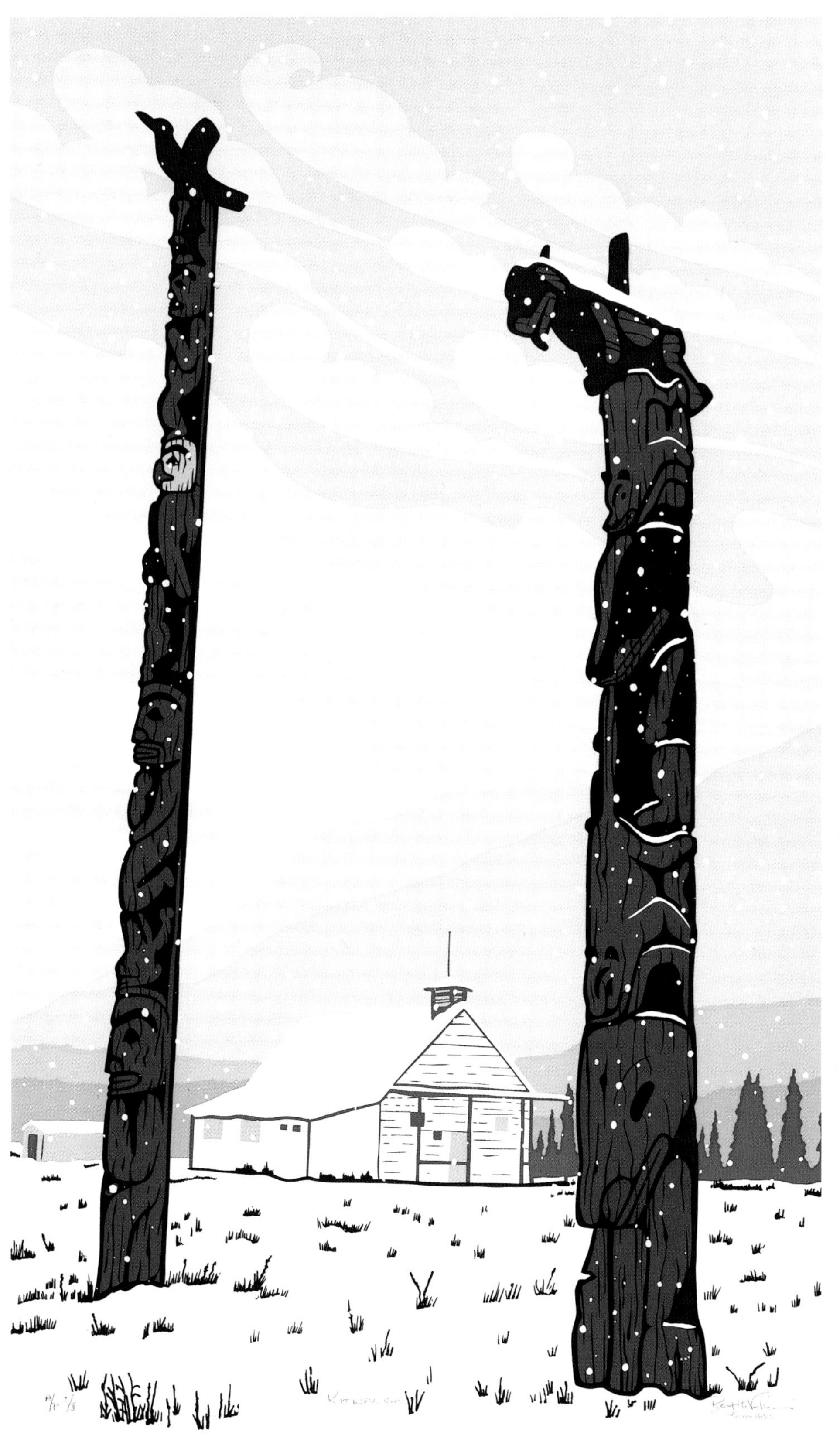

KITWANGA

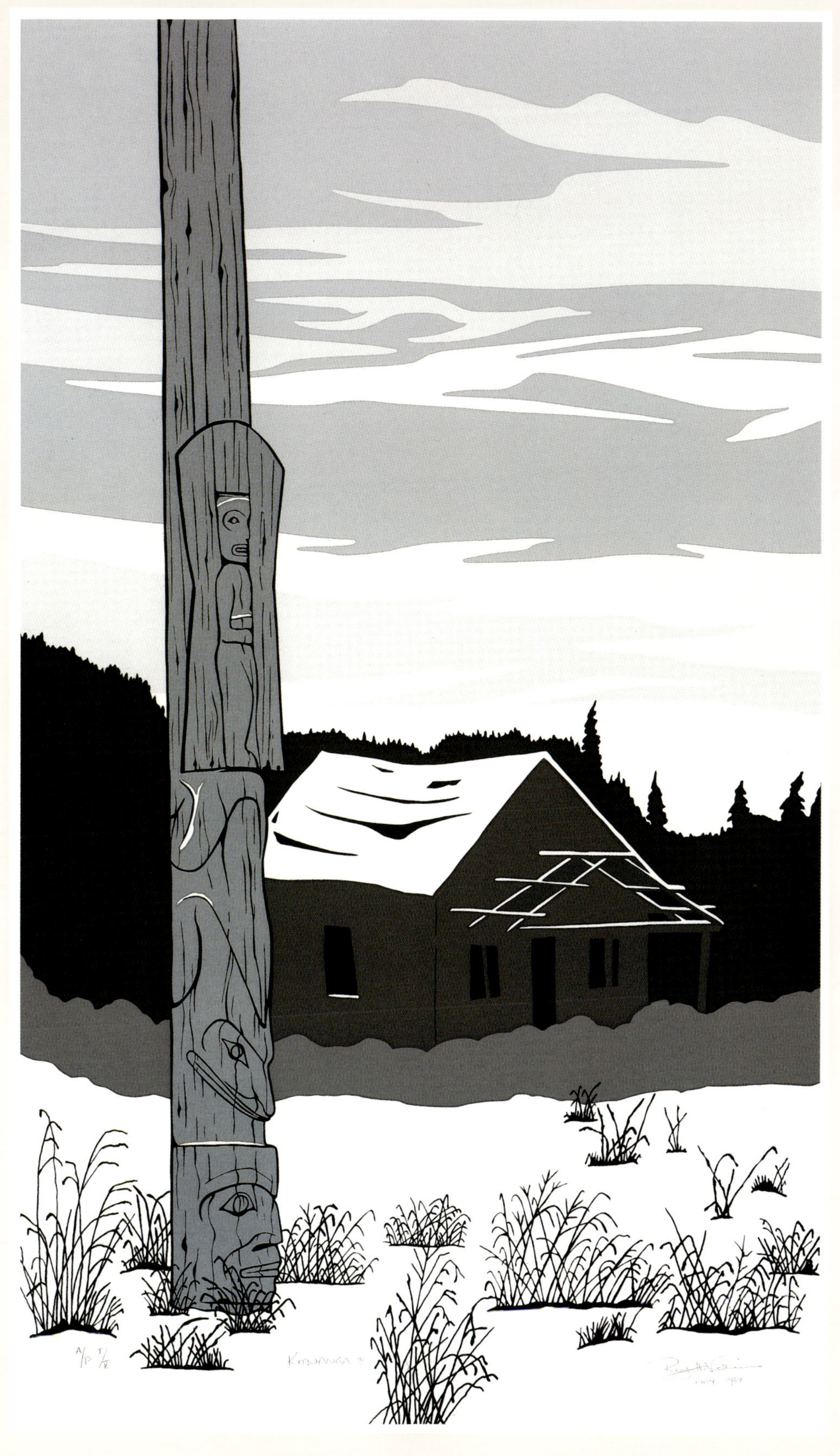

KITWANGA II

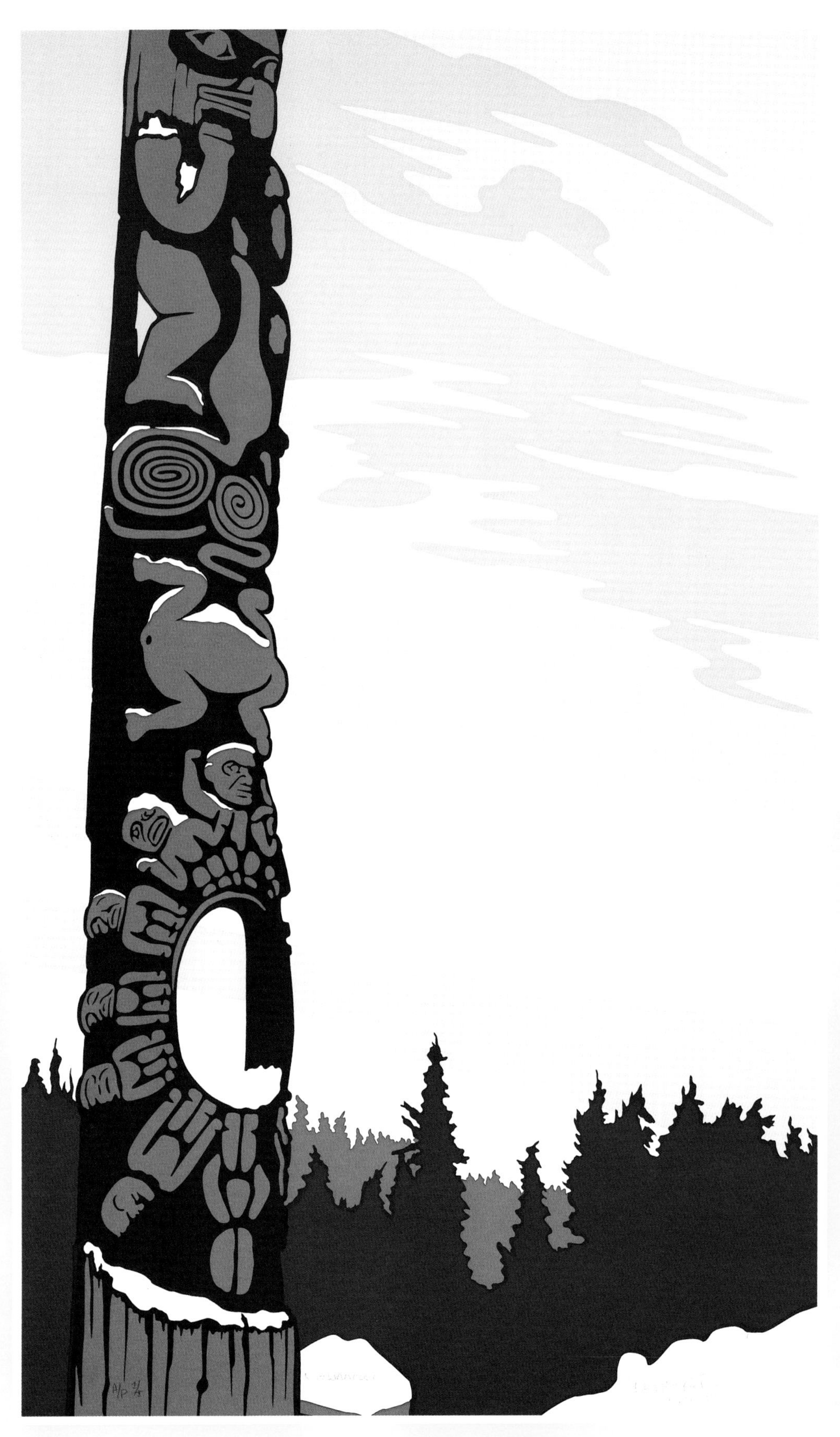

KITWANCOOL

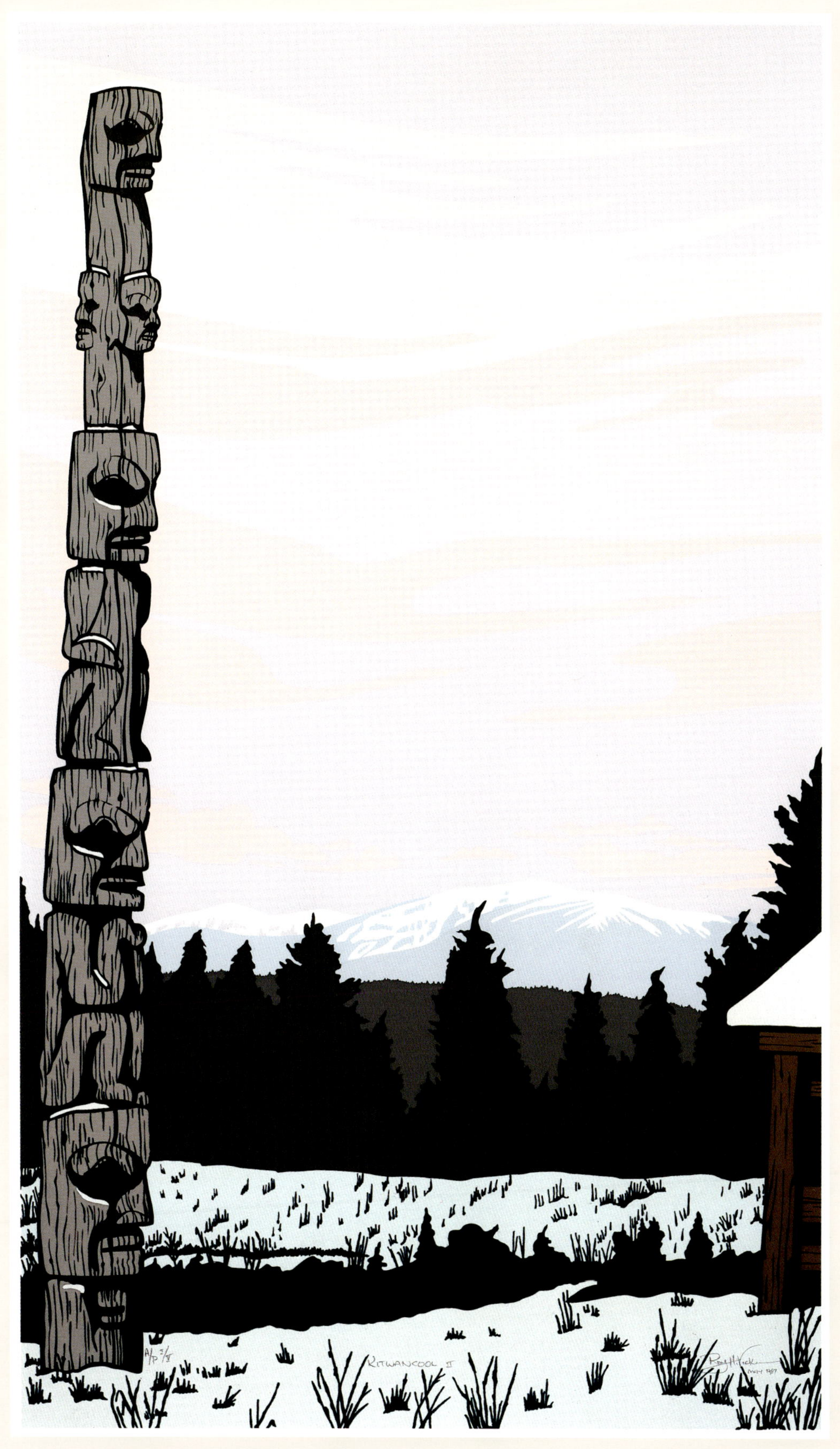

KITWANCOOL II

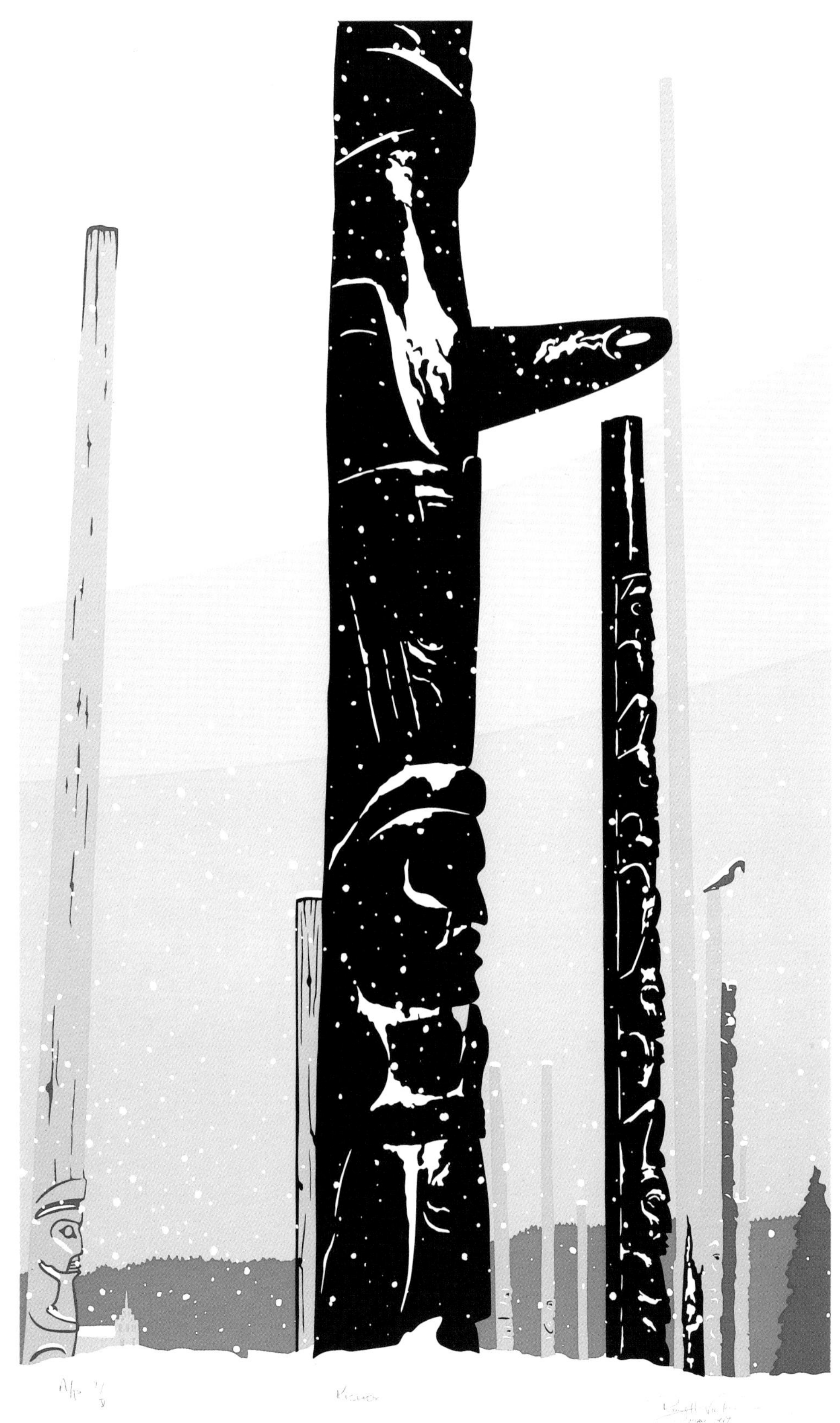

KISPIOX

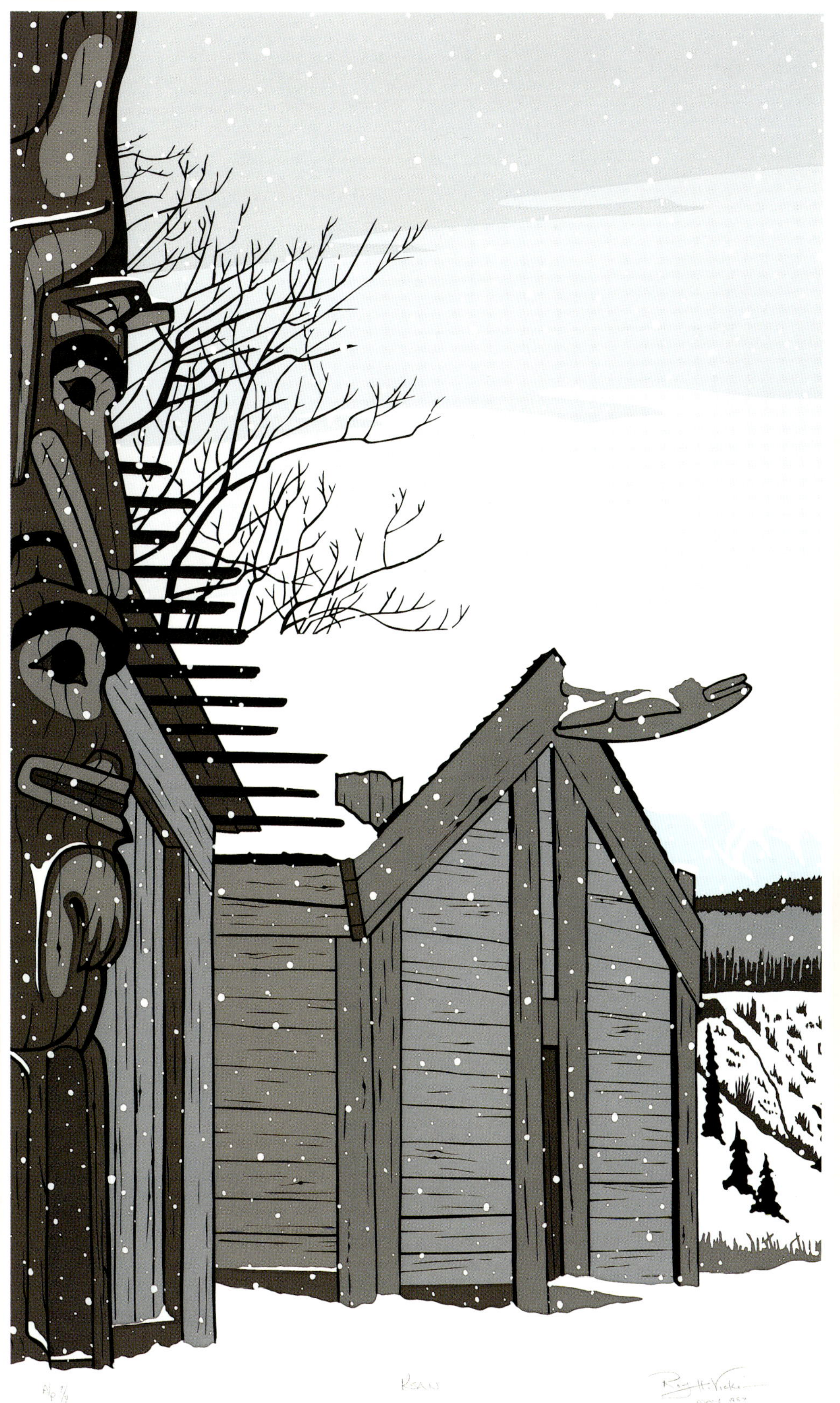

KSAN

THE TWO OF US

To walk in harmony with the world is one of the greatest pleasures in life. The special feeling that your life is quite possibly a contribution to the world you live in—that you may be able to enrich the life of another, can bring much satisfaction to your soul.

The desire to share that harmony with a mate must be the single, largest driving force in a human being. Love is the greatest experience.

Throughout my life, I have had the privilege of being in the company of a few who share this harmonious bond of love. There is actually an aura around them. I was always left with the hope that I, too, could have that treasure of true love. Thousands of words have been penned in poetry, prose and song by and about those who search for that special loving experience. It must be the nearest thing to heaven in this world.

My search ended in Victoria. I met my wife Rhonda in the Art Gallery there. My desire to give her an original painting led to THE TWO OF US.

(Released February, 1987)

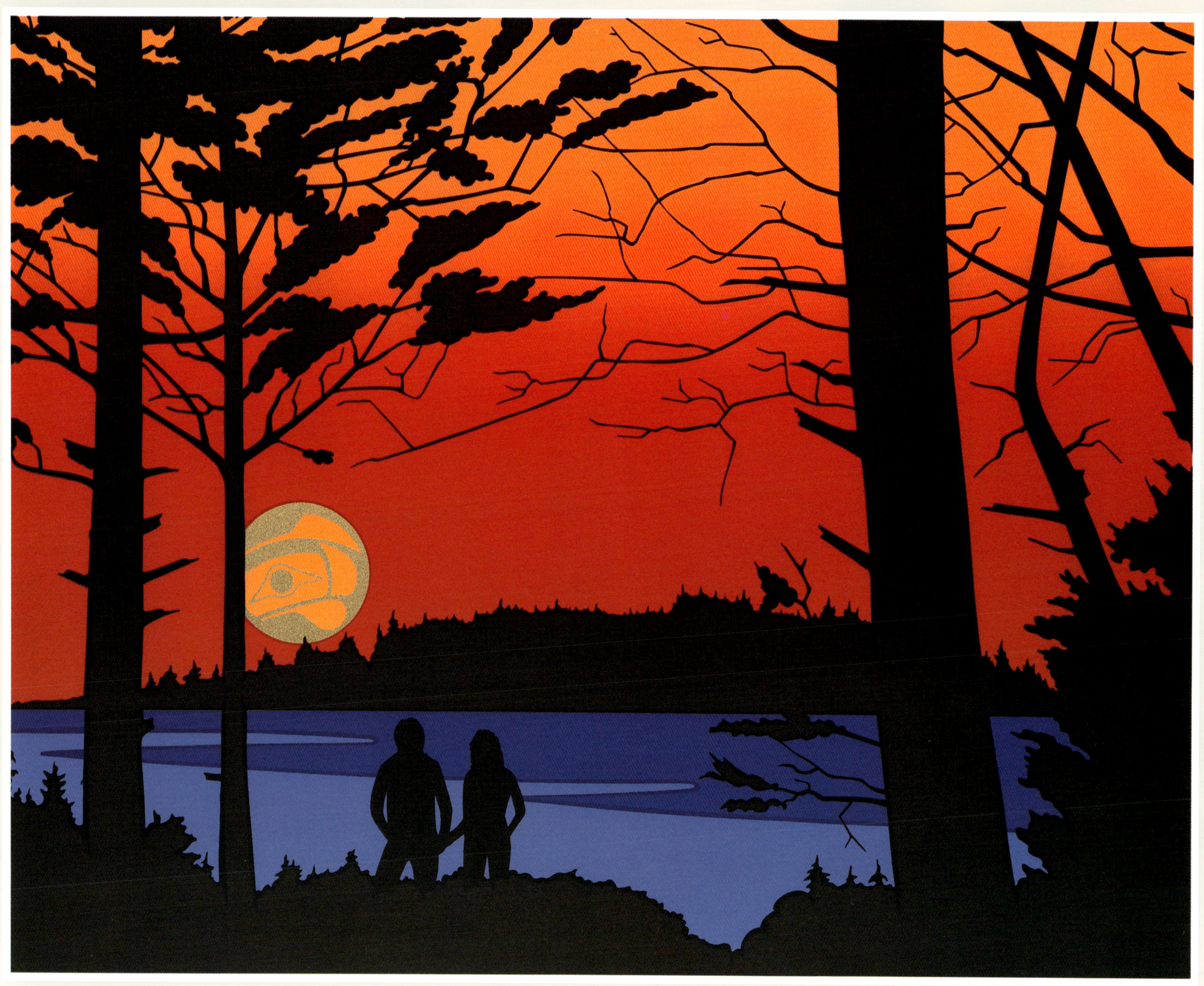

LOOK TO THE MOUNTAIN

The Skeena River valley and its mountains will hold forever a special place in my heart. On a recent photographic expedition to the Gitksan Indian villages which surround Hazelton, this image came to my mind. It caused me to recall the first verse of Psalm 121 from the Bible . . . "I will lift up mine eyes unto the hills, from whence cometh my help".

(Released May, 1987)

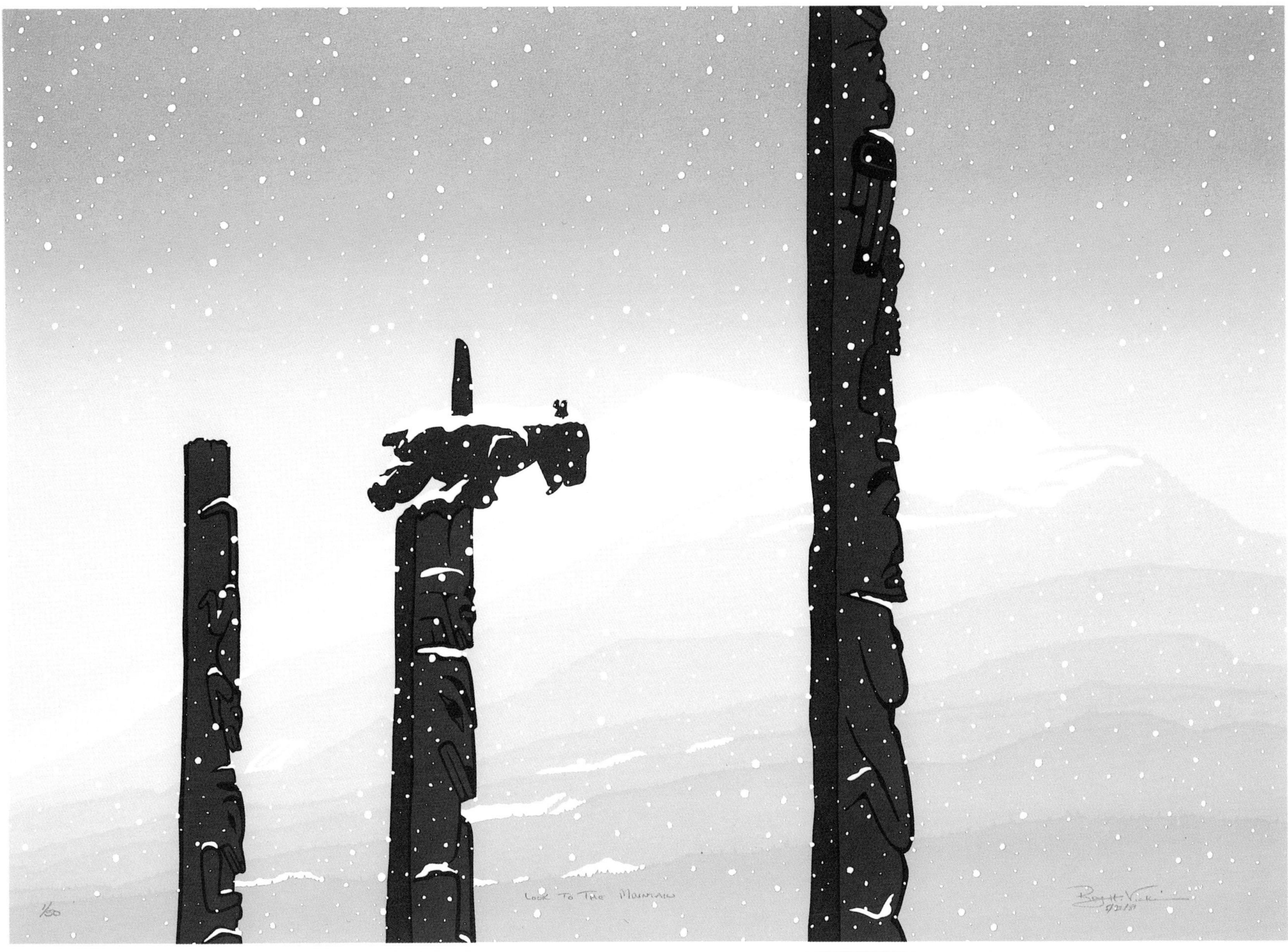

A MEETING OF CHIEFS

'Stegyawden', a Tsimshian Indian name meaning 'painted goat', is a mountain located on the Skeena River near Hazelton, British Columbia. The mighty Skeena itself is known to its first travelers, the Tsimshian Indians, as K'sian, meaning 'juice from the clouds'.

Many stories and legends are told of Stegyawden and K'sian. One in particular refers to the legendary village of Temleham, located at the base of Stegyawden on the banks of K'sian. So powerful and influential were its people, and so majestic, spiritual and beautiful were the surroundings, that the village of Temleham became known to all Indian nations as a very important and proper place to meet. Chiefs from all West Coast Indian nations would travel many perilous miles to congregate at Temleham.

Tlingit, Haida, Tsimshian, Bella Coola, Kwakiutl, and Nuu Cha Nulth—all would attend. Many elaborate and impressive feasts were held. Friendships and alliances developed and differences were settled.

Temleham was appropriate. It was the location that the ancients had chosen and created to serve as a place of peace, a meeting place for all nations.

In the swirling mists of the mighty K'sian, one can, even today, sense the presence of those wise chiefs. Their spirit and wisdom lives on, and their beautiful West Coast of Canada still serves today as a majestic and spiritual meeting place, a proper setting for A MEETING OF CHIEFS.

(This painting was commissioned by the Province of British Columbia on the occasion of the Commonwealth Heads of Government Meeting in Vancouver in October, 1987. The original painting was presented to Her Majesty Queen Elizabeth II by the Honourable William Vander Zalm, Premier of the Province of British Columbia. Limited edition prints were presented by the Provincial Government to the Commonwealth Heads of State.)

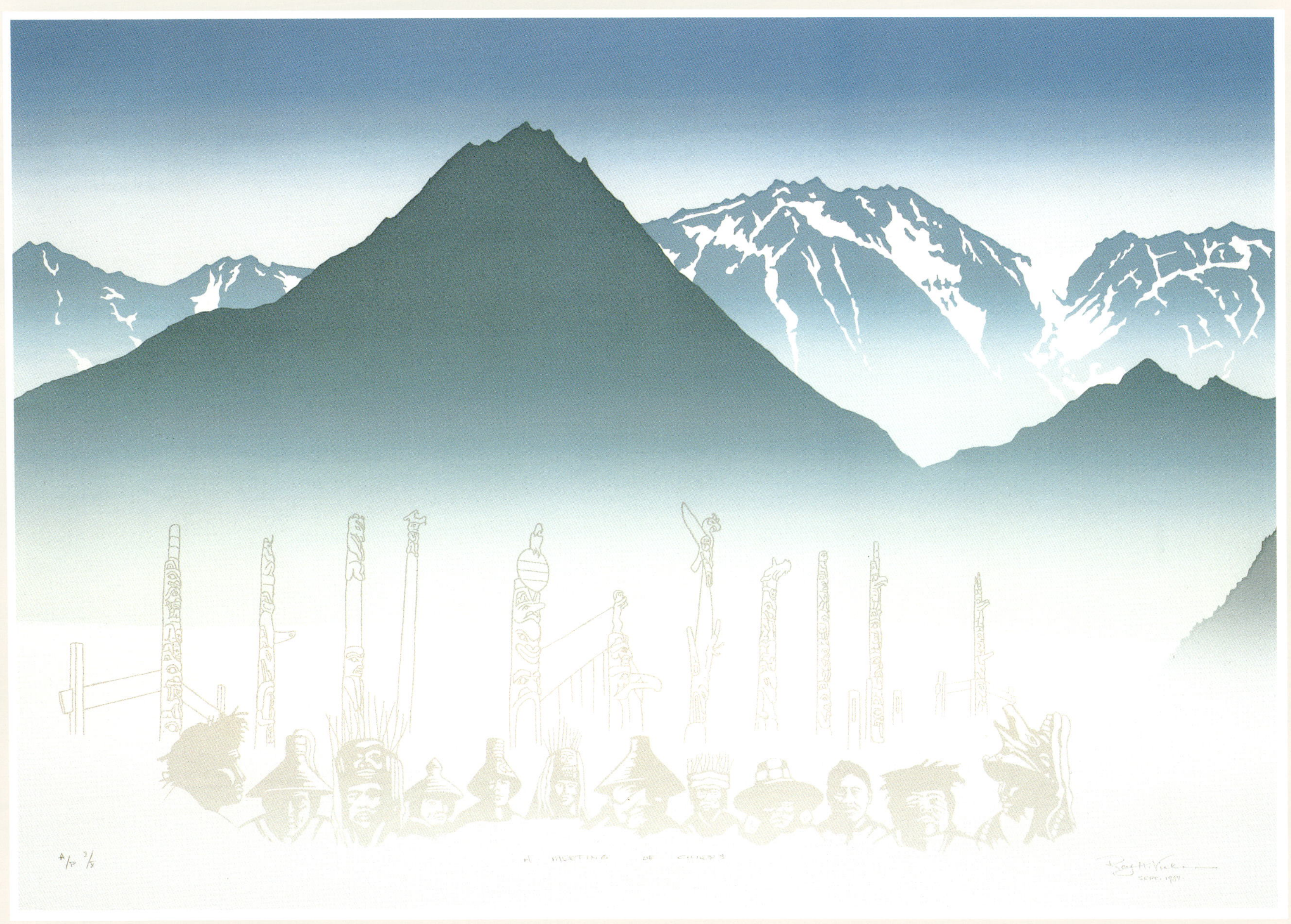
A MEETING OF CHIEFS

GUARDIAN OF THE PASS

Even as we flew over the lush valleys and deep gorges carved below us, I could feel the bristle of anticipation. We were now only feet above a huge expanse of white, a glacier miles long stretching before us. The remote, vast and rugged area that is the West Coast of British Columbia had engulfed us for more than an hour now. Our destination was Owikeeno Lake, a land that takes you back in time.

My friend, and very necessary guide on this trip, was Ted Walkus, hereditary chief of the Owikeeno tribe at Rivers Inlet. He had told me of an old legend of his people, of a powerful guardian who had protected his ancestral village when their village site had been at the north end of Owikeeno Lake. The settlement is presently found on Owikeeno River just before it empties into Rivers Inlet on the Pacific Ocean.

His story was of 'The Guardian of the Pass', a huge stone eagle at the narrows of Owikeeno Lake. It is said that the eagle would oversee all who travelled through the narrows. Those of good will were allowed to pass; those who came as enemies would be crushed by his enormous stone wing.

The cruel, clean glacier dropped sharply below us. We were now suddenly thousands of feet above a long, green finger of water. Within minutes, we were taxiing on the choppy, glacial waters of Owikeeno Lake.

The plane turned into the wind and there before us was the stone eagle. The narrows of Owikeeno Lake are only a few hundred yards wide and the guardian strikes an imposing figure as he watches you pass below. He is so prominent, so real. I was glad I had come as a friend.

I could feel his eye watching and see his wing poised to strike. We were friends, however, and allowed to go about our business.

There was excitement within me as I photographed the scene. I sensed the painting already—a feeling of urgency, a story to be told. I could feel the presence.

We finished, turned into the wind—the cool lonely wind of the West Coast. We took to the air. I can still sense being watched.

Perhaps they are true, those legends of thousands of years. Perhaps the stone eagle really is 'THE GUARDIAN OF THE PASS'.

(Released September, 1987)

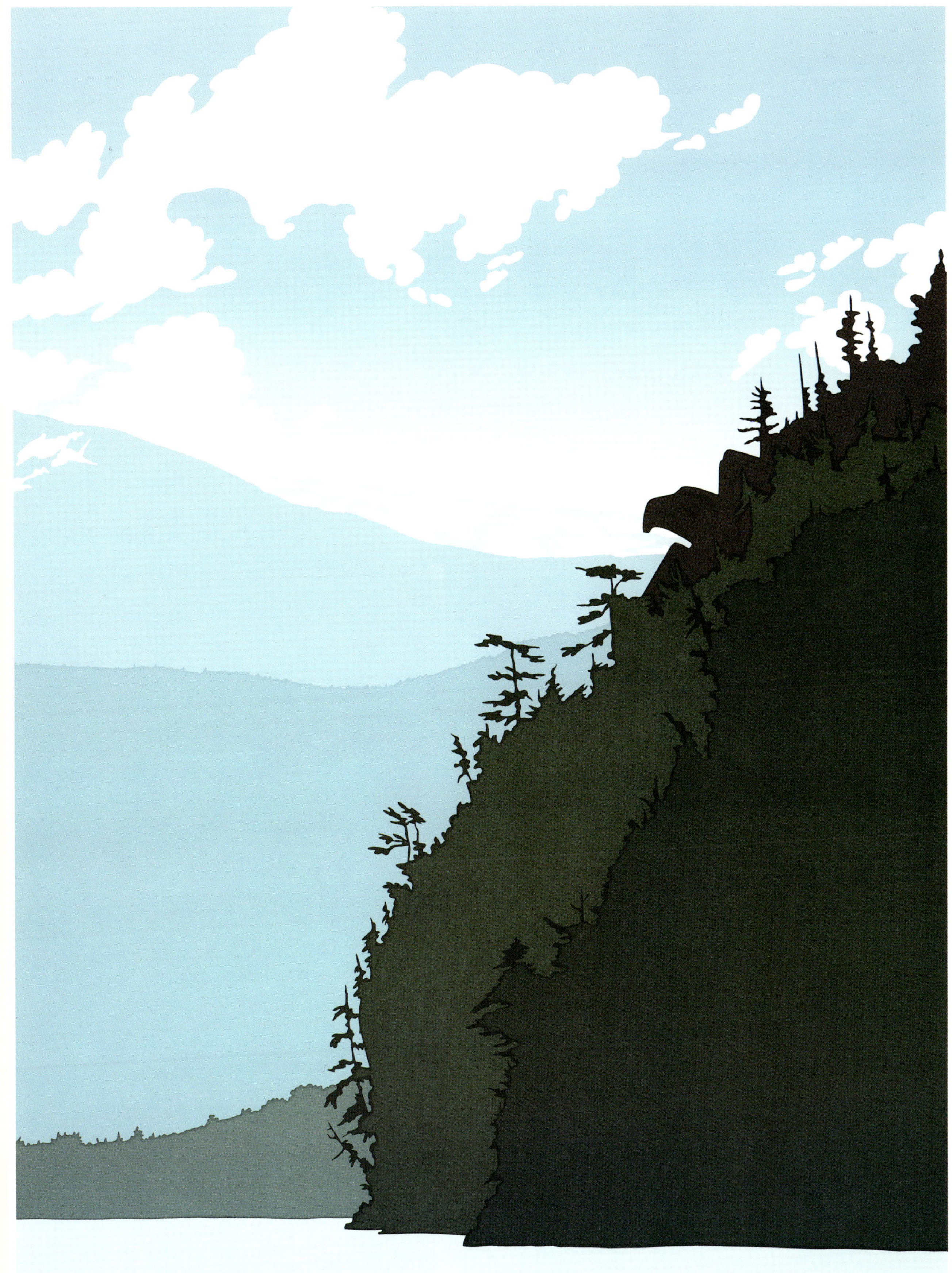

A/P

GUARDIAN OF THE PASS

Roy H. Vickers

1987.

OWIKEENO

A beautiful summer day and a flight from Tofino to Owikeeno Lake at the head of Rivers Inlet. Such was the inspiration for two paintings. The first painting was of a formation of rock called 'Guardian of the Pass' which was completed and printed in September 1987.

The day in the Indian Village of Owikeeno with my wife and three close friends was very special. We were shown how to catch sockeye by a friendly man from the village. And, as usual, an attempt was made to catch the legendary Rivers Inlet chinook. As fate would have it, a brisk westerly wind blowing up the inlet from the ocean turned us back to the comfort and protection of the village.

We spent the day visiting with the people and taking time to give a short lesson to a few eager students at the school.

During our tour through the village we came upon the only sculpture in the village—a granite, mortuary eagle figure erected by a famous chief of the village. The stone eagle triggered thoughts of the carvers at the turn of the century who would create the originals of this and many other stone carvings seen in villages and graveyards of the northwest. It seems that the wealthy chiefs desired stone masons to reproduce the wooden sculptures in granite and stone so that they would exist through the ages.

This rendition of OWIKEENO shows the eagle mortuary as I think it was carved rather than the way it looks today. OWIKEENO is a tribute to those master sculptors of the Northwest Coast Indians, and a reminder for me of a most inspirational summer day with my wife and friends in OWIKEENO.

(Released November, 1987)

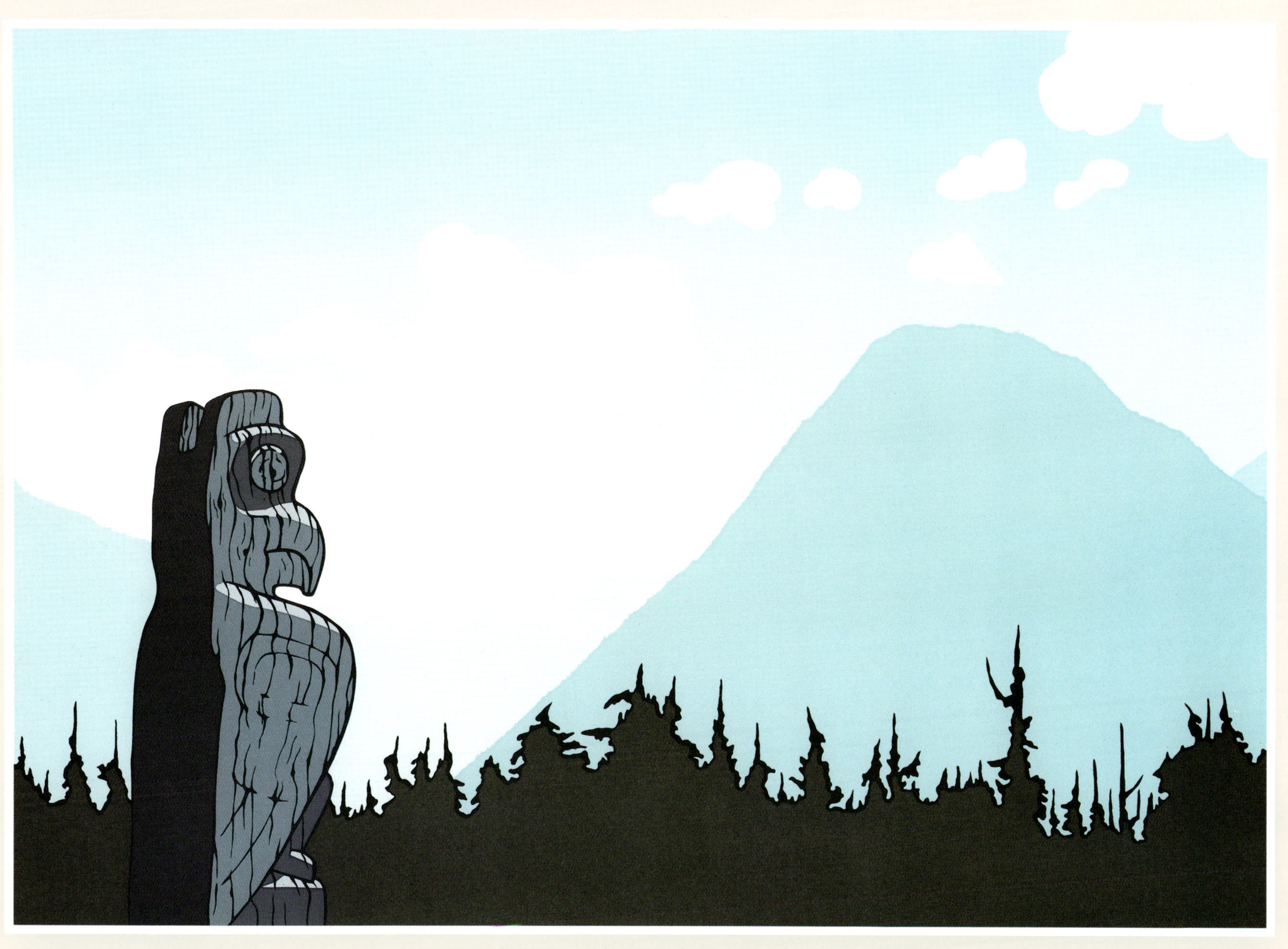

WINTER SOLSTICE

Another year was coming to an end, causing me to reflect on the wonders of this village of Tofino, and on some of the individuals who live here. I was reminded of the many inspirations for me in this area, and came to realize that I wanted to create a work reminiscent of the harbour and of beautiful Meares Island.

Reflecting over the events of the year, it seemed to me to be the year of the Northwest Coast Indian canoe. There was the Haida canoe that travelled the coast from Expo 86 to the Queen Charlotte Islands, and Gilwa, the canoe carved and paddled from Bella Bella to Vancouver. Here in Tofino, there is the Martin family who have carved a number of canoes of the West Coast style. I myself have begun a project that will hopefully see a number of Bronze canoes made from a bowl that I carved and gave to my wife Rhonda.

The wonderful year of 1987, the best year of my life, seemed to dictate the necessity for me to paint a scene of the moon of the WINTER SOLSTICE rising over Mount Colnett on Meares Island, with a canoe from the nearby village of Opitsaht being paddled into Tofino Harbour.

(Released December, 1987)

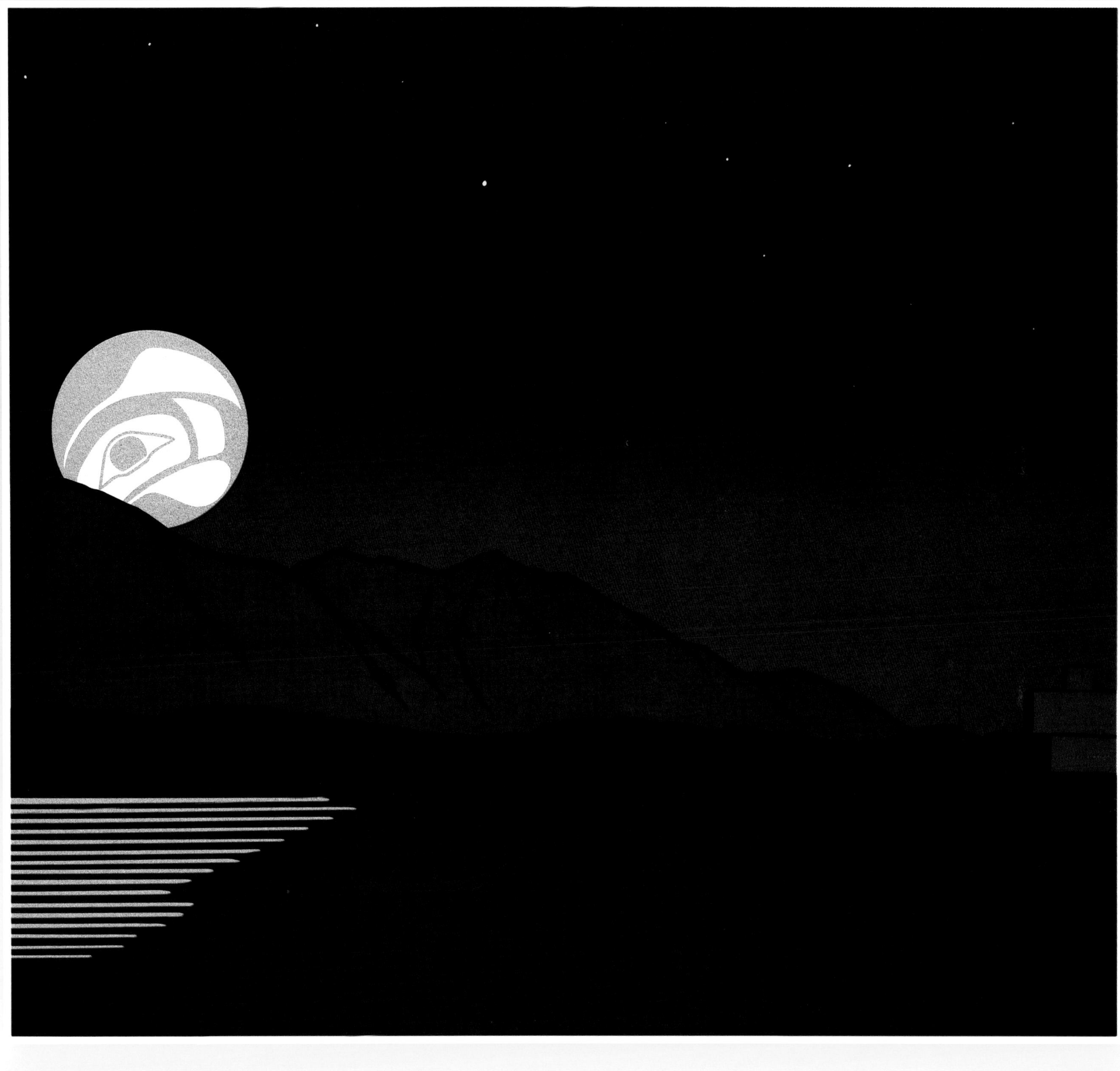

FIVE VIEWS OF VICTORIA

This series of five scenes of Victoria is the completion of a trilogy of works that represent three stages of my life—childhood, youth and adulthood. 'Portholes to the Past' was a series of five favourite village scenes on the coast where I enjoyed my childhood. 'The Group Of Seven' included seven village scenes from the Skeena River area near Hazelton where I spent my youth. This brings me to the third and final group of works and the city of Victoria where I grew up.

Suffice it to say, my years of growing up in Victoria were difficult, and I like to think that I am a better person as a result. Victoria saw the emergence of a somewhat shy and quite introspective young man who longed for the less complicated life of youth and childhood. I often felt like the world was closing in on me or life was demanding more than I could give. There were times when I just felt lost.

During those difficult times I sought solace in a quiet place. Other times I looked for a place that was familiar to ease a sometimes overpowering sense of nostalgia.

Upon returning to Victoria to research the work on this Victoria series, many of those feelings, the joys and pains of growing up swept over me. I found myself coming to grips with and understanding a little more about myself. In that continued process of learning and growing, I enjoy more of life and can also return to the happiness of youth.

It is with the mixed emotions of nostalgia, relief, joy, and freedom that I share these FIVE VIEWS OF VICTORIA.

(Released March, 1988)

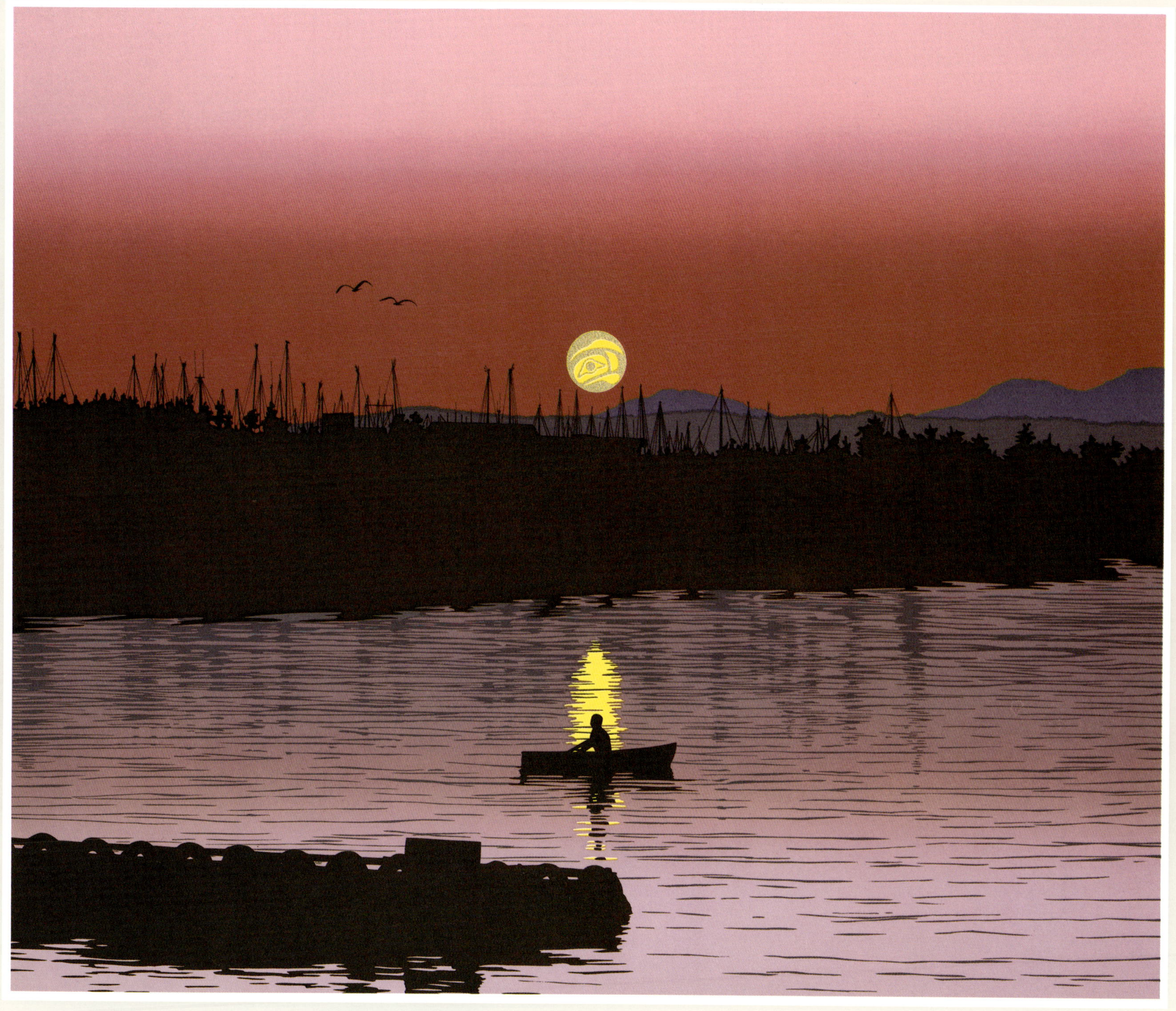

FISHERMAN'S WHARF

As a descendant of thousands of years of seafarers, it is natural for me to want to be near the ocean. I love the salt sea air, cedar pilings, and the song of a seabird. The hustle and bustle of the docks as fishermen prepare for a season of hard work always gets my heart beating faster. FISHERMAN'S WHARF has always been one of my favourite spots in Victoria.

COMING HOME

As the children of a fisherman, it seemed like our father was never home, and we missed him. During the school year, Mom taught and we learned, but Dad was always away fishing.

There were times when the entire family could be together though. The summer holidays found Mom and Dad and all the children on the boat. We shared the memory that those were the happiest times. For the most part, however, we resigned ourselves to the fact that Dad always had to be away fishing. But, we always looked for that day of excitement when he would be COMING HOME.

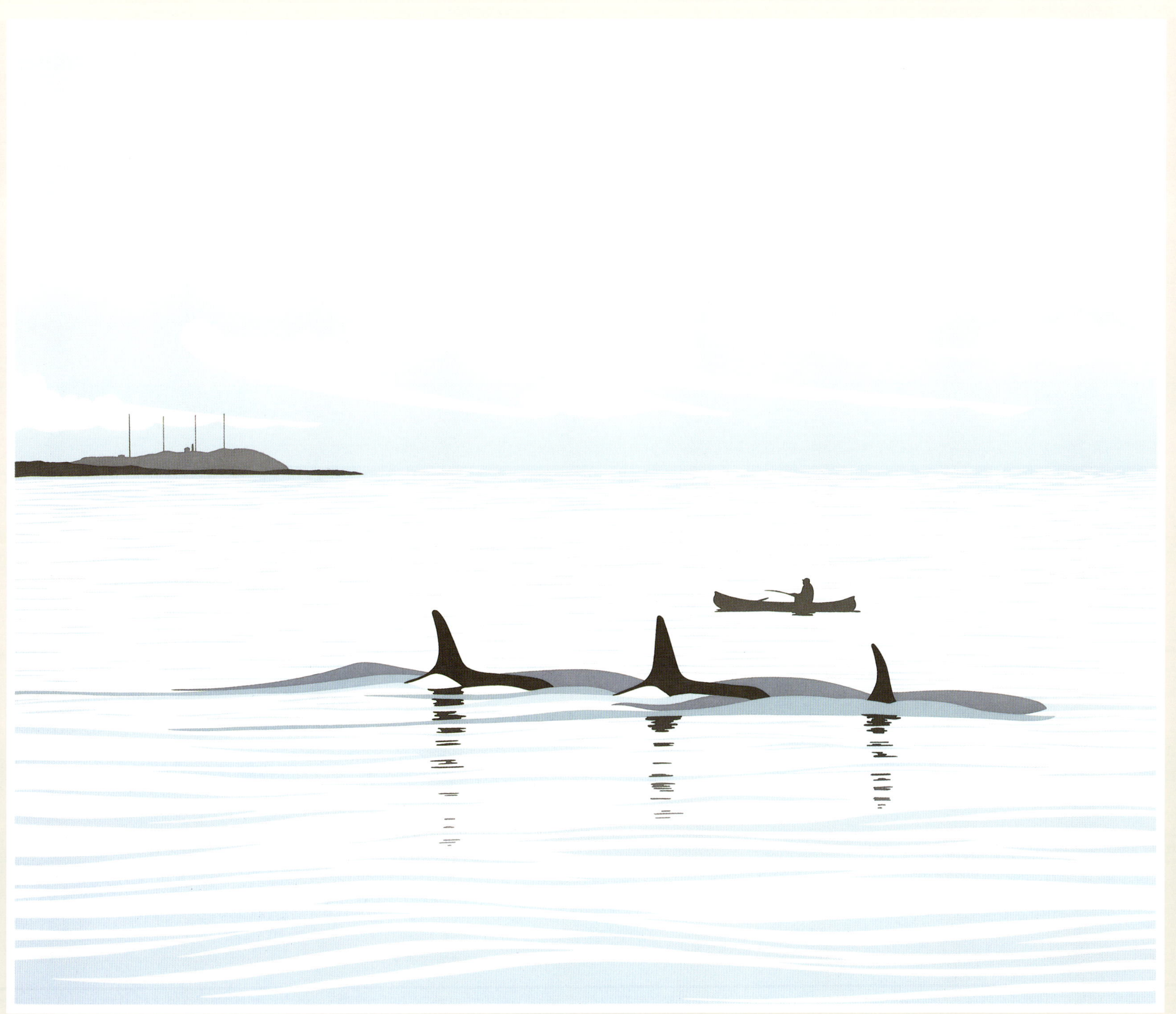

TRIAL ISLAND

I have friends whose relatives were the keepers of the lighthouse and weather station on TRIAL ISLAND which allowed me a number of opportunities to visit.

As we sat one day and visited over coffee, I was struck by the familiarity of the ocean view and the isolation from the city. I realized that being isolated from city life felt good to me, and so I enjoyed Trial Island even more.

Another visit found me in the centre of a pod of orcas and the thrill of being so close to these animals, as I had been before, was exhilarating.

This scene of the canoe and the killer whales was inspired by a photograph that a friend had taken from his equally thrilling encounter. Thank you, Phil!

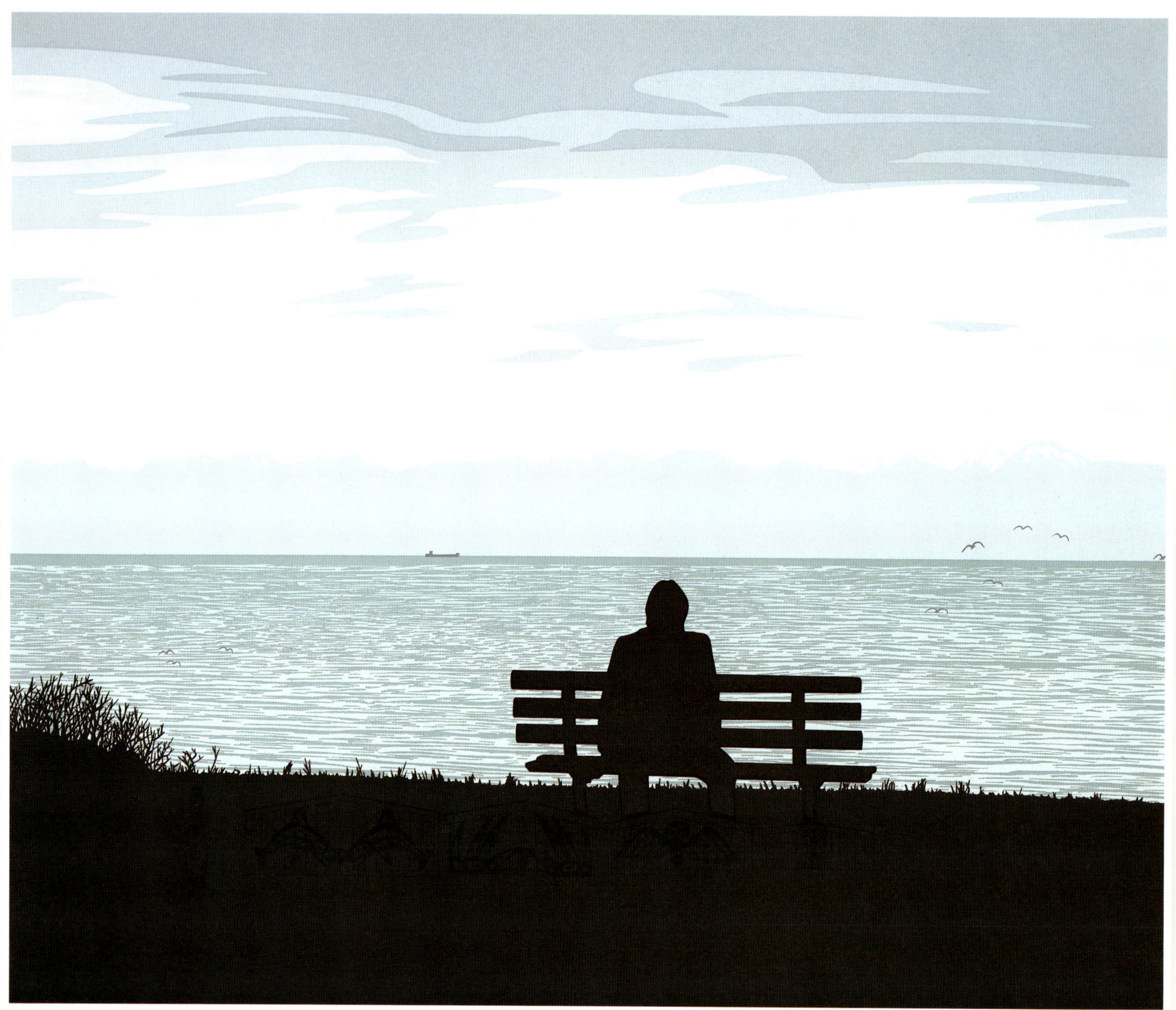

WHERE IS KITKATLA?

This scene was the first that came to mind when I set to work on this project. So many times I sat in solitude overlooking the ocean, wondering who I was and why in the world I was in this city. WHERE IS KITKATLA? I felt so lost, so alone and extremely nostalgic. Gazing at the ocean reminded me of Kitkatla. Lifting my eyes to the Olympic Mountains I was reminded of Hazelton and the Skeena Valley.

Today when I visit Victoria, as I often do, I realize that Kitkatla is always with me. My self portrayal is of a man in contemplation, sitting on a park bench in Victoria, with feet firmly fixed in the village of Kitkatla. The four houses are the four tribes of my village—Raven, Whale, Eagle, and Wolf. And thus, the question is answered by the painting.

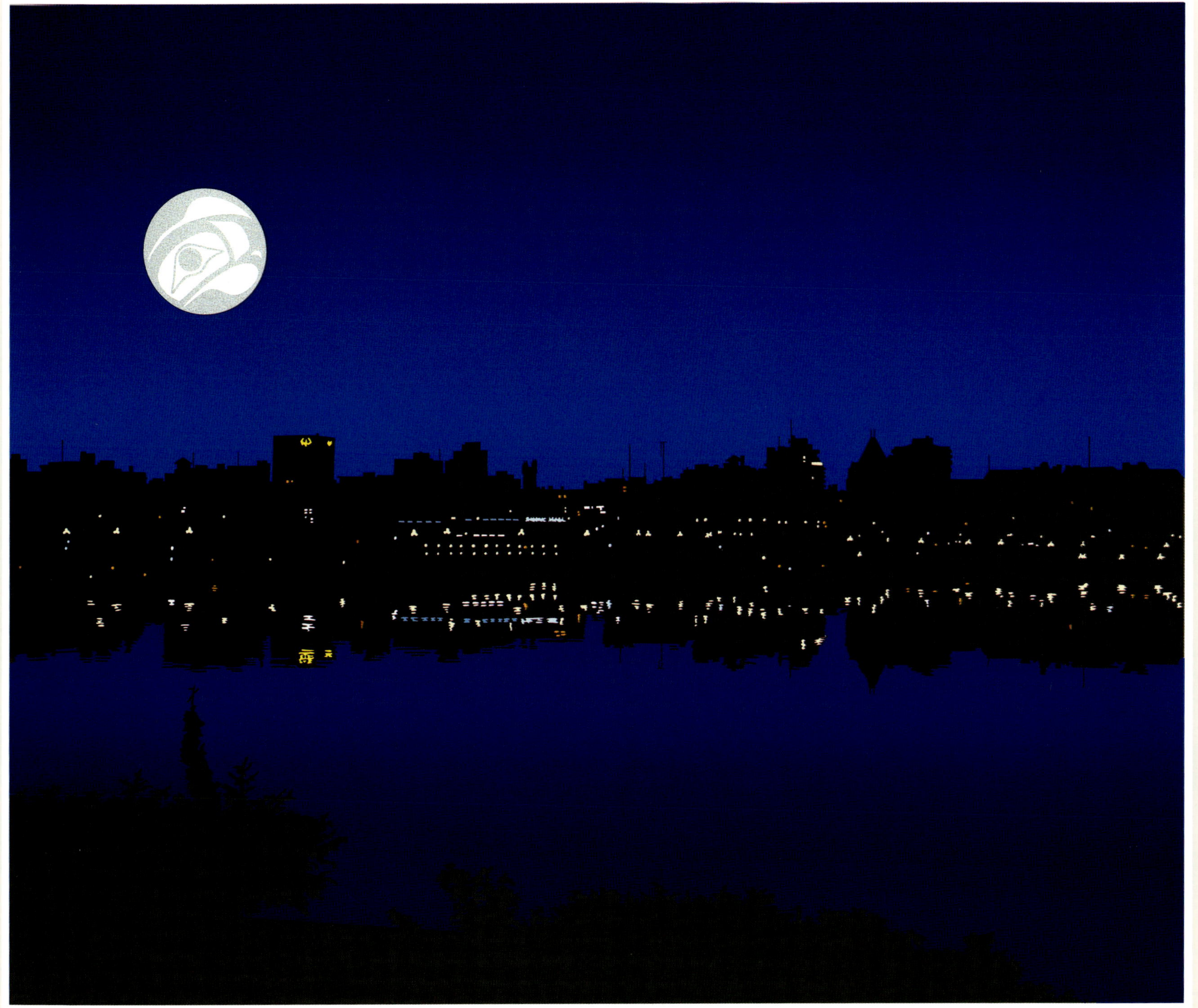

INNER HARBOUR

Victoria, with its array of flowers and protected harbour is one of the most beautiful cities I have ever seen. Many scenes flood my mind upon reflection—fireworks on New Year's Eve, the blessing of the fleet of fishing boats before they put to sea, and the excitement of the Swiftsure Races or the Victoria to Maui Race of open ocean sailboats.

An experience that I enjoy most is standing with Rhonda in the hush of the evening, the scent of a million flowers in the night air, gazing at the reflections of the INNER HARBOUR.

WINTER PERCH

How do two people do one painting? In the case of Ed Hill and myself, it was a simple matter of matching student with teacher: the teacher directing and demonstrating, and the student listening, watching and performing according to that direction.

The image of WINTER PERCH was first conceived by Ed. The rough sketches caught my imagination. Using my own style, I could see a fine finished piece, and it would be a prime opportunity to teach that style to Ed in the process.

Ed's final sketch showed far too much detail, and lines too sharp for my liking, so we agreed to change it by simplifying it. Branches were no longer just branches—they became the hiding place of eagles, cormorants and whales. The viewer fills out the eyes, beak and feathers of the eagle. Leaving much of the detail to the viewer's imaginative eye is a part of my style that I enjoy very much.

The final sketch was completed by myself and then Ed began painting the background. Three tries and sixty hours later found the background 'bleed run' finished to both our satisfaction.

The last lesson, colour mixing, provided a point of argument for us, but as is proper, the teacher won out. We let the subtle grey work, allowing the viewer to fill in the detail. We let the snow pile high on the branch to provide highlight. There was no need for two tones on the branch—the mind's eye would take care of that. These efforts gradually blended together, and Ed went to work to complete the painting.

Utilizing only four colours, sharp clean lines and depth created by the bleed run of the background, I had put all of my lessons into one work, and Ed had been an integral part of the entire process.

WINTER PERCH is more than a solitary eagle overseeing his snowy domain. The sketching, painting and printing of this piece is the result of two men collaborating—one teaching and one learning. It is affirmation for the teacher of his student's work. It is also the kind of experience that has helped make two men the best of friends.

(Released March, 1987)

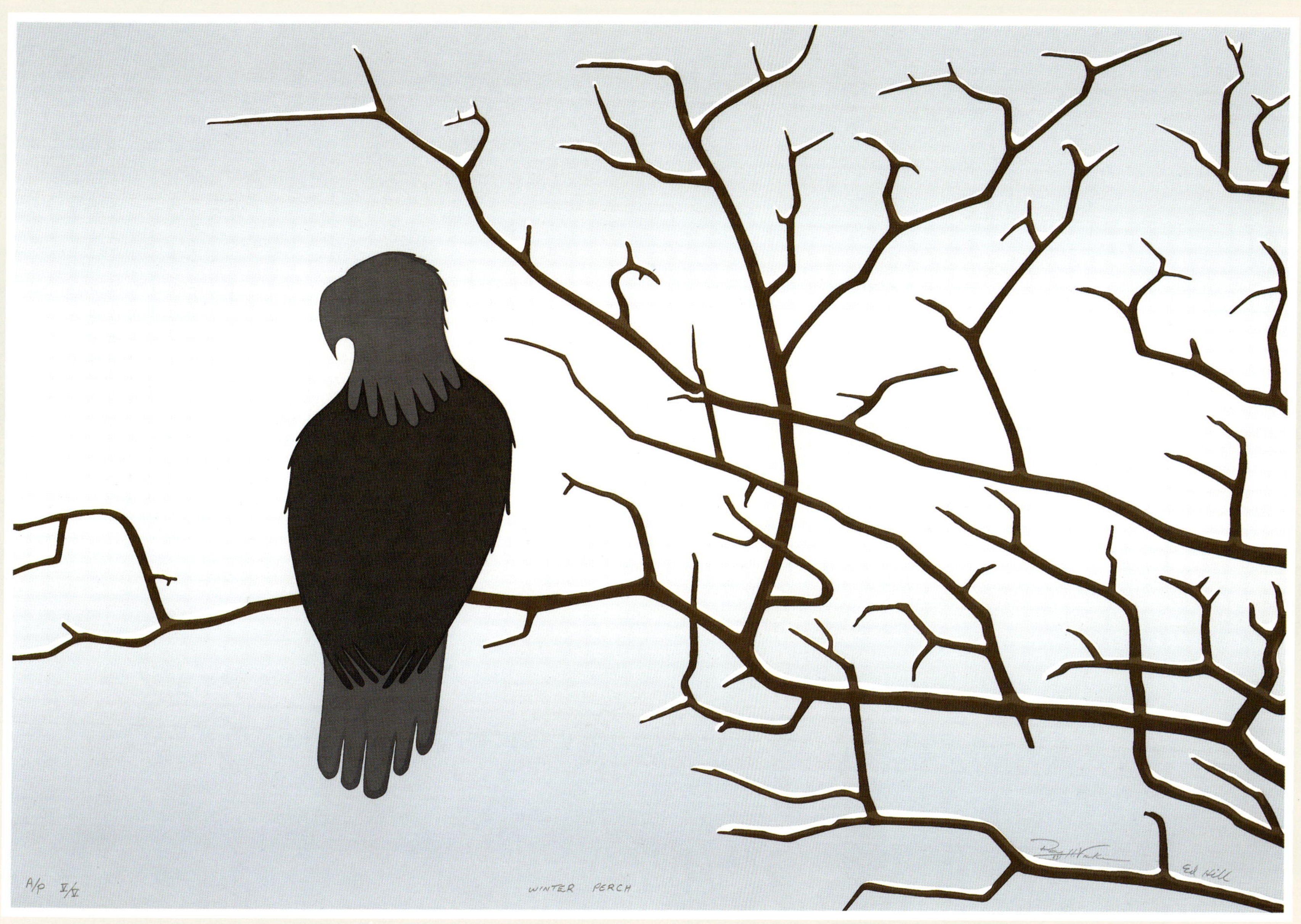
A/P V/V
WINTER PERCH
Ed Hill

THE IMAGES

CANADIAN CATALOGUING IN PUBLICATION DATA

Vickers, Roy Henry, 1946-
Solstice

ISBN 0-9693485-1-7 (trade ed.)

1. Vickers, Roy Henry, 1946- 2. Painting, Canadian—British Columbia. 3. Painting, Modern—20th Century—British Columbia. I. Title.
ND249.V34A4 1988a 759.11 C88-091346-0

Designers: Roy Henry Vickers, Alex Green, Ken Budd
Editor: Ken Budd
Typesetting and Pre-press Production: Zenith Graphics Ltd.
Binder: North-West Books Co. Ltd.
Printer: Metropolitan Press Ltd.

Produced by:
Ken Budd, Executive Producer
SummerWild Productions
#2202 - 1275 Pacific Street
Vancouver, B.C. V6E 1T6
Phone (604) 681-0015

Published by:
EAGLE DANCER ENTERPRISES LTD.
P.O. Box 527, Tofino, B.C., Canada V0R 2Z0
Phone (604) 725-3235 Fax (604) 725-4466

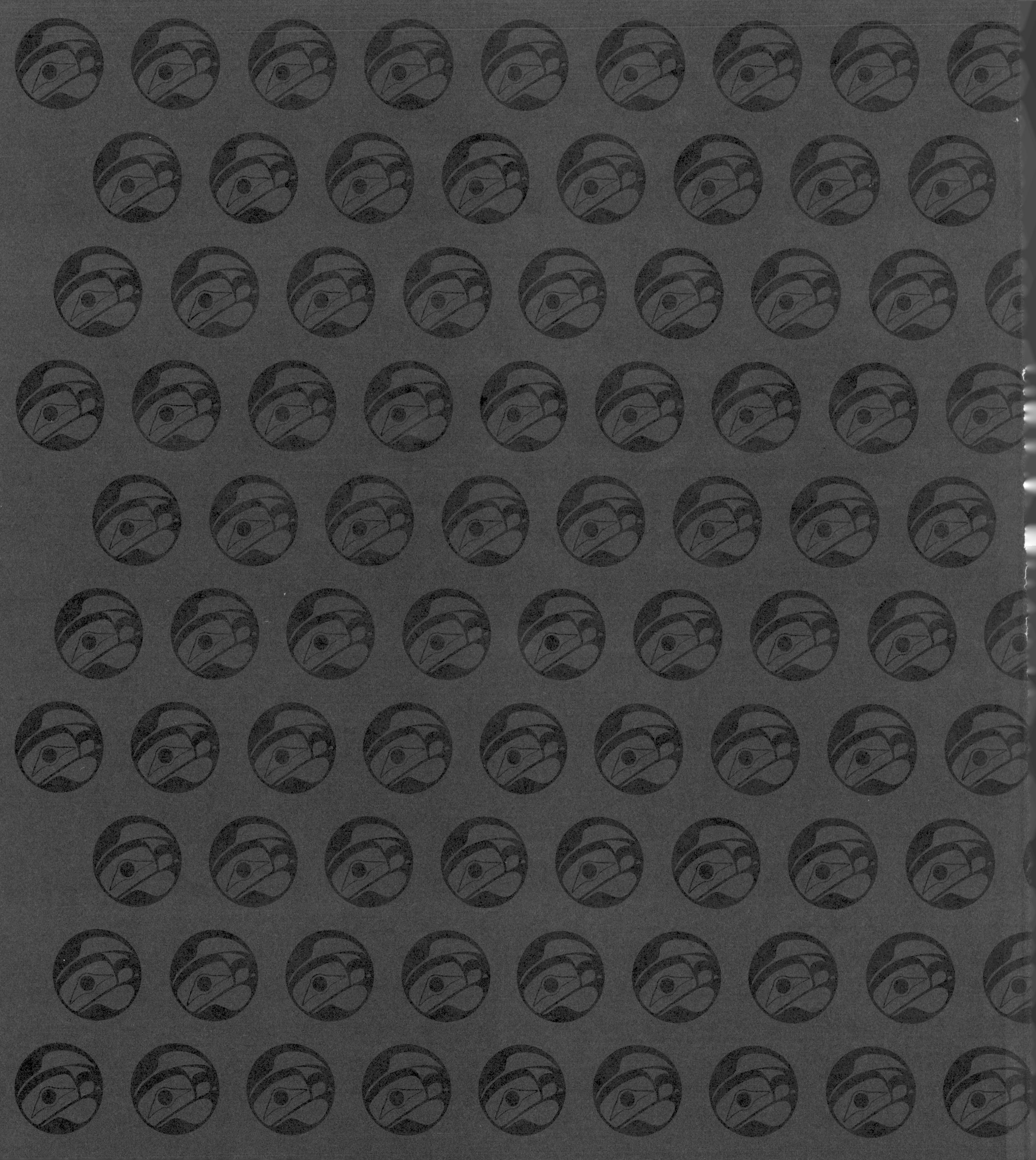